HOLLYWOOD
SPECTATORSHIP

Changing Perceptions of Cinema Audiences

Edited by
Melvyn Stokes and Richard Maltby

 Publishing

First published in 2001 by the
British Film Institute
21 Stephen Street, London W1P 2LN

The British Film Institute promotes greater understanding of,
and access to, film and moving image culture in the UK.

Cover design: ketchup
Cover image: Anthony Hopkins as Hannibal Lecter in
The Silence of the Lambs (Jonathan Demme, 1991)

Set by Alden Group Ltd, Osney Mead, Oxford

Printed in Great Britain by St Edmundsbury Press, Suffolk, United Kingdom

British Library Cataloguing-in-Publication Data
A catalogue record for this book is available from the British Library

ISBN 0–85170–810–2 (pbk)
ISBN 0–85170–811–0 (hbk)

Contents

Notes on Contributors

Gregory D. Black is Director of American Studies and Professor of Communication Studies at the University of Missouri-Kansas City. He has published *Hollywood Censored: Morality Codes, Catholics, and the Movies* (Cambridge University Press, 1994) and *The Catholic Crusade Against the Movies, 1940–75* (Cambridge University Press, 1997). He is co-author of *Hollywood Goes to War: How Politics, Profits and Propaganda Shaped World War II Movies* (Free Press, 1987) and is currently writing a book on anti-war films.

Alain J.-J. Cohen is Professor of Comparative Literature at the University of California-San Diego, where he teaches cinema, semiotics and psychoanalysis. He has published many articles on, among others, Eisenstein, Godard, Hitchcock, Kubrick, Lynch, Marker, Scorsese and Welles, foregrounding in particular methods of film analysis, the rhetoric of violence in contemporary US cinema and the aesthetics of the filmic image. He recently produced a one-hour documentary on California artist Russell Forester.

Amy M. Davis has recently completed a doctoral dissertation on representations of women in Disney animated films. She has taught at University College London, where she helped to organise the 1998 Commonwealth Fund Conference on American history exploring Hollywood and its Spectators. She has served as editorial assistant for this series.

Jane M. Gaines is Associate Professor of Literature and English and Director of the Film and Video Programme at Duke University. She is the author of *Contested Culture: The Image, the Voice and the Law* (University of North Carolina Press, 1991) and *Fire and Desire: Mixed Race Movies in the Silent Era* (University of Chicago Press, 2001).

Mark Jancovich is Senior Lecturer and Director of the Institute of Film Studies at the University of Nottingham. He is the author of *Horror* (Batsford, 1992), *The Cultural Politics of the New Criticism* (Cambridge University Press, 1993) and *Rational Fears: American Horror in the 1950s* (Manchester University Press, 1996). He has co-edited *Approaches to Popular Film* (Manchester University Press, 1995) and *The Film Studies Reader* (Arnold, 2000). He is currently editing *Changing Channels: Television in the Digital Age* and *The Horror Film Reader* and writing up the results of an AHRB-funded research project on film consumption in cities.

Barbara Klinger is Associate Professor and Director of Film and Media in the Department of Communications and Culture at Indiana University. She is the author of *Melodrama and Meaning: History, Culture, and the Films of Douglas Sirk* (Indiana University Press, 1994). She has published articles in *Cinema Journal*, *Screen* and *The Velvet Light Trap*. She is currently working on a book about cinema spectatorship in the home.

Richard Maltby is Professor of Screen Studies and Head of the School of Humanities at Flinders University of South Australia. He is the author of *Hollywood Cinema: An Introduction* (Blackwells, 1995), *Dreams for Sale: Popular Culture in the Twentieth Century* (Harrap, 1989) and *Harmless Entertainment: Hollywood and the Ideology of Consensus* (Scarecrow, 1983), as well as numerous articles and essays. *'Film Europe' and 'Film America': Cinema, Commerce and Cultural Exchange, 1925–39* (Exeter University Press, 1999), which he co-edited with Andrew Higson, won the Prix Jean Mitry for cinema history in 2000. He is currently writing *Reforming the Movies: Politics, Censorship, and the Institutions of the American Cinema, 1908–39.*

G. Tom Poe is Associate Professor of Communication Studies at the University of Missouri-Kansas City. He has published articles relating to audience reception of politics in the classical Hollywood film in the *Journal of Dramatic Theory and Criticism* and *Film History.* He is currently writing a book about audience reaction to Hollywood's Cold War 'chillers'.

Gianluca Sergi is Senior Lecturer in Media and Cultural Studies at Staffordshire University. He has published extensively in the area of film sound, including articles in the *Journal of Film and Television* and chapters in *Contemporary Hollywood Cinema* (Routledge, 1998) and *Screen Acting as Art and Performance* (Routledge, 1999). He is currently writing an article on music in film and researching a book on contemporary film sound.

Martin Shingler lectures in film and radio at Staffordshire University. He is co-author (with Cindy Wieringa) of *On Air* (Arnold, 1998) and has published articles in *Screen,* the *Journal of American Studies* and the *Journal of Radio Studies.* He contributed a chapter on Bette Davis to *Screen Acting* (Routledge, 1999) and is currently co-editing a book on the languages and protocols used by contemporary broadcasters on different kinds of radio.

Janet Staiger is the William P. Hobby Centennial Professor of Communication at the University of Texas-Austin. She is co-author of *The Classical Hollywood Cinema: Film Style and Mode of Production to 1960* (Columbia University Press, 1985) and author of *Interpreting Films: Studies in the Historical Reception of American Cinema* (Princeton University Press, 1992), *Bad Women: Regulating Sexuality in Early American Cinema* (Minnesota University Press, 1995), *Perverse Spectators: The Practices of Film Reception* (New York University Press, 2000) and *Blockbuster TV: Must-See Sitcoms in the Network Era* (New York University Press, 2000).

Melvyn Stokes teaches American history and film history at University College London, where he has been the principal organiser of the Commonwealth Fund Conference in American History since 1988. His co-edited books include *Race and Class in the American South since 1890* (Berg, 1994), *The Market Revolution in America* (University of Virginia Press, 1996), and *The United States and the European Alliance* (Berg, 1999). He is co-editor (with Richard Maltby) of *American Movie Audiences: From the Turn of the Century to the Early Sound Era* (BFI, 1999) and *Identifying Hollywood's Audiences: Cultural Identity and the Movies* (BFI, 1999). He is currently writing a book about *The Birth of a Nation.*

Preface

This is the third of a series of four volumes dealing with the reception of Hollywood films. The first, *American Movie Audiences*, is devoted to the exploration of how differing American audiences responded to films and the film-going experience from the beginning of the century to the early sound era. It also examines the varying ways in which audiences were perceived, either by movie exhibitors or those regarding themselves as champions of the prevailing morality and culture.

The second volume, *Identifying Hollywood's Audiences*, explores two major themes: first, what Hollywood knew (or thought it knew) about its audiences from the 1920s to the 1990s, and the effects of this knowledge; second, what audiences made of the films they viewed and the meanings they constructed from them.

The present volume seeks to test the validity of theoretical, text-based constructions of spectatorship in the light of either historical evidence on how films were actually received by audiences and critics or the changing patterns of exhibition encouraged in recent years by technological change.

We should like, once again, to offer our thanks to Andrew Lockett, Head of Educational Publishing at the BFI, who first conceived the idea of the series; to Robert C. Allen and Janet Staiger for their help and support for the project from the beginning; to Amy M. Davis for her work as editorial assistant on the series; and to Leigh Priest who has prepared the index for each volume.

The series itself had its origins in a Commonwealth Fund Conference held at University College London on the theme 'Hollywood and its Spectators'. We would like to express our gratitude and acknowledge financial support in organising this conference from the Commonwealth Fund, Graduate School and Friends of University College London, the British Academy, the London University Institute of United States Studies, the Royal Historical Society, the History Faculty of Cambridge University, the British Film Institute, W. W. Norton and Company and Oxford University Press.

Melvyn Stokes and Richard Maltby
December 2000

Introduction
Historical Hollywood Spectatorship

Melvyn Stokes

This book is made up of a series of essays by film studies scholars on the theme of Hollywood spectatorship. Its main purpose is to question the dominance of theoretical views of spectatorship across the field as a whole. In particular, it seeks to test the validity of theoretical, text-based constructions of spectatorship either against evidence from historical sources on how film texts were actually received by audiences and critics or in the light of the changing exhibition circumstances brought about by modern technological changes.

Theoretical definitions of cinema spectatorship have been at the heart of film studies for much of the last three decades. The interest in such definitions arose originally for several reasons, one of the most crucial of which was the events of May 1968 in France. 'Les évènements' were less important for what they were (student protests and mass demonstrations together with – sometimes coinciding – strikes and industrial unrest) than for the critical reappraisal of society and politics that accompanied them. A key text in this reappraisal was Guy Debord's *The Society of the Spectacle* (1967), in which it was argued that traditional forms of human communication had given place, in modern society, to the contemplation and consumption of images. After Debord and the events of May 1968, it was considerably harder to regard film-viewing as an innocent activity. Indeed, as Judith Mayne has observed, it now came to seem 'ideologically suspect', with critics perceiving it as reflecting 'a passive and complicitous acceptance of society as it was'.[1]

Much of the best theoretical work of the late 1960s and early 1970s in France dealt with the issue of ideology expressed by – and implicated in – systems of representation. A crucial publication in this field was Louis Althusser's essay, 'Ideology and Ideological State Apparatuses'.[2] Althusser contended that the existing capitalist order was preserved partly by the state apparatus (government, police, courts, prisons and the army), but also partly by what he called 'ideological state apparatuses' (ISAs). Such apparatuses included institutions such as the churches, schools, the family, the legal and political system, trade unions, and communications and cultural media. While the state apparatus operated mainly through repression, the ISAs functioned predominantly through ideological means. Ideology itself, according to Althusser, was 'the imaginary relationship of individuals to their real conditions of existence'. The task of ISAs was to invite or 'interpellate' individuals to accept whatever 'subject' position – a constructed, imaginary sense of self – was most appropriate in order to reproduce the mode of production and thereby preserve the dominance of the ruling class.[3]

Althusser's insistence that ideology had a 'material existence' (p. 165) encouraged the view that it could be analysed in similar terms, as an effective means of structuring social relationships. Many film critics believed that the ideology behind mainstream cinema was a particularly appropriate field for analysis of this kind, since cinema enjoyed an 'emblematic quality', embodying so many of society's hopes, myths, fears and fantasies.[4] Examining how the cinema operated as an ideological mechanism for the interpellation of subjects might clear the way to its mobilisation as a major instrument of social change.

Reflecting the dominant intellectual currents of the time in France, writers dedicated to this objective began with the assumption that the best – indeed the only – means of examining the cinema's ideological operations was to focus attention on filmic texts and the ways in which those texts constructed spectators. There were two main approaches to this task. The first, derived from Saussurean semiotics, attempted to demonstrate how the theoretical spectator was implicated in the operations of filmic texts by various modes of signification. While itself dealing with literature rather than film, Roland Barthes's *S/Z* (1970), a detailed textual analysis of a short novel by Balzac, offered a deeply appealing model for this type of endeavour. By the mid-1970s, however, there was an increasing recognition that the linguistic preoccupations associated with the first approach were 'failing to account for the psychic effects of the cinema on the spectator'.[5] A second approach, therefore, foregrounded the use of psychoanalysis – most notably, Jacques Lacan's ideas on how subjects are constructed – in order to explain how filmic texts address and position (still theoretical) spectators.

The text reigned supreme in French film writing of this period in part because of the traditional practice of 'close reading', in part because of the structuralist ascendancy, and in part because of the customary Marxist conception of film as a means of changing ways of thinking in 'progressive' directions (or, alternatively, of reproducing and disseminating 'false consciousness'), now strengthened and reinforced – albeit in a somewhat different direction – by Althusser's work. The two best-known journals, *Cinéthique* and *Cahiers du cinéma,* attempted to expose the manner in which mainstream cinema assisted in the ideological operations of capitalism. Unlike its competitor, however, *Cahiers du cinéma* did not accept that all films simply represented the ideology of the capitalist ruling class. It identified some classical Hollywood texts as 'subversive', in the sense that they contained inherent cracks and contradictions that actively invited fresh readings with (at least) the potential to damage and disrupt the dominant ideology.[6]

Thus far, the concept of a textually constructed spectator, positioned or interpellated in ideological terms, has been considered only from the point of view of French film theorists. The late 1960s and the 1970s, however, saw the rapid expansion of film studies in Britain and the United States.[7] Many of those who practised the new discipline were as politically engaged as their French counterparts.[8] The influential British journal *Screen,* for example, similarly launched itself into an attempt to theorise the role of ideology in subject formation on the basis of a combination of Althusser's reinterpretation of Marxism, semiotics and psychoanalysis. The spread of the debates surrounding these subjects into the American and British academy encouraged the development of new issues and perspectives. *Screen*'s publication of Laura Mulvey's famous article, 'Visual Pleasure and Narrative Cinema' (1975), for example, foreshadowed a growing interest in questions of female spectatorship.[9]

The fact that most practitioners of the new discipline of film studies in Britain and the United States started in other fields – most notably literary studies, philosophy and art history – deeply influenced their approach to film. As Robert Sklar has noted, in the early days of film studies most of these fields had fallen 'deeply under the thrall of contemporary European theories, Marxist and non-Marxist'.[10] Unusually, Sklar himself had trained as a historian before transferring his professional allegiance to cinema studies. The difference between the main concerns of many historians at this time and the priorities of their academic counterparts in cinema studies and its associated fields could not have been more striking. French historians of the *Annales* school and British social and cultural historians such as E. P. Thompson and Raymond Williams attempted to construct a new version of the past in which previously marginalised groups (the working class, women, ethnic and racial minorities) were not only foregrounded, but presented as active agents in the struggle to win control over their own lives and circumstances. Spreading to the United States as the 'new' social history, this movement privileged the life and actions of 'ordinary people'. Usually seen as an expression of left-wing political commitment, it offered a complete contrast to the (also left-wing) preoccupations of contemporary film studies scholars. While historians sought to draw a picture on the basis of empirical evidence of how 'real' people had once lived and fought to acquire agency, film theorists set about explaining how highly theoretical spectators were ideologically positioned (for the most part passively) by the cinematic apparatus.

The continuing engagement with the issue of the textually constructed spectator not only emphasised the difference between film studies and history but also encouraged an increasing contrast with one of film studies' parent disciplines: literary studies. During the 1970s, studies of 'historical, concrete instances' of the reception of literary texts began to proliferate in both Europe and America, often inspired by the work of such German reception theorists as Hans Robert Jauss.[11] In contrast, most practitioners of film studies preferred to ignore completely the issue of how movies were received in historical terms, treating films essentially as if they 'had no audiences or were seen by everyone and in the same way'.[12] While this made film studies itself rather unusual as a discipline, the distrust of empirical studies of movie reception was deeply engrained, reflecting both the theoretical orientation of the field in general and an awareness among many American film scholars of the history of audience research of this kind and the uses made of such research.

Audience issues – who went to the movies, how they behaved while watching films and what were the subsequent effects of the movies they had seen – were already salient in political discourse in the United States during the early twentieth century. Many native-born middle-class 'progressives' were concerned by the large numbers of working-class, often immigrant men and women who patronised big-city nickelodeons. Early cinema became a site of political struggle as reformers endeavoured to impose middle-class social controls over the lives and behaviour of working-class and ethnic movie-goers. This attempt expressed itself in campaigns directed at either censoring the content of films themselves[13] or at controlling and making 'safe' the environment in which movies were shown. Both these considerations seemed of particular importance, so far as progressive reformers were concerned, in relation to children, whom they saw as the most vulnerable and impressionable part of the movie audience.[14]

One profound effect of the anxieties articulated by many American middle-class reformers over the cinema was an initial attempt to use social scientific methods to measure the parameters of its influence on audiences. Indeed, it is hardly an exaggeration to say that modern mass communications research in the United States had its origins in these anxieties. Reflecting the concerns of contemporaries, moreover, most of the early research of this kind was made up of surveys of the movie-going practices of schoolchildren. Surveys were conducted in a number of localities – Portland, Oregon (1915), Iowa City (1916), Providence, Rhode Island (1918), Evansville, Indiana (1923), Chicago (1926) and, more ambitiously, in seventy-six cities (and including a total of 23,000 high-school students) by the Russell Sage Foundation, the National Board of Review of Motion Pictures and Associated First National Exhibitors in collaboration in 1923.[15] At the end of the 1920s, an even more elaborate series of investigations into movie-going habits and the ways in which movies ostensibly influenced attitudes and behaviour was financed by the Payne Fund. While not all of the eleven studies actually published focused on children, a high proportion did, and these findings were popularised by journalist Henry James Forman in his book entitled *Our Movie-Made Children*.[16]

Most of the survey investigations in the first four decades of American cinema reflected the fact that movie attendance was a highly political subject. Such surveys began as a result of concerns over the social composition of audiences and the nature of their response to the new medium. They soon began to focus primarily on children. Since, in their findings, they tended to 'prove' that the cinema exerted a strong influence on the attitudes and behaviour of movie-goers, they were often cited by people demanding movie censorship or self-regulation.[17] This association with élitist class assumptions and a fundamentally conservative political agenda explains much of the later mistrust of empirical investigation on the part of film studies scholars who have, in the main, been motivated in their discussions of spectatorship by the desire for 'alternative cultures and political identities which refuse to comply with dominant ideology'.[18]

A further source of the distrust of empiricism in film studies was the other main tradition of audience research: the attempt of the film industry itself to investigate its clients in order to further its understanding of its own market, and thereby its profitability. One of the great self-propagated myths of the movie industry was that Hollywood knew little about its audience.[19] As one movie industry executive, summarising the conventional wisdom, commented in 1954: 'we have usually worked in the past on the thesis that if we stand in the dark and throw a rock and hear a crash, we've hit the greenhouse. This is not an altogether dependable method. It means that if you don't hear a crash, you may no longer be in the motion picture business'.[20] However, George Gallup's growing interest in the motion picture industry and the founding of his Audience Research Institute (ARI) in 1940 and the subsequent appearance of Leo Handel's Motion Picture Research Bureau signalled the effective start of Hollywood's infatuation with modern market research and its 'scientific' sampling techniques and questionnaires. During the 1940s, ARI surveys encouraged RKO to change the plots of films to appeal to men as well as women, to aim to reach 'lowbrow' rather than 'highbrow' audiences, and to target in particular young movie-goers.[21] The operations of pollsters such as Gallup were greatly undermined by their failure to predict Harry Truman's victory in the 1948 presidential election, and for some years afterward

Hollywood turned its face against such techniques.[22] But, as Thomas Doherty has suggested, the research done in the 1940s demonstrating that teenagers and young adults went most frequently to the movies had the eventual effect – when reinforced by later evidence – of persuading the movie industry of the late 1960s and early 1970s to target its products primarily at a youthful (and predominantly male) audience.[23]

In the minds of many film studies practitioners, therefore, empirical studies were tainted either by their association with conservative political discourses or by the ways in which they had warped Hollywood itself. They did not, moreover, offer any real means of understanding either the subjectivity of individual spectatorial response or what shaped the nature of that response. Investigators only learned 'what spectators thought they saw or felt or believed'. As Janet Staiger pointed out, earlier work of this kind had involved little more than noting 'spots on people's faces'. Such visible signs had provided information 'that symptoms are manifest but not much about the organism that produced these spots'.[24]

In spite of these drawbacks, there were signs already evident in the 1980s that abstract theories of spectatorship might, at some stage, need to be reconsidered in the light of accounts of the individual and collective response of 'real' spectators (i.e. viewers) to the cinematic experience. This was especially obvious on the part of feminist film writers. Laura Mulvey's essay of 1975, in which she contended that the spectatorial position offered by the 'classical' Hollywood cinema was a 'masculine' one, with female spectators alienated and essentially ignored by a cinematic institution deeply imbued with patriarchal values, prompted a veritable avalanche of work in which feminist film scholars (including Mulvey herself) attempted to demonstrate how a more mobile and less victimised form of female spectatorship might, at least in theory, exist. At times, a number of these writers expressed regret that no serious attempt had been made to link textually constructed female spectators with 'real' viewers. In a 1984 article on 'Women's Genres', for example, Annette Kuhn suggested rethinking the relationship between the two categories. Respondents to a questionnaire on female spectatorship in 1989 repeatedly drew attention to – or expressed frustration with – the continuing division between theories of the subject and real social and historical spectators. In the same year, Tania Modleski, while not herself in agreement with the viewpoint concerned, summarised the approach of those 'dissenters' who maintained that '*Screen*'s psychoanalytically informed theory, concerned largely with describing the ways subjects are "constructed" by popular film texts, tended to ignore actual social subjects'.[25]

Early attempts within feminist film studies to deal – in Judith Mayne's words – with 'the sneaking suspicion that theorists of the subject have left aside the problem of the relationship between constructions and contradictory people by discarding the people' for the most part concentrated on attempts to conceptualise theoretical and 'real' spectatorship in ways that demonstrated more clearly the relationship between the two. This was apparent, for example, in several of the contributions to a collection of essays edited by E. Deidre Pribram in 1988.[26] It was also clear in the work of Miriam Hansen. Spectatorship, according to Hansen, should be thought of as a mediation between the theoretical spectator and his/her real counterpart. Because such spectatorship was historically constructed, it also varied over time. Moreover, Hansen believed, it was necessary to complicate the question of spectatorship even further by considering another issue: the influence of the 'social, collective, experiential dimension' of cinema-going on individual viewers.[27] In a book-length study of 1991, Hansen analysed American movie spectatorship of the silent era from both theoretical and historical perspectives. Spectatorship, she argued, was a conscious construction of the early film industry, which regarded it as a means of integrating socially and ethnically diverse audiences into a new mass culture of consumption. Among other things, this meant replacing the big-city nickelodeon, with its working-class, ethnic audience, variety format and customary sociability, with theatres where spectators drawn from various levels of society were both absorbed in, and subordinated to, the narrative taking place on screen. Despite such efforts, Hansen believed, there may well have been a gulf between what was intended to happen and the response of real, historical audiences. Using the notion of 'oppositional' or 'counter public spheres' developed by Oskar Negt and Alexander Kluge as an extension of Jürgen Habermas's original conception of the public sphere, she found evidence suggesting that early cinema did allow for the emergence of such an alternative social sphere by providing some groups, notably immigrants and women, with a new kind of space in which they could negotiate imaginatively between the images and discourses introduced on screen and their own experiences of life in an increasingly industrial society. 'Active' spectatorship of this type, of course, offered a major contrast to the kind of spectatorship the film industry itself was attempting to achieve.[28]

Since textually constructed spectatorship was regarded as being fundamentally male, it is understandable that feminist film scholars endeavouring to establish and comprehend a female spectator should be interested in going beyond what Hansen termed 'the psychoanalytic-semiotic framework' in order also to examine 'culturally specific and historically variable aspects of reception'.[29] But there were additional reasons for feminist and other film scholars to move away from the issue of how subjects were created by texts in order to focus on how viewers received such texts and the meanings they created from them. In recent literary studies, the increasing salience of the idea that meaning was not something inherent in texts, but was created through the interaction between the text and a particular reader led to a growing number of 'ethnographic' surveys examining the reception of texts or kinds of texts by readers, each with a distinct social and cultural identity, in specific historical circumstances. Jacques Leenhardt, for example, explored the different responses of French and Polish readers to two novels, concluding that each group interpreted them differently as a result of various factors arising from their respective national cultures.[30] In a study that would later often be cited by film studies practitioners as a model of how to reconceptualise the question of reception, Janice Radway examined the manner in which a group of keen female readers of romance novels both constructed their favourite genre and justified their enthusiasm for fiction of this kind.[31]

A second important factor encouraging a new interest in audiences has been the rise of British cultural studies, which emerged in response to a diverse group of influences: ongoing British debates over the nature of Marxism, Saussurean semiotics, the writings of Richard Hoggart, Raymond Williams and E. P. Thompson, together with the Marxist revisionism of Althusser and Antonio Gramsci. Gramsci saw the dominance of the capitalist mode of production and the supremacy of the ruling class as hegemonic: they were not imposed by force so much as secured by the consent of the populations concerned. Yet that consent was itself the product of negotiation and struggle. Cultural practices and texts were deeply embedded in power relationships as a consequence of their important role in ideological interpellation, and as a result they became a principal site of economic, social and political conflict. Proponents of cultural studies, therefore, were dedicated to the attempt to comprehend the political context in which cultural texts and practices were produced. They were also intent on understanding the ways in which readers and audiences actively created meanings from the interaction in specific contexts between cultural products and their own social and cultural identities. A key work in cultural studies was the publication in 1980 of Stuart Hall's essay on 'Encoding/Decoding', outlining three main ways in which readers produce meanings ('decodings') from cultural texts. According to Hall, such decodings were of three kinds: dominant (accepting the ideology concerned), negotiated (accepting or rejecting features of the prevailing ideology in order to shape the text to the reader's own needs) or oppositional (firmly opposed to the prevailing ideology).[32] Decodings themselves were shaped by the class, ethnic and gender characteristics of the readers concerned, and the varied contexts in which reception occurred.

One major example of the cultural studies approach has been the attempt to explore, by ethnographic methods, how audiences 'read' the television programmes they watch. Studies of this sort typically pay considerable attention to the social factors that shape individual viewers' readings of particular texts and also foreground the influence of viewing practices on the groups to which they belong. David Morley's pioneering 1980 analysis of audiences for the BBC current-affairs programme *Nationwide* demonstrated how specific subgroups advanced different readings of the programme in ways reflecting their social, educational and cultural backgrounds and the institutions to which they belonged.[33] Morley's investigation was followed by a steady stream of others, a significant number of which were devoted to the long-running American soap opera, *Dallas*. Ien Ang published her influential study of how *Dallas* was received in The Netherlands in 1985. Eight years later saw the appearance of Tamar Liebes and Elihu Katz's analysis of the varying ways in which the show was interpreted by viewers from differing ethnic and cultural backgrounds.[34]

Ethnographic work on television audiences helped to draw the potentialities of this kind of research to the attention of film scholars. It seemed particularly useful to feminists eager to escape the passive role so often ascribed to women in text-based studies of spectatorship. In 1988, influenced by the cultural studies approach, Jacqueline Bobo published an ethnographic investigation into how black female spectators reacted to *The Color Purple* (1985).[35] Subsequent years saw the appearance of two other important studies of particular female movie audiences: Helen Taylor's 1989 work on British and American fans of *Gone With the Wind* (1939) and the meanings they created for themselves from the film; and Jackie Stacey's 1994 analysis of the place of female Hollywood stars in how a sample of British women remembered the 1940s and 1950s.[36] Ethnographic investigations became steadily more popular in the second half of the 1990s: the contributions by Annette Kuhn, Thomas Austin, Martin Barker and Kate Brooks, Annette Hill and Brigid Cherry in the previous volume of this series were, for example, all based on researches of this sort.[37]

The last few years have also seen the emergence of an alternative view of how films come to be interpreted by spectators. Like their colleagues in ethnography, practitioners of 'reception studies' assume that film texts have no innate, essentialist reading. Instead, they argue that differences in the way in which movies are interpreted are historically based, and therefore change over time. These varying interpretations reflect the context of exhibition, including the influence of prevailing political, social and economic conditions, the interests and expectations of readers, and the manner in which they construct their own identities in terms of gender, race, class, nationality and sexual orientation. Since there are no immanent meanings and since it is clearly impossible to find out the position of every individual spectator, the objective of reception studies is, according to Janet Staiger, to try to establish 'not the so-called correct reading of a particular film but the range of possible readings and reading processes at historical moments'.[38] In *Interpreting Films* (1992), Staiger advanced her own view of why it was essential to develop what she termed 'a historical materialist approach to reception studies'. Such an approach would, she maintained, shed considerable light on 'how politics and culture interweave'. By making it possible 'to trace possible dominant and marginal interpretative strategies available historically', and thereby illuminate 'what is and what is not used', it would act as a useful aid 'for understanding historical processes and the struggle over the meaning of signs'.[39]

In her own work, Staiger has endeavoured to understand how viewers or critics make sense of films and the manner in which the meanings they create are historically contingent. As a result, she does not believe in broad-ranging theoretical frameworks in reception studies, since these will never be able to contain the rich complexity and multiplicity of the reception process. This is a theme she develops in the first chapter of Part One of this book, taking as her main focus the subject of audience talk at the movies. Staiger cites evidence provided by Judith Mayne and Miriam Hansen to show that early movie-goers engaged in lively discussions and debates while films were being shown, thus complicating the issue of how films were actually received. The conventional wisdom, however, holds that talk of this kind on the part of audiences largely ended with the coming of sound. Staiger herself draws attention to exceptions to this rule among fans of *The Rocky Picture Horror Show* (1975), adolescent movie-goers during World War II and members of teenage film-going parties in the 1950s. African-Americans engaging in 'call and response' at times also 'talk back' at the screen. It may be argued that these examples are drawn primarily from minority groups, but Staiger also finds evidence from a variety of exhibition settings – from World War II soldiers at the front through Bogart revivals during the 1960s to contemporary male stag parties – that white middle- and working-class men also engage in talk at movie theatres and, at times, that this habit has been encouraged by movie theatre managers. Imposing boundaries of audience identity or time-period, therefore, Staiger argues, does not help in creating a general theory of audience reception. She uses the example of 'movie talk' to emphasise an additional point: that the reception experience is not synonymous with the time spent watching a film. Viewing a film (with or without talk in the auditorium) is often followed by discussions of it in which spectators rework the text and ascribe new meanings to it.

In the next chapter, Mark Jancovich deals with the historical significance of definitions of genre. He points out that these definitions vary from period to period, in common with understandings of which films belong to the genres concerned. Such variations occur because of the differing ways in which the genres concerned are constructed by critics, audiences and those who produce them. The constructions themselves are unstable: following Pierre Bourdieu, Jancovich perceives them as a reflection of ongoing struggles for cultural authority and power between varying taste formations. Reviews, which provide some sense of the manner in which audiences are supposed to talk about films, play a significant role in these struggles, being products and champions of specific taste formations. To demonstrate how such processes can operate, Jancovich analyses the reception of *The Silence of the Lambs* (1990). Although many reviewers saw the film as offering the pleasures of a horror movie, they acknowledged the low cultural status of the latter and at the same time tried to legitimate the new movie by underlining the differences between *The Silence of the Lambs* and most other horror films (particularly those of the 'slasher' kind). They focused especially on the aesthetic qualities of the film (something already foregrounded in the movie's promotional material) and its sexual politics (the 'feminism' of character Clarice Starling, reinforced by the reputation of Jodie Foster, the actress who played her).

Martin Shingler applies the historical-materialist approach advocated by Janet Staiger to the reception of *All About Eve* (1950). In this film, the principal character, played by Bette Davis, abandons her career in order to embrace domesticity and motherhood. While this was a familiar pattern in American society after World War II, as women increasingly retreated from (or were driven out of) the workforce, it represented a major change in Davis's own star image as an energetic, ambitious and independent woman. As Shingler demonstrates, however, at the time of its release the film circulated within a particular set of social and cultural discourses. On the one hand were the pseudo-scientific arguments of Marynia Farnham and Ferdinand Lundberg, who believed that women should not compete with men in the marketplace and ought to confine their efforts to the areas to which they were best suited: home and family. On the other hand, writers like Margaret Mead and Mary McCarthy argued against the imposition of such limitations. *All About Eve* seemed to support the first of these positions and, therefore, in recent years has often been seen as a typical example of retrogressive gender politics on the part of 1950s Hollywood. Yet, Shingler suggests, it is at least possible that the film was open to different male and female readings. While men may have regarded the film as supporting what was both a social trend and a dominant ideology, women – knowing more of Bette Davis and her films – may well have seen her character's renunciation of career in favour of husband and home as ironic and unbelievable. Adopting a diachronic as well as synchronic approach, Shingler also looks at the very different ways in which *All About Eve* was received in the 1960s and 1970s, as it acquired a whole new range of meanings through its appropriation by gay audiences.

It is hardly ever easy to predict with accuracy which films will succeed with a mass audience and which will not. 'Why', writes Bruce A. Austin, 'do some films "catch on" with the public so quickly, others more slowly, and others not at all?'[40] Disney's *Fantasia* (1940), the subject of Amy M. Davis's chapter, falls into the second of Austin's categories. Poorly received at the time of its first release, it survived to become, by the early 1990s, one of the best-known and highest-grossing films ever made. Moreover, Davis maintains, the meaning of the film changed over time as a consequence of the promotional discourses attached to it. Perceived in 1940 as an experimental attempt to combine animation and classical music, it was marketed primarily to adults rather than children. With its expensive new sound system ('Fantasound'), *Fantasia* was exhibited as a roadshow attraction in a strictly limited number of locations. Davis argues that it was the failure of this strategy (partly as a result of the lack of advertising for the film), rather than any reluctance on the part of Americans to accept 'high culture' through the medium of the mass market, that accounted for the film's initial lack of success. The marketing strategy remained essentially unchanged in subsequent reissues but, aided by growing publicity on TV, the film finally earned back its original cost by the 1960s. Increasingly regarded as a 'classic' (and thus itself now part of 'high culture'), *Fantasia* also eventually profited greatly from the fact that parents who had once seen it in theatres were now buying it on video for their children.

In the next two chapters, Gregory D. Black and G. Tom Poe explore the extent to which critical 'talk' generated by institutions of censorship or government informs or limits the interpretative possibilities available to audiences. Black deals with the changing discourses over film censorship and 'permissible' entertainment existing within the Catholic Church. By the second half of the 1950s, two distinct but overlapping debates had emerged on these issues. One concentrated on whether – and by what right – Catholics should be forbidden from attending certain films by the Legion of Decency, the rating organisation established by the American Roman Catholic Church in 1934. The second debate was that conducted within the Legion of Decency itself over the issue of what was acceptable in terms of movie entertainment. As Black points out, the Legion itself was in many respects a curious organisation: while almost no one in Hollywood (apart from Howard Hughes) was prepared openly to defy it, at least before the 1950s, it was not well regarded within the Catholic hierarchy and exercised little real control over Catholic movie-going. By the late 1950s and early 1960s, however, the Legion of Decency itself was finding the task of classifying films an increasingly difficult one, reflecting the more and more complex range of opinion within the Church itself over what was or was not permissible in movie entertainment. This may have reflected the growing anti-censorship climate in the US in the wake of the supreme court's decision in *Burstyn v. Wilson* (1952). It may also have been influenced by the slightly more liberal line on the cinema advanced in a papal encyclical of 1957. Most important of all, however, Black contends, was change within the Legion itself: the 1957 addition of a Board of Consultors with a membership of up to a hundred drawn from priests and lay members of the Church. The new consultors reflected the growing changes both in the Church itself and the world outside (on some films, priests now found themselves more liberal than their lay colleagues). Movies that would formerly have been condemned out of hand now found themselves the subject of vigorous debate. By analysing divisions within the board (and among Catholic reviewers) over such films as *Splendor in the Grass* (1961) and *Lolita* (1962), Black shows how consensus on what was 'moral' entertainment had collapsed within the Church even before the further liberalisation of attitudes stimulated by Vatican II.

In his chapter, Poe examines the debates, both public and private, relating to *On the Beach* (1959), Stanley Kramer's film dealing with the subject of a nuclear holocaust. There were, Poe argues, many kinds of spectatorship surrounding the film, including representatives of the Production Code Administration who negotiated details of the script, Legion of Decency members who (to opposition from parts of the hierarchy) accepted it, government officials who expressed anxiety over its political effects, political commentators who assessed the film's actual impact, film critics and entertainment reporters, theatre-going audiences and those who at least read about the controversy swirling around it even if they did not see the film itself. Hailed by Nobel laureate Linus Pauling as potentially 'the movie that saved the world', *On the Beach* provoked little comparable enthusiasm on the part of official Washington. Members of the Eisenhower administration worried that the film's grim depiction of nuclear annihilation would undermine support for military expenditure and civil defence programmes. To counter this, they had briefings prepared by State Department and Pentagon personnel on how to handle questions on the scientific accuracy of the movie. The substance of these briefings found its way into speeches by military and civil defence officials, into some press reports and into a number of hostile reviews. But, Poe believes, the government's ability to influence how spectators reacted to the film proved in the end very limited. *On the Beach* was a relative commercial failure, but for other reasons.

While the essays in Part One of this volume re-examine concepts of spectatorship in the light of historical accounts of audience reception, those in Part Two engage directly with the theoretical paradigm of spectatorship which has dominated film studies in recent decades. From the late 1960s onward, Christian Metz was probably the most influential figure in the evolution of the new field, partly – as Judith Mayne has pointed out – because his own intellectual evolution, starting with semiotics and moving on to psychoanalysis, closely reflected the development of the discipline as a whole.[41] In his essay 'The Imaginary Signifier' (1975), Metz analysed the notion of the screen as mirror from a Lacanian perspective. The principal difference between a screen mirror and a real mirror, he observed, was the fact that movie spectators could not see themselves in the screen mirror. Yet this was not a problem, Metz argued, because the spectator had sufficient experience with mirrors (or the mirror phase) that she or he did not need to see her or his own body on screen in order to make the images there intelligible.[42]

Jane M. Gaines, in her essay for this volume, interrogates Metz's comments on 'mirroring' from the point of view of race formation, basing her arguments on an analysis of James Baldwin's recollections of movie spectatorship in *The Devil Finds Work* (1976). As a young African American, Baldwin found that the all-white films he saw offered no images that were actually like himself (and thus could be used as a basis for easy identification). Instead, he sought to create an identity for himself on the basis of a fundamental misrecognition, appropriating selected features of the white female stars he saw in these movies, most notably Joan Crawford and Bette Davis. In part, this represented an attempt to transform the screen into his own mirror. By redefining Crawford as 'black' and focusing on the fact that he and Davis both had similar 'frog eyes', Baldwin demonstrated the possibility of such a transformation (and, at the same time, suggested the possible interchangeability of racial categories). In part also, however, it was a recognition of the limits to such identifications (the screen can never be a true mirror). Baldwin, in the end, saw himself and Davis as united not by colour (at one stage he described her as neither white nor black but green) but by the fact that, in their ugliness, both were essentially 'strange'. As Gaines points out, in Baldwin's definition of himself and Davis as 'strange', there is at least a hint of Baldwin's own later camp personality. Modern queer theory assumes that identities are invariably invented rather than just received or given. Baldwin himself, as a young film spectator, made use of an eclectic process of appropriation from white female stars in order to help construct an adult identity that was both black and homosexual.

Gianluca Sergi points out that most studies of movie spectatorship are almost entirely concerned with the visual: the processes by which images are consumed. But spectators are listeners as well, and the ways in which they listen may be seen to have a considerable impact on the meanings they construct from the filmic experience. This has become particularly true over the last three decades, as Hollywood, responding to a range of factors – new technology, the enthusiasm of younger directors and, in particular, the perceived commercial necessity of appealing to the 15 to 30 age group – has encouraged the introduction of new sound systems into movie theatres. Whereas the spectator had previously been placed before a filmic space (the screen), she or he was now placed inside one. A combination of new technology, advanced cinema architecture (to meet acoustic demands) and expressive (rather than reproduced) sound turned modern movie theatres into three-dimensional 'sonic playgrounds' where 'super-listeners' could become actively involved in making sense out of the proliferation of aural sensations around them. As Sergi comments, this view of the spectator as an active listener – creating meanings from a diversity of sounds arising from several distinct soundtracks – contrasts greatly with the theoretical spectator of much recent film writing, who has usually been depicted as a passive figure positioned in front of the screen by the cinematic apparatus. Moreover, Sergi notes that spectators watching films at home, while often able to enjoy cinema-like sound, have the potential to be even more active, since they have the freedom to manipulate nearly all aspects of a film's soundtrack.

While the notion of a cinema at home is not a new one – one million American households already owned movie cameras in 1948[43] – it is only in recent years, with the advent of cable and satellite TV and the introduction of VCRs, laserdiscs and DVDs, that home has become the main locus of movie-watching. Instead of the experience of watching films on a big screen in a darkened public theatre, most Americans now view them in the private sphere of their own homes. This has meant, of course, that classical notions of film spectatorship have become increasingly irrelevant and outmoded. In her chapter for this volume, Barbara Klinger contributes to a reappraisal of the whole notion of spectatorship by repositioning the modern spectator as a connoisseur. Deliberately focusing on the élite collector building a film archive for exhibition on the most technically advanced equipment, Klinger demonstrates how the modern cinephile differs from the figure once apotheosised by Metz and other psychoanalytical film theorists. Unlike earlier collectors, the present-day connoisseur prizes the new above the old. Subscribing to a 'hardware aesthetic', he (in this group it is usually he) judges films not on the basis of their artistic qualities, their relation to particular directors or genres, or favourable critical evaluations but mainly as vehicles for the performance and assessment of the latest exhibition technologies. Recognising the importance of film collectors in economic terms, the industry has targeted them as a niche audience, addressing them as movie 'insiders' and offering special 'collector's or 'limited' editions of movies. Even if the films concerned are old 'classics', however, the modern connoisseur still expects them to conform to today's rigorous standards of technical quality. As films have moved from the public to the private sphere, therefore, abandoning their role as abstract artefacts to become household objects, the nature and preoccupations of their spectatorship have also changed.

The development of theoretical notions of spectatorship in the late 1960s and after was characterised by two crucial ironies. Although initially inspired by French theorists, it was from the beginning primarily concerned with American spectators for classical

Hollywood. Furthermore, since classical Hollywood (at least as defined as a system of production) is generally thought to have come to an end around 1960, its spectatorship had already receded well into the historical past before its reappearance as a focus of scholarly debate. Alain J.-J. Cohen, in the last chapter of this book, explores the implications for now traditional notions of 'the spectator' of the recent technological innovations that have expanded access to film in exponential ways. The early twentieth century witnessed the initial attempts to construct a film spectatorship that would understand narrative conventions and become involved in the fictional world depicted on screen. This was the spectatorship, positioned by the cinematic apparatus, that would later be investigated and mapped by Metz and other film writers. Yet, even while this work of theorising spectatorship was under way, an alternative view of the spectator was beginning to emerge among, in particular, a number of European directors. These men and women, themselves highly knowledgeable as spectators of Hollywood cinema, wove intertextual fragments of that cinema into their own work, anticipating to an extent the possible later emergence of a 'hyper-spectator'. As Hollywood evolves into a 'virtual' Hollywood of creations and products, Cohen contends, the original constructions of classical spectatorship seem increasingly outmoded. He suggests the necessity of theorising a new kind of spectator: the virtual or hyper-spectator. Like the original spectator, the hyper-spectator is very largely a product of technological change, in this case the advent of new modes of film exhibition, including cable and satellite TV, VCRs, laser-discs and DVDs, and new processes such as digitalisation.

Cohen, in effect, announces the death of the classical spectator, and his/her replacement by a new figure representing a further extension of the kind of connoisseur viewer described by Barbara Klinger in Chapter 10. Unlike the classical spectator, the hyper-spectator is not predominantly passive, having acquired – through new technologies – the ability both to enter and shape (as well as be shaped by) the filmic universe encountered in hyper-space. At the dawn of the twenty-first century, therefore, as classical Hollywood retreats still further into history, the form of spectatorship associated most closely with it is in the process of being replaced by something more self-consciously indeterminate, in the form of the eclectic movements of hyper-spectators through what increasingly comes to appear as an electronic version of Borges's library.

Notes

1 Judith Mayne, *Cinema and Spectatorship* (London and New York: Routledge, 1993), p. 5.
2 Louis Althusser, 'Ideology and Ideological State Apparatuses (Notes Towards an Investigation)', in *Lenin and Philosophy*, trans. Ben Brewster (London: New Left Books, 1971), pp. 127–86. Robert Sklar would later write that this essay 'probably had more impact on the concept of "history" in the fledging years of cinema studies than all the works of the world's historians piled on end'. Sklar, 'Oh! Althusser!': Historiography and the Rise of Cinema Studies', *Radical History Review*, vol. 41 (spring 1988), reprinted in Robert Sklar and Charles Musser (eds), *Resisting Images: Essays in Cinema and History* (Philadelphia: Temple University Press, 1990), p. 13.
3 Althusser, 'Ideology and Ideological State Apparatuses', pp. 124, 127–8, 131–2, 136–8, 141–2, 146, 153, 160, 162–3, 169, 171.
4 Mayne, *Cinema and Spectatorship*, pp. 20–1.

5   Robert Stam, 'Contemporary Film Theory', in Gary Crowdus (ed.), *The Political Companion to American Film* (Chicago: Lakeview Press, 1994), p. 78.

6   The best-known effort to apply these ideas was the detailed analysis of the text of *Young Mr Lincoln* (1939). See 'John Ford's *Young Mr Lincoln*: A Collective Text by the Editors of *Cahiers du Cinéma*', trans. Helen Lackner and Diana Matias, *Screen*, vol. 13, no. 3 (autumn 1972), pp. 5–44.

7   In the United States in 1967, only 200 colleges offered film-related courses; by 1977, the number had grown to more than a thousand. Robert C. Allen and Douglas Gomery, *Film History: Theory and Practice* (New York: McGraw Hill, 1985), p. 27.

8   On the adoption of Althusserian views in cinema studies in Britain, see Jane Gaines, 'White Privilege and Looking Relations: Race and Gender in Feminist Film Theory', *Cultural Critique,* no. 4 (autumn 1986), pp. 62–3.

9   Laura Mulvey, 'Visual Pleasure and Narrative Cinema', *Screen,* vol. 16, no. 3 (autumn 1975), pp. 6–18.

10 Sklar, '*Oh! Althusser!*', p. 13.

11 Jostein Gripsrud, 'Film Audiences', in John Hill and Pamela Church-Gibson (eds), *The Oxford Companion to Film Studies* (Oxford: Oxford University Press, 1998), p. 209.

12 Robert C. Allen, 'From Exhibition to Reception: Reflections on the Audience in Film History', *Screen,* vol. 31, no. 4 (winter 1990), p. 348.

13 Two major cities (Chicago and New York) and three states (Pennsylvania, Kansas and Ohio) had already established censorship boards before the outbreak of the World War I. In 1909, the movie industry itself encouraged the creation of the New York Board of Motion Picture Censorship, later known as the National Board of Review of Motion Pictures.

14 See, for example, Jane Addams's comments on children attending the five-cent theatres where movies were shown: Addams, *The Spirit of Youth and the City Streets* (New York: Macmillan, 1909), pp. 75–6, 86–7, 93. On the role of children in reformist debates of the time, see Roberta Pearson and William Uricchio, ' "The Formative and Impressionable Stage": Discursive Constructions of the Nickelodeon's Child Audience', in Melvyn Stokes and Richard Maltby (eds), *American Movie Audiences: From the Turn of the Century to the Early Sound Era* (London: BFI, 1999), pp. 64–75.

15 Garth Jowett, 'Giving Them What They Want: Movie Research Before 1950', in Bruce A. Austin (ed.), *Current Research in Film: Audiences, Economics and Law,* vol. I (Norwood, NJ: Ablex, 1985), pp. 23–8; Richard Koszarski, *An Evening's Entertainment: The Age of the Silent Feature Picture 1915–28* (Berkeley, CA: University of California Press, 1990), pp. 28–30.

16 Henry J. Forman, *Our Movie-Made Children* (New York: Macmillan, 1933). See also Werrett W. Charters, *Motion Pictures and Youth* (New York: Macmillan, 1933).

17 Most of the Payne Fund Studies were published in 1933. The Production Code (Hollywood's system of self-regulation) established in 1930 was appreciably tightened in 1934 and a Production Code Administration set up.

18 Mayne, *Cinema and Spectatorship,* p. 99.

19 As Richard Maltby has argued in a previous volume of this series, Hollywood knew more about its audiences than this scenario suggests. See Maltby, 'Sticks, Hicks and Flaps: Classical Hollywood's generic conception of its audiences', in Melvyn Stokes and

Richard Maltby (eds), *Identifying Hollywood's Audiences: Cultural Identity and the Movies* (London: BFI, 1999), pp. 23–41.

20 C. A. Palmer, 'Commercial Practices in Audience Analysis', *Journal of the University Film Association*, 6 (spring 1954), p. 9.

21 Susan Ohmer, 'The Science of Pleasure: George Gallup and Audience Research in Hollywood', in Stokes and Maltby (eds), *Identifying Hollywood's Audiences*, pp. 68–70.

22 Ibid., p. 76.

23 Thomas Doherty, *Teenagers and Teenpics: The Juvenilization of American Movies in the 1950s* (Boston: Unwin Hyman, 1988), pp. 62–5, 230–4.

24 Janet Staiger, 'The Handmaiden of Villainy: Methods and Problems in Studying the Historical Reception of a Film', *Wide Angle*, vol. 8, no. 1 (1986), p. 21.

25 Annette Kuhn, 'Women's Genres', *Screen*, 25, no. 1 (January–February 1984), pp. 18–28; Janet Bergstrom and Mary Ann Doane (eds), *Camera Obscura*, 20–1 (1989), special issue on the spectatrix; Tania Modleski, 'Some Functions of Feminist Criticism, or the Scandal of the Mute Body', *October*, 49 (1989), p. 4.

26 E. Deidre Pribram (ed.), *Female Spectators: Looking at Film and Television* (London: Verso, 1988).

27 Miriam Hansen, untitled, *Camera Obscura*, 20–1 (1989), p. 169.

28 Miriam Hansen, *Babel and Babylon: Spectatorship in American Silent Film* (Cambridge, MA: Harvard University Press, 1991), especially pp. 8, 61–2, 70–6, 83, 99, 114–20.

29 Ibid., p. 5.

30 Jacques Leenhardt, 'Towards a Sociology of Reading', trans. Brigitte Navelet and Susan R. Suleiman, in Suleiman and Inge Crosman (eds), *The Reader in the Text: Essays on Audience and Interpretation* (Princeton, NJ: Princeton University Press, 1980), pp. 205–24.

31 Janice Radway, *Reading the Romance: Women, Patriarchy and Popular Culture* (Chapel Hill, NC: University of North Carolina Press, 1984).

32 Stuart Hall, 'Encoding/Decoding', in Stuart Hall, Dorothy Hobson, Andrew Lowe and Paul Willis (eds), *Culture, Media, Language* (London: Hutchinson, 1980), pp. 128–38.

33 David Morley, *The 'Nationwide' Audience: Structure and Decoding* (London: BFI, 1980).

34 Ien Ang, *Watching 'Dallas': Soap Opera and the Melodramatic Imagination* (London: Methuen, 1985); Tamar Liebes and Elihu Katz, *The Export of Meaning* (Cambridge: Polity Press, 1993).

35 Jacqueline Bobo, '*The Color Purple*: Black Women as Cultural Readers', in Pribram (ed.), *Female Spectators*, pp. 90–109.

36 Helen Taylor, *Scarlett's Women: 'Gone With the Wind' and Its Female Fans* (London: Virago, 1989); Jackie Stacey, *Star Gazing: Hollywood Cinema and Female Spectatorship* (London: Routledge, 1994).

37 Kuhn, ' "That Day Did Last Me All My Life": Cinema Memory and Enduring Fandom'; Thomas Austin, ' "Desperate to See It": Straight Men Watching *Basic Instinct*'; Martin Barker and Kate Brooks, 'Bleak Futures by Proxy'; Annette Hill, 'Risky Business: Film Violence as an Interactive Phenomenon'; and Brigid Cherry, 'Refusing to Look: Female Viewers of the Horror Film'; all in Stokes and Maltby (eds), *Identifying Hollywood's Audiences*, pp. 135–203.

38 Staiger, 'The Handmaiden of Villainy', p. 20.

39 Janet Staiger, *Interpreting Films: Studies in the Historical Reception of American Cinema* (Princeton, NJ: Princeton University Press, 1992), pp. 15, 93.

40 Bruce A. Austin, 'The Motion Picture Audience: A Neglected Aspect of Film Research', in Austin, *The Film Audience: An International Bibliography of Research* (Metuchen, NJ: Scarecrow Press, 1983), p. xxxiv. Besides a number of additional articles on audiences, Austin has also published *Immediate Seating: A Look at Movie Audiences* (Belmont, CA: Wadsworth, 1989).

41 Mayne, *Cinema and Spectatorship,* p. 39.

42 Christian Metz, *The Imaginary Signifier: Psychoanalysis and the Cinema,* trans. Celia Britton, Annwyl Williams, Ben Brewster and Alfred Guzetti (1975; Bloomington, IN: Indiana University Press, 1982).

43 Allen, 'From Exhibition to Reception', p. 350.

PART ONE

Talking Pictures: The Reception of Hollywood

1
Writing the History of American Film Reception

Janet Staiger

This chapter is part of a sequence of reflections about theoretical and historiographical issues in writing the history of American film reception. In an essay entitled 'Modes of Reception', I have argued against a tendency in film studies to create two large categories of texts or exhibition situations, to pit those against each other, and then to make vast claims about spectator effect from that binary opposition.[1] Although such broad generalisations may have had an initial schematic purpose in the study of American film, they do not hold up historically. Instead, the entire history of cinema in every period, and most likely in every place, witnesses several modes of cinematic address, several modes of exhibition and several modes of reception. Moreover, any individual viewer may engage *even within the same theatre-going experience* in these various modes of reception.

A second essay, 'The Perversity of Spectators', provides an alternative system for examining the modes of reception to the binary oppositions I am criticising.[2] Based on the work of Russian formalists, Meir Sternberg, David Bordwell and Kristin Thompson, the system summarises and expands upon what these scholars have claimed to be the reception activities for a narrative film of the 'classical' type.

Research on actual viewers of classical films, however, suggests that they engage in an extensive variety of activities which do not conform to predictions postulated by formalist critics of spectators and readers. For example, film scholars often criticise *The Big Sleep* as having an incoherent plot. At the time of the film's release, reviewers also described the plot as confusing, but suggested that the violence (they tended to count the number of murders), sexual innuendo and their pleasure in watching Humphrey Bogart and Lauren Bacall provided more than adequate compensation. Some of these writers viewed the film's disconnected narrative positively, comparing its effects to experiences of nightmares or opium smoking.[3] Research on viewers of romances and melodramas shows that consistency in characterisation does not matter to their audiences. Studies of gay viewers of Judy Garland movies or male adolescent viewers of horror films indicate that people do not always make same-sex identifications. Viewers ignore endings of films and fantasise alternative outcomes, or propel secondary characters into the focal points of the narration or choose to identify with the villain instead of the hero. Camp and 'paracinema'[4] viewers have more interest in *mise-en-scène* and excessive acting than in verisimilitude. Instead, they enjoy the process of 'dishing'[5] the text and reading in 'ironic detachment'.[6] In summary, for nearly every expectation about normative readings of classical texts, a 'perversion' can be found.

The system, then, is useful for noting types of strategies in richer detail than the triad of preferred, negotiated and resistant readings. Additionally, one could also track the receptions of a film across a period of time. An example of such a tracking is contained in my book, *Interpreting Films*.[7] One chapter analyses the political and aesthetic debates around *The Birth of a Nation* over a period of fifty years, describing how the debates surrounding the film in 1915 became transformed in the World War II era as the film continued to be shown despite protests.

Another angle on this system is its potential function in studying discourses around a culture event in which a film might participate. In 'Taboos and Totems', instead of studying a full set of discourses around the film *The Silence of the Lambs*, I explore how a segment of gay male readers used the film to try to 'out' its star, Jodie Foster, as a lesbian.[8] My interest here was not in surveying all the receptions of the film but in how the film could be appropriated by a specific group for a political act of resistance against what they perceived was the possibility of reading the serial killer as a homosexual.

In this chapter, I want to take up the broad problem of studying media reception. Most scholars of reception construct arguments that create boundaries around the reception experience, considering only the time a viewer is engaged with the text. Such a strategy regards the text as an artefact that determines the behaviour of the audience. If the film is a classical Hollywood narrative, then the viewer adopts a voyeuristic reception mode, becoming absorbed in the plot and identifying with the characters. If, however, the film is a text of spectacle and visual or aural stimulation, the viewer takes up an exhibitionist mode of reception and responds critically or with distraction. Some scholars go on to argue that the latter type of film is popular (of the people), modern or postmodern, with the classical film usually labelled 'bourgeois' or pre-modern.[9] The boundaries constraining the audience in this theoretical framework are the stylistic practices of the text. This argument is, however, deeply problematic. If the text were, in fact, determining in the way suggested, all of the perversions, changes and appropriations described above would be impossible.

Even those film scholars who argue that the viewing context can improve the possibility of a wider range of readings or audience experiences themselves construct new boundaries, as I shall discuss below. The two boundaries constructed by contextual theorists on which I shall focus are historical time-periods (pre-sound, sound/classical, post-classical) and audience identities (class, race, ethnicity, age, sexual orientation, gender). In the concluding part of the chapter, I shall also consider a third boundary embedded in many contextual studies, which is constructed around the assumption that the time spent watching the film is the context of the event.

Talking in the Theatre

In an important and under-recognised essay published in 1982, Judith Mayne argues that the immigrant experience in the nickelodeon may have been more complex than scholars had previously understood. She posits that, while the immigrant was being familiarised with American culture and consumerism through the 'shopping window' of the screen, the collective experience within the theatre should also be considered as a potential force for promoting resistance to industrialisation and, for women, to the patriarchal home.[10] The nickelodeons bestowed on immigrants an unprecedented status as worthy consumer. Moreover, the exhibition site functioned as a mediation between public and private spheres. Descriptions by contemporary writers such as Mary Heaton

Vorse in 1911 indicate a lively exchange of audience commentary and debate at the exhibition site, and Mayne argues that such an exhibition context increases the complexity of the movies' reception.[11]

Miriam Hansen has developed Mayne's original idea by drawing on German theories of the public sphere, but she also combines Mayne's observations about the nickelodeon scene with binary text-determinant reception theories.[12] This results in Hansen constructing a bifurcated history, in which exhibition situations that permit a 'public sphere' dialogue among the participants have some potential for contemplative, distractive viewing, while exhibition situations that close down this dialogue reduce spectators to an absorbed, identifying viewing position. Hansen places great weight on the effect of the arrival of mechanically synchronised sound, which permitted on-screen diegetic dialogue. The screen's commanding talk shuts down the audience's chat. That Hansen sees this as seminal is reinforced in her discussion of recent viewing situations, where she states that the effects of watching films in homes in 'institutionally less regulated viewing situations' has had some effect on increasing talk in ordinary movie theatres.[13] The question I want to ask is: is this claim about the effects of the ability to talk during a movie an appropriate dividing line in the theorisation of audiences and media reception? What do we know about talking in the American film theatre? Did the arrival of sound cut off talk? Were some audience groups who would like to have continued to chat constrained by other audience members who prohibited community dialogue? Were the contemplative, distractive opportunities shut down and reduced to an absorbed, identifying experience?

We do know that talk by minority groups has occurred during some types of screenings. A famous example of this phenomenon, the screenings of *The Rocky Horror Picture Show*, started during the transitional post-classical period, which Hansen describes as a time in which opportunities for a public-sphere experience were renewed. *The Rocky Horror Picture Show* opened in New York City in 1975. By 1976, 'counterpoint dialogue' had started. Although it still persists, *The Rocky Horror Picture Show* scene has come to serve a different minority group. Once a haven for urban gay men, the current audience is predominantly young adolescent males, and dialogue lines once extolling sexual freedom and gender-bending are less common while homophobic and misogynist remarks are common.[14]

The Rocky Horror Picture Show, however, came out of a wider party scene in the New York underground cinema movement of the 1960s. From the early 1960s, through the Warhol media events at the Dom in St Marks' Place in 1966 and beyond, the late-night taboo-breaking exhibition situation was an environment appealing to non-conformist but often white, and usually male, hipsters and sexually liberated people. Often with a liberal to leftist agenda, but not necessarily non-sexist, films such as *Flaming Creatures* (1963), *Chelsea Girls* (1966–7), and *Cocks and Cunts* (1963–6) challenged not only heterosexual, monogamous mores but very often taboos against interracial sexuality. Accounts of these screenings make it clear that they were quite rowdy, with people vocally expressing their judgements of the films. Smoking and ingesting illicit drugs helped contribute to a casual viewing context.[15]

This underground scene was not the scene of the classical film, so it does not serve as an example of talk during the watching of classical films. The New York hip scene did, however, have *its* own precedents in situations in which classical Hollywood films were screened. This context is the teenage film-going parties of the 1950s, where attendance at drive-ins or even four-wall theatres featuring showmanship gimmicks promoting grade-B horror and thriller films scarcely encouraged an absorbed, identifying spectator.[16] Accounts of the audiences encountering the surprise of buzzers under their chairs suddenly going off during *The Tingler* (1959) or a skeleton flying across the auditorium at the climax of *House on Haunted Hill* (1958) suggest some exhibitors of Hollywood movies were interested in a much more lively experience than the quiet that was expected at other 1950s screenings.[17] They also remind us that the dialogue activity for *Scream* (1996) is nothing new.

In fact, such teen-screening (and screaming) parties even pre-date the 1950s. During World War II, adolescent and pre-adolescent audiences were identified as a major problem for theatres. With a scarcity of day-care centres and more funds available to youth as a consequence of the war economy in which jobs were now available to them, kids attended the movie theatres more often, stayed later (often to midnight even on week nights), and had no parental supervision. 'Juvenile delinquency' became a commonly reported complaint in relation to young audiences. In Indianapolis, juveniles were 'slashing seats, breaking light globes and committing other acts of vandalism'. Chicago exhibitors reported smoking damage, screens 'riddled with pins till they look like waffles', and kids dropping things from the balcony. Moreover, 'sex crimes have been committed in dark houses with insufficient help to patrol them properly'. Managers witnessed mothers dropping off children under the age of six and then heading off to shop.[18] Our image of 1940s audiences as quietly engrossed in the most recent Hollywood film needs to be revised by inserting many more adolescents and pre-teens into the theatres and questioning the presumed 'silence' that existed there.

Several groups including minorities have, then, used the exhibition site as a public space not only to talk to one another (an important aspect of community and the public sphere) but also to talk back to the screen. Groups served by this community space

A Nickelodeon audience

include gays and straights, sexual and political liberals, conservatives and teenagers. Many of the members of these groups are marginalised by age, although studies also suggest that they are typically white and often middle class.[19]

Talk at theatres is not, however, confined to the white and middle- or working-class adolescent or young urban male. A less-studied but important example is the 'call-and-response' talk common among African-American audiences. In a description of two recent screenings, Kevin L. Carter describes black audience commentary about *Independence Day* (1996), starring Will Smith:

> On screen, as a huge alien spacecraft hovers threateningly over downtown Los Angeles, weirdos and trendies party on the roof of an LA skyscraper and excitedly await the aliens' arrival. MAN and WOMAN in audience respond to the images on screen.
>
> Man: Look at that. Do you notice one thing? There aren't any black people up there! We aren't stupid enough to stay around waiting for no aliens.
> Woman: They'd be on the way out of there.
> Man: I know I'd be out of Dodge.[20]

While the reference to the western genre by this male audience member suggests how astute audiences can be about what they are seeing, this remark can be seen as no more than an example of resistant commentary among two audience members. Carter cites another example of 'call-and-response' that is surely expressed by its speaker for reasons other than being a contemplative, distracted or 'oppositional' viewer:

> Scene 2: Interior, local movie theatre, weeknight showing of 'Eraser'. VANESSA WILLIAMS has just made a harrowing escape from some BAD GUYS and is panicked. The FEDS assure her that, even though she's risking her life to put the BAD GUYS in jail, she'll be protected.
>
> Fed: Don't worry, you'll be fine.
> Williams: No, I'm not going to be fine.
> Man in audience: Vanessa, you'll always be fine![21]

Carter continues his discussion by suggesting that not all African-Americans appreciate call-and-response. One 15-year-old female told him: 'I think it's one of the rudest things someone can do … It makes it very hard for a listener to hear what's going on in a movie.'[22] This reaction, as well as other studies of African-American audiences, suggests that class – or gender – identity may produce divisions within the wider racial–ethnic identity.[23]

The examples of talk described so far might be characterised as belonging to members of minority groups, albeit of different kinds. Is it possibly the case that the most obvious non-minority group – white, heterosexual, adult, middle-class males – are listeners who sit silently at the movies? Once over the troublesome teen years, do they become responsible bourgeois viewers? The answer is: not in all cases. In some particular circumstances, this audience will talk at the movies.

One such particular circumstance is the all-male stag party or exploitation movie which some white, heterosexual, adult, middle-class (and working-class) men attend. Now I have only attended one stag-movie party with a mostly male audience, but silence was the last thing any of them wanted. Teasing, joking and general verbal showing-off were the prevalent behaviours – possibly because, if quiet had occurred, the sexual tension and potential homoerotic possibilities might have become too apparent. Other people's informal accounts to me of these events, moreover, suggest that my experience was typical.

Another example of this group of people talking during movies is while watching Hollywood movies at the front during World War II. Research by Bill Fagelson indicates that soldiers indulged in the same kind of cynical 'call-and-response' backtalk to Hollywood movies that I have described as characterising the response of some African-Americans.[24] Moreover, the content of the backtalk can be linked to the soldiers' broader context. Often their verbal comments criticised what the men considered were the unrealistic movie representations of the war conditions. They also resented male stars who escaped induction into the service.

Both of these occasions for talk by the most 'dominant' audience group might be explained by their exhibition situations – illicit stag movie-parties or rag-taggle, *ad hoc* screenings at the front. And the former group of movies certainly does not suggest any kind of 'classical' text. Yet, evidence does exist from differing periods that talk by this dominant group occurred at least occasionally in 'classical' exhibition situations in which appropriate behaviour was expected. According to Richard Jewell, at the preview screening of *The Magnificent Ambersons* (1942) in Pomona, California, 'the audience detested the picture, laughing in the wrong places, talking back to the screen and decrying its "artiness" in their preview card comments'.[25] In 1965, the *New York Times* reported that, at revivals of Humphrey Bogart films, the audience 'shouts the dialogue'. The audience members themselves are described by the reporter as 'collegiate and post-collegiate – a welter of dungarees, war-surplus coats and tweed jackets with a scattering of beards, mustaches and students in motorcycle boots'.[26]

The hypothesis that classical Hollywood exhibitors took the exhibition scene totally seriously and as something to be preserved inviolate is also questionable. During the supposed heyday of the classical film in the 1930s and 1940s, movie houses were used as community halls in which exhibitors promoted movie-going by prizes for games, and in addition they displayed their civic responsibility by soliciting for bond drives. Although the audience might settle down for the main feature, a lively 'public-sphere' environment was not excluded but actually encouraged. Moreover, even the main feature could be interrupted if audience preferences required. Arthur Frank Wertheim has observed that the radio comedy *Amos 'n' Andy* was so popular in the early 1930s that 'motion picture theaters installed loudspeakers in lobbies and stopped whatever film was being shown so that fans could hear the program over a radio placed on the stage'.[27]

While many writers during these years complained about interference from people's talk, not all white, middle-class bourgeois men supported the 'quiet-during-the-movie' mode of spectating. The progressive poet and democrat Vachel Lindsay argued in the late 1910s for a 'conversation theater':

I suggest suppressing the orchestra entirely and encouraging the audience to talk about the film … With Christopher Morley … I was trying to prove out this [thesis]. As the orchestra stopped, while the show rolled on in glory, I talked about the main points in this book, illustrating it by the film before us. Almost everything that happened was a happy illustration of my ideas. But there were two shop girls in front of us awfully in love with a certain second-rate actor who insisted on kissing the heroine every so often, and with her apparent approval. Every time we talked about that those shop girls glared at us as though we were robbing them of their time and money. Finally, one of them dragged the other out into the aisle, and dashed out of the house with her dear chum, saying, so all could hear, 'Well, come on, Teresa, we might as well go if those two talking *pests* are going to keep this up behind us'. The poor girl's voice trembled. She was in tears. She was gone before we could apologize or offer flowers.[28]

Lindsay went on to suggest that, if the reader planned to follow his suggestion, perhaps he should sit toward the front of the auditorium so that only those he was talking to – and 'Little Mary' Pickford – would hear what was being said.

This example upsets the stereotypical view of American film reception. Middle-class, white men are urging talking during the film, albeit quietly and so as not to bother other people, while working-class women attempt to constrain Lindsay and Morley's behaviour with the classic tactic of the scathing gaze. They did in 1918 what we do today. I concede that the reason the women want the men to stop talking here is because they cannot become absorbed in the romance unfolding before them. And I will also accept the fact that talk disrupts the illusionistic experience. But these sets of etiquette at the movies seem unconvincingly aligned with audience identities or with historical time-periods. I have already provided examples of differing audience identities talking through all historical periods of the classical Hollywood film at several types of films – the horror, the thriller, the war movie, the male melodrama and the romance. The boundaries of audience identity or historical time-period are inadequate as dividing lines to carve up history unilaterally and support a general theory of audience reception.

Significantly, a recent study of the movement toward a quiet, attentive audience mode implies that, while listening intently may be a bourgeois protocol, the configuration of relations may be different from what has been posited by film scholars arguing that middle-class norms managed to shut down talk in the film theatres in order to position people to attend fully to films which were reproducing them as ideological subjects. James H. Johnson, in *Listening in Paris,* asks why the Parisian audiences became silent at musical events. During the reign of Louis XV, from 1715 to 1774, the expected behaviour of the aristocracy was to circulate throughout the theatre, conversing with friends and occasionally enjoying the spectacle of the machinery, dancing and the *filles d'opéra* (the women dancers). Johnson writes that one 'young nobleman explained to his guest that listening to the music with focused attention was "bourgeois". "There is nothing so damnable", he went on, "as listening to a work like a street merchant or some provincial just off the boat"'. Johnson comments that, 'For these spectators, attentiveness was a social *faux pas*'.[29]

Johnson concludes that while listening attentively became the dominant convention (as the bourgeoisie replaced the aristocracy as the principal audience at the theatre), the move to silence during the show was also a consequence of changes in the physical features of the hall (related to the politics of the French Revolution), the musical and theatrical qualities of the works, and altered desires and expectations about aesthetics. In the mid-eighteenth century, music was supposed to be so obvious that careful listening was not required. Toward the end of the century, aesthetics and musical trends moved toward emphasising emotionalism and personalised connections to the spectacle. Expectations of audiences and appropriate behaviour might now include crying during an opera. By the early 1800s, 'Grand Opera was spectacle, an updated mix of revolutionary-era scenes of masses crowding the stage and Napoleonic glitter'.[30] The props and costumes were more realistic but also varied and plentiful; 'hair-raising dénouements' were praised; and the music was powerful and percussive. So much was going on in the theatres that the new audience of the bourgeoisie needed to pay attention. While Johnson connects silence in the auditoria with the bourgeoisie, spectacle, stimulation and melodrama also all drove that choice. It is a choice away from talk, but it is the aristocracy who had been the talkers – pandering to their vanity, showing off and gossiping among their peers.[31]

Johnson's observation also reminds us that talk-as-talk is not necessarily talk of the serious kind implied by the phrase, 'the public sphere'. What determines talk in the theatre? Certainly the context, and not the text. Who is watching, what the occasion is and whether the situation is serious or play – all of these matters seem pertinent. But audience identity or exhibition situation (such as mechanically synchronised sound) will not always match up with a listening or a talking audience. More importantly, if the question relates to the potential for progressive or conservative audience effects, looking at *what is being said* matters too. Praising talk in the theatre is all very well, but a lot of talk is not talk that promotes democratic discussion, intelligent dialogue or a progressive critique of the movie's plot. As I pointed out at the start of this chapter, the boundaries of audience identity and historical time-period do not help to write the history of American film reception nor, as I have detailed here, does the existence or nonexistence of talk in the auditorium. Thus, how do we write the history of American film reception? We avoid binaries; we consider history as more complex and contradictory; we study in depth the context of the theatres; and, most significantly, we figure out what people are thinking, feeling and saying.

Beyond Talking in the Theatre

I suggested a third boundary may also be limiting the writing of reception history: assuming that the time spent watching the film is the context of the event. Some scholars of reception write as though 'experiencing' the text stops at the end of the show. Even if the audience has been perfectly bourgeois and quiet during the movie, talk happens afterwards, often in great quantity. To analyse the ideological, cultural and personal effects of film-viewing, considering post-movie talk by spectators is exceptionally important. Here, the work of cultural studies and analysis of fandom contributes to writing the history of American film reception.

Beyond presumed normative reception activities

Terminology based on film and television viewing, but applicable to other types of text.

Physical and expressive activities during the event

Extent of this will depend on contextual factors such as:

- site of event: four-wall theatre, exploitation house, drive-in, party, bar viewing night, home
- genre of the text
- social mix/dynamics: all-male stag party; adolescent males in a group with women; broadly-viewed social ritual (such as televised wedding or funeral).

Activities:
- meta-talking – discussion of the narration and text-as-text
- talking to characters
- talking to 'author'
- talking with companions such as
  - bringing them up to date on the events
  - explaining character motives
  - translating cultural ambiguities
- repeating memorised lines of dialogue from film (repeat viewers)
- expressing affective and emotional states – laughing, crying, screaming, becoming aroused
- performing social roles – expressing terror or fortitude in face of horror
- walking out temporarily or permanently.

Reception activities after the event
- Viewers and other viewers – discussion of the text with others
  - social interaction, bonding
  - cultural forum' – discussion, debate
  - fan or 'cult' involvement – more systematic or intensive exchange about the text:
    - commentary – opinions of pleasure, displeasure, 'dishing'
    - speculation – gossip and predictions, possibly using extra-textual information
    - request for and diffusion of information
- Viewers and characters and/or stars
  - extra-cinematic practices include
    - attempting to resemble the physical features of the character and/or star
    - imitating the character's and/or star's actions
    - copying the star so as to become the star
  - write letters to character and/or star
  - attempt to get physically close to star
  - fantasise – from repetitive daydreams to accounts of paranormal encounters
- Viewers and the production of new materials
  - dislocate characters into new worlds
  - insert oneself into the story
  - building on an emotional crisis in the original narrative
  - create sexual stories between characters
  - Narratives
    - recontextualise the story

- expand the series timeline
- refocalise the character
- realign the moral world
- shift the genre
- combine diagetic worlds
- creation of songs, videos, academic articles, etc.
- Viewers, the textual world and the real world
  - name children, pets, etc. after aspects of the textual world
  - take trips to places used in the textual world
  - collect materials related to the text and its makers
- Viewers and personal significance
  - use information in film to guide behaviour in everyday life
  - use films in personal memory as signposts to life's experiences
  - organise collected or created materials to stimulate memories of text, star, meanings in scrapbook, fan newsletters, fanzines, web pages
- Go to see the film again, perhaps bring others to 'initiate' them.

Chart 1, '*Beyond* Presumed Normative Reception Activities', outlines some of these considerations. The first half of the chart, 'Physical and Expressive Activities During the Event', lists possible external features of the spectator's activities during the movie. The second half of the chart, 'Reception Activities After the Event', seeks to break the boundary of the film-viewing event as the end of the reception process.[32] The chart lists external activities that are not traditionally thought of as making meanings but which obviously feed into the individual's viewing experience. Thus, on one side, an activity during the film of 'meta-talking' – discussing with a co-spectator what is occurring – would have consequences on an interpretation. On the other side, expressing sudden terror or laughing out loud indicates an affective and emotional state being experienced.

This chart does not attempt to explain why these activities occur, nor does it suggest that all activities occur for the same reasons. Affective and emotional state expressions may be better explained by psychological theories; sociological theories are more suited for much of the talk and some of the physical behaviour. Yet both types of theories probably should be marshalled to account for any specific case being studied.

The second half of Chart 1 is a provisional attempt towards outlining what other researchers and I have described about post-movie meaning-making. This is not the place to discuss whether or not what is made 'after' the movie is more or less accurate to some 'faithful' idea of the original movie any more than what is made during the event is the 'true' interpretation. I assume that anyone working in reception studies has already forsaken belief in some immanent meaning to the text. What matters in either case (interpretations existing during or after the film) are the uses that the meanings have for people.

The second half of Chart 1 supplies some ideas about the possibilities of dialogue and connection among spectators by which 'talk' continues to process the text, reworking it for the use of the spectator. Part of that spectatorial use seems clearly to be personal, but other use values are social – the creation of communities of people who use the text as the object through which to construct networks of attachment, discovery, and, sometimes, authority and power.

While most studies of fans emphasise the positive features of exchange and empowerment from interests in often marginal objects of pleasure, I would point out that scholars may need to shift their presumptions even here – although not all the way back to the days when fans were considered pathological spectators. Without going that far, I would argue that some fans and fan communities might benefit from more critical social theory. The fan's attention to capturing the physical garments of a star or creating a website with the most hits bespeaks of desires of power and control. Like talk in the theatre, fan behaviour should not be automatically categorised as progressive, and, like exhibition-site behaviour and, indeed, movies themselves, fandom cannot easily be bifurcated into good and bad. The historian's responsibility is to provide adequate description and thoughtful evaluation.

To write the history of American film reception requires avoiding unnecessary and unproductive boundaries that prevent scholars from considering a wide variety of factors that might explain what the relations are between spectators and films. The boundaries of the text as stimulus need to be removed. The boundaries of the audience identity and the historical time-period also have to be questioned as scholars seek evidence of a variety of exhibition experiences during times presumed to 'contain' spectators from being intelligent and thoughtful – or just plain silly – viewers of the films. Scholarship also needs to avoid the boundary of the event of movie-going itself. Working and reworking a text continues far beyond the walls of the movie theatre.

I suggest that reception scholarship should move away from a decade/period model of film exhibition to a set of practices that cross the years of film-going. Scholarship *should* note class practices, perhaps related to presumptions of taste such as 'high' and 'low'. These class practices, however, need to be checked against the meanings being made. Ethnic and gender practices should also be tracked for patterns, but not unreasonably homogenised. Scholarship should also investigate not just the event of film-going but the continual making and remaking of the interpretations and emotional significances through the lives of the individuals. Here the work on popular and cultural memory offers important research and theory to pursue. The use of a film such as *Gone with the Wind* to pin down the 'meaning' of someone's life at a particular moment in her existence will be part of the history of American film reception. Finally, scholarship must avoid correlating political effectivity with specific behaviours. The event as a whole – within its historical context and its historical consequences – must be considered to produce any kind of evaluative claims about whether the meanings made are progressive or conservative, and for whom. Ideological evaluations should also avoid universalisations. Talk is far from being always progressive even in the public sphere. Talk can be quite incendiary. It can, however, also be binding and supportive.

Notes

1   Janet Staiger, 'Modes of Reception', in André Gaudreault, Germain Lacasse and Isabelle
    Raynauld (eds), *Cinema: A Hundred Years Later* (Quebec, Canada: Editions Nota Bene,
    1999). The trends are observed in the work of Tom Gunning, Miriam Hansen, Timothy
    Corrigan and others following in their footsteps. See Tom Gunning, 'The Cinema of
    Attraction: Early Film, Its Spectator and the Avant-Garde', *Wide Angle*, vol. 8, no. 3/4

(1986), pp. 63–70; Tom Gunning, ' "Primitive Cinema" – A Frame-Up? Or the Trick's on
Us', *Cinema Journal*, vol. 28, no. 2 (winter, 1989), pp. 3–12; Tom Gunning, ' "Now You
See It, Now You Don't": The Temporality of the Cinema of Attractions', *The Velvet Light
Trap*, no. 32 (1993), pp. 3–10; Tom Gunning, 'Tracing the Individual Body:
Photography, Detectives, and Early Cinema' in Leo Charney and Vanessa R. Schwartz
(eds), *Cinema and the Invention of Modern Life*, (Berkeley, CA: University of California
Press, 1995), pp. 15–45; Miriam Hansen, *Babel and Babylon: Spectatorship in American
Silent Film* (Cambridge, MA: Harvard University Press, 1991); Miriam Hansen, 'Early
Cinema, Late Cinema: Permutations of the Public Sphere', *Screen*, vol. 34, no. 1 (spring
1993), pp. 197–210; Timothy Corrigan, *A Cinema without Walls: Movies and Culture
after Vietnam* (New Brunswick, NJ: Rutgers University Press, 1991).

2 Janet Staiger, 'The Perversity of Spectators: Expanding the History of the Classical
Hollywood Cinema', in Ib Bondebjerg (ed.), *Moving Images, Culture and the Mind*,
(Luton, England: University of Luton Press, 2000). pp. 19–30.

3 Bosley Crowther, ' "The Big Sleep" Warner Film in which Bogart and Bacall Are Paired
Again, Opens at Strand', *New York Times*, 24 August 1946, p. 6; 'Brog', 'The Big Sleep',
Variety, 14 August 1946, n.p.; 'The New Pictures', *Time*, 26 August 1946, p. 95; James
Agee, 'Films', *The Nation*, 163 (31 August 1946), p. 250; Manny Farber, 'Journey into the
Night', *The New Republic*, 23 September 1946, p. 351; 'The Big Sleep', *Daily Variety*, 52,
no. 48 (13 August 1946), p. 3; Herb Sterne, 'The Big Sleep', *Rob Wagner's Script*, 32, no.
739 (28 September 1946), pp. 12–13.

4 'Paracinematic' viewers are spectators who enjoy 'paracinema', a mode of film form and
style described by David Bordwell in *Narration in the Fiction Film* (Madison, WI:
University of Wisconsin Press, 1985). The term is applied by Jeffrey Sconce to spectators
in his ' "Trashing" the Academy: Taste, Excess and an Emerging Politics of Cinematic
Style', *Screen*, vol. 36, no. 4 (winter 1995), pp. 371–93.

5 'Dishing' is an American term for 'trashing' a text, pointing out all of its faults.

6 For an extensive discussion of these behaviours, see Staiger, 'The Perversity of
Spectators'.

7 Janet Staiger, *Interpreting Films: Studies in the Historical Reception of American Cinema*
(Princeton, NJ: Princeton University Press, 1992).

8 Janet Staiger, 'Taboos and Totems: Cultural Meanings of *Silence of the Lambs*', in Jim
Collins, Hilary Radner, and Ava Collins (eds), *Film Theory Goes to the Movies* (New
York: Routledge/American Film Institute, 1993), pp. 142–54.

9 Tom Gunning tends to use more formalist, 'defamiliarisation' language; Miriam Hansen
draws on Brechtian language. See citations above.

10 Judith Mayne, 'Immigrants and Spectators', *Wide Angle*, vol. 5, no. 2 (1982), pp. 32–41.

11 Mary Heaton Vorse, 'Some Picture Show Audiences', *Colliers*, 24 June 1911, pp. 441–7.

12 Hansen, *Babel and Babylon*; Hansen, 'Early Cinema'. Hansen is careful to suggest that
the public sphere of the nickelodeons does not perfectly fit the definition of Habermas's
public sphere; rather it is ambiguous, with both progressive and conservative features.

13 Hansen, 'Early Cinema', p. 198.

14 Based on my own observations in 1979 versus today.

15 J. Hoberman and Jonathan Rosenbaum, *Midnight Movies* (New York: Harper & Row,
1983), pp. 40–3; David McReynolds, ' "The Flower Thief" – Invalid or Incompetent

[Letters to the Editor]', *Village Voice*, 7, no. 40 (26 July 1962), p. 13; Andy Warhol and Pat Hackett, *POPism: The Warhol '60s* (New York: Harper & Row, 1980), p. 49.

16 Mary Morley Cohen, 'Forgotten Audiences in the Passion Pits: Drive-In Theatres and Changing Spectator Practices in Post-War America', *Film History*, vol. 6, no. 4 (winter 1994), pp. 470–86; Staiger, 'Modes of Reception'.

17 William Castle, *Step Right Up! … I'm Gonna Scare the Pants Off America* (New York: G. P. Putnam's Sons, 1976), pp. 136–59. I thank Alison Macor for her research which introduced me to Castle's antics.

18 'Late Pix Menace to Kids?', *Variety*, 14 October 1942, p. 7; 'Curfew Spreads', *Motion Picture Herald*, 5 December 1942, p. 9; 'Curfew Cutting Grosses But Towns Want Strict Juve Delinquency Curb', *Variety*, 25 August 1943, p. 7; 'Zoot-Suited Juveniles Run Amok in Detroit Theatres and Niteries', *Variety*, 23 November 1943, p. 7; 'Parents' Responsibility', *Variety*, 14 November 1945, p. 9; 'Chi Theatre Vandalism Up', *Variety*, 21 November 1945, p. 7.

19 On the midnight movie and *Rocky Horror* audiences see: Hoberman and Rosenbaum, *Midnight Movies*, pp. 1–76, 174–213; Bruce A. Austin, 'Portrait of a Cult Film Audience: *The Rocky Horror Picture Show*', *Journal of Communications*, vol. 31 (1981), pp. 43–54.

20 Kevin L. Carter, 'Black Audiences Don't Watch, They Talk to Movies', *Austin American-Statesman*, 26 July 1996, p. E6.

21 Ibid.

22 Ibid.

23 Thomas Cripps, '*Amos 'n' Andy* and the Debate Over American Racial Integration', in John E. O'Connor (ed.), *American History/American Television: Interpreting the Video Past* (New York: Ungar, 1983), pp. 33–54; Norman F. Friedman, 'Responses of Blacks and Other Minorities to Television Shows of the 1970s about Their Groups', *Journal of Popular Film and Television*, vol. 7, no. 1 (1978), pp. 85–102; Jacqueline Bobo, '*The Color Purple*: Black Women as Cultural Readers', in E. Deidre Pribram (ed.), *Female Spectators: Looking at Film and Television* (London: Verso, 1988), pp. 90–109; Cheryl B. Butler, '*The Color Purple* Controversy: Black Woman Spectatorship', *Wide Angle*, vol. 13, nos. 3/4 (1991), pp. 62–9.

24 Bill Fagelson, seminar paper, University of Texas at Austin, autumn 1997, forthcoming in *Cinema Journal*.

25 Richard B. Jewell, 'Orson Welles, George Schaefer, and *It's All True*: A "Cursed" Production', *Film History*, vol. 2, no. 4 (1988), p. 330.

26 'Old Bogart Films Packing Them In', *New York Times*, 28 January 1965, n. p.

27 Arthur Frank Wertheim, *Radio Comedy* (New York: Oxford University Press, 1979), p. 48. Thomas Doherty also discusses the behaviour of audiences for classical Hollywood films, and the ways in which exhibitors and movies themselves accommodated that behaviour, in 'This Is Where We Came In: The Audible Screen and the Voluble Audience of Early Sound Cinema', in Melvyn Stokes and Richard Maltby (eds), *American Movie Audiences: From the Turn of the Century to the Early Sound Era* (London: BFI, 1999), pp. 143–8.

28 Vachel Lindsay, *The Art of the Moving Picture*, rev. ed. (New York: Liveright, 1970, originally published in 1922), pp. 217–18.

29 James H. Johnson, *Listening in Paris: A Cultural History* (Berkeley, CA: University of California Press, 1995), p. 31.

30 Ibid., p. 250.
31 Also see John F. Kasson, *Rudeness and Civility: Manners in Nineteeth-Century Urban America* (New York: Hill and Wang, 1990). Kasson suggests refinement of manners implied physical control of emotions; yet restraint of physical expression does not necessarily conflict with the pleasures in having those feelings.
32 This chart is indebted to a massive amount of research by many fine scholars. I apologise to those I have failed to recognise in the following list: Denise Bielby and C. Lee Harrington, 'Reach Out and Touch Someone: Viewers, Agency, and Audiences in the Televisual Experience', in Jon Cruz and Justin Lewis (ed.), *Viewing, Reception, Listening: Audiences and Cultural Reception* (Boulder, CO: Westview Press, 1993), pp. 81–100; John Champagne, ' "Stop Reading Films!": Film Studies, Close Analysis, and Gay Pornography', *Cinema Journal*, vol. 36, no. 4 (summer 1997), pp. 76–97; John Fiske, *Television Culture* (London: Methuen, 1987); Stephen Hinerman, ' "I'll Be Here With You": Fans, Fantasy and the Figure of Elvis', in Lisa A. Lewis (ed.), *The Adoring Audience: Fan Culture and Popular Media* (New York: Routledge, 1992), pp. 107–34; Henry Jenkins, *Textual Poachers: Television Fans and Participatory Culture* (New York: Routledge, 1992); Jackie Stacey, *Star Gazing: Hollywood Cinema and Female Spectatorship* (London: Routledge, 1994); Helen Taylor, *Scarlett's Women: 'Gone With the Wind' and Its Female Fans* (New Brunswick, NJ: Rutgers University Press, 1989); Jennifer C. Waits; 'United We Dish: The Construction of Reality in the Melrose Update Community', Popular Culture Association Conference, San Antonio, TX, March 1997; and the numerous papers from undergraduate and graduate students in the department of Radio–Television–Film at the University of Texas at Austin.

2
Genre and the Audience: Genre Classifications and Cultural Distinctions in the Mediation of *The Silence of the Lambs*

Mark Jancovich

In a recent article on *film noir*, James Naremore has commented on the difficulty of *defining* the term. This difficulty, he argues, arises because the definition 'has less to do with a group of artefacts than with a discourse – a loose evolving system of arguments and readings, helping to shape commercial strategies and aesthetic ideologies'.[1] Not only have understandings of *film noir* changed, but in the process specific films and film-makers have acquired different meanings in relation to the term. *The Lost Weekend,* once regarded as a central reference point in early discussions of *film noir,* has been completely excluded from later constructions of the field.

As Naremore argues, it is not so much the case that a group of texts simply exist in some relation to one another, however obscure that relation might be, but that 'the Name of the Genre ... functions in much the same way as the Name of the Author'.[2] He cites Michel Foucault's analysis of 'the author function' to substantiate the parallel between these systems of classification. For Foucault, the author function creates 'a relationship of homogeneity, filiation, authentification of some texts by use of others'.[3] But this technique of classification does not simply identify some pre-existing essence. Instead, it produces what it purports to identify. It is the product of a desire and projection, of a need to believe that there is 'a point where contradictions are resolved, where incompatible elements are at last tied together or organised around a fundamental original contradiction'.[4]

As a result, and as Andrew Tudor has also argued, the pursuit of the 'Factor X' that defines a specific genre is both essentialist and ultimately futile. Naremore and Tudor both argue that genres are not defined by a feature that makes all films of a certain type fundamentally similar; rather, they are produced by the discourses through which films are understood. While Naremore considers how the meaning of the term *film noir* changes historically, Tudor defines the horror genre as 'what we collectively believe it to be', and sets out to study historical shifts in the patterns of those films understood to belong to the genre, and in the social concerns that have been expressed by and about them.[5]

Both types of work provide vital contributions to the study of genre and illustrate the point that genre definitions are not simply of academic interest, but have far greater currency and significance. Both also emphasise that genre definitions are produced more by the ways in which films are understood by those who produce, mediate and consume them, than they are by the internal properties of the films themselves. The historical focus of these two critics tends to obscure one problem, however. Both authors presuppose the existence of a collective consensus – about the definition of particular genres within any given period. But such a collective consensus may not have actually existed. We need, therefore, to study not only how definitions of genre change over time, but also how they operate within the intense struggles between different taste formations that are present at a given historical moment.

Differences in taste are never neutral. The varying definitions of any given genre used by different social groups do not imply a pluralistic ideal of variety and heterogeneity. Ien Ang has observed that it is not the *fact* of differences but 'the meanings of differences that matter', and that these meanings 'can only be grasped ... by looking at their contexts, social and cultural bases, and impacts'.[6] Issues of cultural authority and power are normally inextricably bound up with the conflict between different taste formations. Pierre Bourdieu has argued that virtually all forms of cultural practice and symbolic exchange, including taste preferences in dress, art or entertainment, give expression to prevailing systems of social and economic domination, and perform a social function by legitimating social differences:

> taste classifies, and it classifies the classifier. Social subjects, classified by their classifications, distinguish themselves by the distinctions they make, between the beautiful and the ugly, the distinguished and the vulgar.[7]

Through such distinctions, and through the discursive positioning of cultural objects in classificatory hierarchies such as genre definitions, the classifier classifies himself or herself. Like other taste distinctions, definitions of genre are seldom free from evaluative prescriptions: both consumers and critics use systems of classification to articulate their preferences, exemplifying Bourdieu's argument that: 'tastes are perhaps first and foremost distastes, disgust provoked by horror or visceral intolerance ("sick-making") of the tastes of others'.[8] When people with an antipathy towards horror films claim that the defining feature of the genre is visceral – 'blood and guts' – they also make a series of other implicit claims: that horror is sick, threatening and moronic in its appeal; and that they distinguish themselves from the people who watch horror films, who are by implication as moronic, sick and potentially threatening as the films they consume. Those making the claim represent themselves by contrast as reasonable, healthy and in a position to define what needs, in Andrew Ross's phrase, to be 'governed and policed as illegitimate or inadequate or even deviant'.[9]

Such conflicts over the definition of a genre occur among both its consumers and its detractors. There are at least three levels at which struggles over the cultural authority inherent in distinctions between genres take place among audiences. One cultural position identifies genre with popular film, and aligns itself with an art cinema which is either seen as 'free' from genre or else as subverting the genres of 'mainstream commercial cinema'. A second position does not reject genre *per se*, but instead constructs hierarchies of genre, by which *film noir*, for example, is likely to be seen as a more 'legitimate' genre than horror, or the western as more important than 'feminine' genres such as the romantic comedy. Even consumers of genres with low-cultural status will often find themselves in competition with one another. As Bourdieu has contended: 'Explicit aesthetic choices are in fact often constituted in opposition to the choices of the groups closest in social space, with whom competition is most direct and immediate'.[10] It is perhaps not surprising that those who seek to distance themselves from the consumers of a particular genre may have a very different sense of the genre from those who were either its untroubled, casual viewers or its enthusiastic fans. There can, however, be violent disagreements among the consumers of a specific genre over their respective constructions of the field, and this constitutes the third level at which struggles over genre definitions take place.

It is common for some horror fans to make a bid for greater legitimacy by distancing themselves from the denigrated image of the gory horror movie and its fans, and to privilege films, such as *The Innocents* (1963) and *The Haunting* (1963), that are said to work through 'atmosphere' and 'suggestion'.[11] In contrast, other horror fans, as represented by such publications as *Fangoria* and *Gorezone,* specifically privilege films of gory 'excess', and present the emphasis on 'atmosphere' and 'suggestion' as a 'cop out', an essentially feminised preference for the predictable, safe and untroubling.

In these debates, notions of authenticity often become central, with each group defining themselves as superior to other fans who are constructed as a mindless, conformist horde associated either with mass, middlebrow culture or with a lowbrow, illegitimate form. By the same process, each group distinguishes between the 'real' and 'authentic' examples of a genre and its 'inauthentic' appropriation. On occasions, this distinction becomes a matter of exclusion from the category. Within horror fandom, there are major disagreements over the status of films such as *Alien* and *Aliens.* For some horror fans, these films are included within the horror canon as works of immense importance, while others exclude them altogether, dismissing them as representing all the impoverishments of the science fiction film. Other groups distinguish vampire literature and films as separate from the general category of horror.[12]

Genres cannot, therefore, simply be defined by the expectations of 'the audience', because the audience is not a coherent body with a consistent set of expectations. Different sections of the audience can have violently opposed expectations. Not only can the generic status of an individual film change over time, it can also be the object of intense struggles at a particular moment. A film which, for some, may seem obviously to belong to one genre may, for others, clearly belong to another genre altogether.

A case in point is Jonathan Demme's *The Silence of the Lambs,* which critics such as Jonathan Lake Crane and Carol Clover identify unequivocally as a horror film.[13] For years, I have done so quite happily as well, but I have gradually come to realise that most of my present-day students find this classification bemusing. While I remember *The Silence of the Lambs* as the first horror film to sweep the major awards at the Oscars, for most of my students the film's status as an Oscar winner defines it as a 'quality drama' – a grouping frequently preferred by people who claim not to like 'genre films'. While this seemed puzzling to me at first, research on the film's promotion established that, even on its initial release, the distributors of *The Silence of the Lambs* had tried to negotiate a special status for the film as distinct from the 'ordinary horror film', capable of appealing to those who identified themselves as far removed from 'the horror fan'. The final part of this essay examines this strategy by analysing the cover story of the March 1991 US edition of *Premiere* magazine, 'A Kind of Redemption' by Fred Schubers.[14]

Before examining this article, however, it is necessary to engage with some of the insights provided by historical reception studies, an approach to the study of film that has placed particular emphasis on the study of subsidiary publications such as reviews, interviews and feature articles. Theoretical accounts of historical reception studies acknowledge that there is no 'immanent meaning in a text' and that 'receptions need to be related to specific historical conditions as *events*'.[15] Janet Staiger, whose book, *Interpreting Films,* provides the most sustained conceptual elaboration of historical reception studies, is critical of types of film studies which assume that meaning is an inherent quality existing in the forms of the text. Staiger insists that meaning is produced by audiences on the basis of the knowledge and discourses they bring to the film, and that each interpretation is therefore an event, an act of meaning production. Reception studies must, therefore, reinsert the film into the system of social relations that sustains it, and analyse not only the material conditions of its production, but also what Bourdieu terms 'the symbolic production of the work, i.e. the production of the value of the work or, which amounts to the same thing, of belief in the value of the work' – a symbolic production undertaken by, among others, the agencies of publicity, criticism and the academy.[16]

According to Barbara Klinger, however, historical reception studies has exhibited a tendency

> to concentrate on single practices within the original moments of reception. Thus, much of this research … has not systematically explored the fuller range of effects that historical context might have on cinematic identity. Films clearly circulate beyond their encounter with any one institutional or social sphere. How can we conceive of the relationship between history and cinema to address this more extensive sense of circulation, to examine the issue of meaning in a *comprehensive*, that is, transhistorical, transcontextual manner?[17]

Klinger also emphasises the need to look not only at how the meanings of a film change over time, but also at the different meanings which a film can have within a specific time-period. Her work expands the horizons of historical reception studies, which has on occasion done little more than practise a historical version of reader-response theory, in which the task of the critic is to unearth the 'appropriate' competences necessary for the interpretation of films. While historical reception studies has been principally concerned to discover how audiences are 'expected' to fill in gaps within texts and what knowledge they are 'required' to bring with them to the interpretation of films, it has shown relatively little interest in the ways in which issues of taste produce not only different readings of a text within a given historical period, but conflicts between the proponents of these different readings.

Klinger's work suggests that it is also necessary to strive for a more complex and nuanced understanding of historical receptions, and the competing discourses which make them possible. In practice, historical reception studies has relied on the analysis of published materials such as reviews, on the grounds that other evidence is often unavailable, while acknowledging that the public status of these artefacts makes them suspect. In her article on *The Silence of the Lambs,* for example, Staiger refers to reviews as *traces* of the event, as ways of reconstructing reception events, while also using them to identify the discourses that *produce* these events. Other critics have seen reviews as providing very different kinds of evidence: Robert C. Allen and Douglas Gomery, for example, point to the agenda-setting function of reviews that may not tell 'audiences what to think so much as ... what to think *about*'.[18] As part of the process of contextualisation by which interpretations are framed and incorporated in struggles between different taste formations, reviews cannot be read as giving automatic or unproblematic access to the ways in which audiences interpret films. Any review, or any other act of criticism, is in itself 'an affirmation of its own legitimacy', a claim by the reviewer of his or her entitlement to participate in the process by which cultural value is defined and distinguished, and thus to take part not only in a legitimate discourse about the film, but also in the production of its cultural value.[19] Reviews cannot, then, simply be taken as *traces* of readings, nor as providing a straightforward access to the discourses that produce interpretations; rather, they give a sense of the very different ways in which people are supposed to 'talk' about films. The importance of distinguishing between the activity of consuming films and the activity of talking about them is clearly demonstrated in Ien Ang's work on *Dallas*. She found that many of those who wrote to her were fully aware of the ways in which their consumption of the show could be judged by others, and constantly positioned what they said about the show in relation to a public discourse on the distinction between legitimate and illegitimate taste, and to what Ang calls 'the ideology of mass culture'.[20]

Articles and reviews can most usefully be understood as one of the ways in which people learn to position themselves within hierarchies of taste. As Klinger contends, reviews

> signify cultural hierarchies of aesthetic value reigning at particular times. As a primary public tastemaker, the critic operates to make, in Pierre Bourdieu's parlance, 'distinctions'. Among other things, the critic distinguishes legitimate from illegitimate art and proper from improper modes of aesthetic appropriation.[21]

Although Klinger is principally discussing the construction of hierarchies of legitimate taste, a similar argument can be made about the role of popular publications in constructing cultural hierarchies and proper modes of aesthetic appropriation in matters of popular taste. In both cases, reviews and feature articles set agendas for audiences by drawing attention to what is taken to be interesting or noteworthy about a film. They also reflect the differing attitudes of different sections of the media to varying taste formations. In the process, they focus their attention on different features and employ wildly different notions of cinematic value.

In her analysis of the reviews of Douglas Sirk's films during the 1950s, Klinger identifies three different and opposed taste formations in operation. The first, which she identifies as 'the liberal sources', routinely ignored mainstream Hollywood product in favour of an avant-garde aesthetic. The second shared tastes similar to those addressed by Universal's sales campaigns for Sirk's movies, while the third was associated with a broadly realist aesthetic related to the upper end of the middlebrow and the lower end of legitimate culture:

> Appearing mainly in East Coast and otherwise urban periodicals and newspapers, these

reviews offered negative evaluations of Sirk's melodramas, in part influenced by a dominant canon of the time that endorsed realism in dramas. This general critical context supervised value judgements for drama, including the adult melodrama, that genre to which Sirk's films belonged at the time.[22]

As Klinger demonstrates, reviews are products of specific taste formations, and also function specifically as gate-keepers or guardians of specific taste formations, mediating between texts and audiences and specifying particular ways of appropriating or consuming texts. As such, they are part of a complex process involving a series of media which we must recognise as neither monolithic nor monological. As both Klinger and Charlotte Brunsdon have shown, the different taste formations which underpin different publications will lead those publications to discuss films, and to address their own readers, in very different ways.[23] There are deep struggles not only *between* many of the media but also *within* specific media. Newspaper and magazine reviewing, for example, embraces very different taste formations with very different agendas: one would hardly expect *Fangoria* or *Gorezone* to share the same terms of reference as, say, *The New Republic* or *Sight and Sound*; indeed, *Fangoria* and *Gorezone* share different taste formations from one another. Examining a range of publications addressing a variety of readerships will reveal very different interests and preoccupations in any given film, and even clarify the contexts within which these publications are themselves meaningful as texts.

Staiger's discussion of *The Silence of the Lambs* clearly demonstrates an interest in discursive struggles over meaning, but her analysis concentrates on reviews of the film in publications addressing a middle-class, educated intelligentsia: the *Village Voice, Los Angeles Times, Wall Street Journal, New Republic, New Yorker, Rolling Stone, Vanguard* and *The Nation*. Within this audience, which corresponds to the first of Klinger's three taste formations, debates about the meaning of *The Silence of the Lambs* had, by the film's fifth week of the release

> solidified into a set of propositions: 1) that whether or not Jonathan Demme had intended to create a homophobic film, the character of the serial murderer had attributes associated with stereotypes of gay men; 2) that in a time of paranoia over AIDS and increased violence directed towards gays in the United States, even suggesting connections between homosexuals and a serial murderer was irresponsible; but 3) that the character of Clarice Starling played by Jodie Foster was a positive image of a woman working in a patriarchal society and, thus, empowering for women viewers.[24]

The struggle that Staiger analyses is, however, also bound up with a debate over the film's cultural and generic status, a debate that was given particular inflection in the different media outlets addressing different taste formations. Attempts to emphasise the status of Starling as a 'positive image' often relied on distinguishing the film from the generic category of 'the slasher movie', while attacks on the film's supposed homophobia usually sought to associate the film with the horror genre in a manner that both drew upon and reproduced assumptions about the genre's status as an example of popular cinema. In contrast to many other critics, Carol Clover does not present *The Silence of the Lambs* as either a radical reversal of the sexual politics of the slasher movie, or as proof of the horror film's inherently reactionary nature. For her:

When I see an Oscar-winning film like *The Accused* or the artful *Alien* and its blockbuster sequel *Aliens* or, more recently, *Sleeping with the Enemy* and *The Silence of the Lambs,* and even *Thelma and Louise,* I cannot help thinking of all the low-budget, often harsh and awkward but sometimes deeply energetic films that preceded them by a decade or more – films that said it all, and in flatter terms, and on a shoestring. If mainstream film detains us with niceties of plot, character, motivation, cinematography, pacing, acting, and the like, low or exploitation horror operates at the bottom line, and in so doing reminds us that every movie has a bottom line, no matter how covert or mystified or sublimated it may be.[25]

It is therefore important to address the ways in which debates over the film's gender politics were bound up with issues of class taste and its legitimating functions, and it is this association which will be the focus of my analysis of Fred Schubers's article in *Premiere.*

When *The Silence of the Lambs* was released in the United States (on St Valentine's Day, 1991) sections of the press scrupulously avoided any direct association of the film with the horror genre. Many reviews established the film's association with horror, but then deflected or neutralised it. In place of generic classifications, reviewers deployed ambivalent adjectives: 'terrifying', 'brutally real', 'chilling', 'macabre', 'dark', and as having 'an atmosphere of Gothic gloom'.[26] Apart from this reference to the Gothic, the only generic identification I have been able to find in reviews and commentary published in mainstream, middle-class or quality publications describes the film as a 'suspenseful drama'.[27]

The Silence of the Lambs was nevertheless associated with the horror genre in reviews which emphasised the 'ordeal' involved in watching the film in a manner that drew directly upon the traditional 'dare' of horror movie promotion. *Playboy,* for example, declared that: 'If you can handle it, *The Silence of the Lambs* is a paralysing suspense drama, the kind of movie to watch by peeking through your fingers … Audiences are likely to sit tight … and gasp with relief when it's over'.[28] *Premiere*'s short review observed: 'If it's a choice between this and chocolates for Valentine's Day, the bonbons might be a better bet, but then again, *The Silence of the Lambs* promises to be so terrifying, you're bound to end up in your sweetheart's arms'.[29]

The main strategy of many of the reviews is simultaneously to present the film as offering the pleasures associated with the horror movie – that it will be gripping, terrifying, shocking, etc. – while also legitimating the film through its distinction from the genre. This sense of distinction is constructed in two main ways: first, through claims about the film's aesthetic 'quality', and, second, through claims about its politics, which are generally defined in terms of feminism.

The first of these strategies can be seen in the article by Fred Schubers, published in *Premiere* in 1991, which tries to negotiate a position for the film by emphasising both the horrific nature of its material and the auteur status of its director, Jonathan Demme:

> The zesty auteur of such recent light operas as *Something Wild* (which did have corrosive later stages) and *Married to the Mob* did not seem temperamentally ideal for novelist Thomas Harris's brutally real, often macabre version of a pair of serial killers who, respectively, skin and consume their victims.[30]

The role of promotional materials in framing the film for reviewers before reviewers frame films for audiences is indicated by the striking similarity between this passage and one which appears in the *Playboy* review, which observes: 'Director Jonathan Demme, more often associated with lightweight fare (*Something Wild* and *Married to the Mob*), brings touches of dark humour as well as cinematic style to this adaptation … of Thomas Harris's novel'.[31] Both passages emphasise Demme's status as an auteur director who is to be taken seriously (so countering one problem) while also stressing that he is known for making light, likeable films (so countering another). On the other hand, they ignore Demme's background in 'exploitation' movies, such as the women-in-prison drama, *Caged Heat,* which he made for Roger Corman.

The Schubers article in *Premiere* also continued this project by presenting Demme's motivations for making *The Silence of the Lambs* as simultaneously aesthetic and political: 'If somebody had asked me if I would be interested in doing a movie about a young woman who goes after a man who mutilates and murders young women, I would have said absolutely not. But the people at Orion said, "We've got this script we're really excited about – just read it"'.[32] Without any attempt at a transition, the article continues: 'Given the choice, says Demme, "I'd much rather see a strong story with a lead character as a woman than the lead as a man. Because the odds are stacked higher against the woman"'.[33] This again emphasises the 'horrific' nature of the materials while maintaining a sense that Demme was attracted to the quality of the script – its 'strong story' – and the presence of a female rather than a male lead, which is at the core of the film's supposedly feminist politics. While many discussions of the film suggested that the presence of a heroic female lead distinguished it from other horror movies, the slasher movie is usually characterised by the presence of a strong female hero, the figure whom Carol Clover identifies as the 'final girl'.[34] In plot terms, the presence of Clarice Starling as the heroic protagonist associates the film with the slasher genre, rather than distancing it.

Other distinctions between *The Silence of the Lambs* and the horror genre were constructed by invoking Demme's auteur status and emphasising his discreet handling of the film's violence. *The Time Out Film Guide* observed: 'Although Demme does reveal the results of the killer's violence, he for the most part refrains from showing the acts themselves; the film could never be accused of pandering to voyeuristic impulses' – a reference to the supposedly voyeuristic nature of the horror film in general, and the slasher movie in particular.[35] Once again, the message was clear: the film could offer the thrills of a horror movie without middle-class audiences either having to feel guilty or questioning their sense of their own distinction from that monstrous other, the troubling and disturbing figure of the slasher movie viewer.

The most overt and sustained way in which these distinctions were constructed, however, was through the star image of Jodie Foster. A particular construction of Foster's star image was used to legitimate the film as a whole and the character of Clarice Starling in particular. By presenting Foster in particular ways, Schubers's article endorses certain readings of Clarice as a character. This process also works reciprocally. Foster is presented as actively investing the character with meaning (strength) and in the process, her own star image and her credentials as an actor are re-established and given an explicitly political dimension. At one point, Schubers informs us that Demme had originally considered Michelle Pfeiffer for the part of Clarice, but that he had soon changed his mind because 'feminist fellow-traveller Demme understood that [Foster's] commitment would give Starling the backbone the part requires'.[36]

This notion of backbone, articulated through an emphasis on professional and political commitment, is central to the image of Foster constructed by the article. Her status as a serious actor is established through an account of her dedication to realism: 'In the service of authenticity, Foster spent several days simulating the life of a trainee

Jodie Foster as Clarice in *The Silence of the Lambs* (1991)

at the FBI in Quantico'.[37] Quite what 'several days' actually amounted to, and quite how 'authentic' it might have made Foster's performance, is not elaborated. Rather, the reader is supposed to relate this information to a concept of acting established through Method performance, demonstrated predominantly by male stars such as Robert De Niro and Dustin Hoffman, who seek to distinguish themselves from the supposed 'inauthenticity' of popular culture – an inauthenticity which is usually associated with feminisation – and to associate themselves with a masculine, legitimate culture.[38] In Foster's case, these notions of commitment and the suggestions of the work involved in constructing the star's performance are given a political dimension through the claim that the performance is itself an act of *political* labour. Some of the film's promotional material structures her performance as part of a broader struggle underpinning Foster's entire career, which arises from her personal and political commitment to feminism. As the *Premiere* contents page states, in *The Silence of the Lambs* Foster 'once again confronts the victimisation of women'.[39] This involves both a rereading of Foster's previous films, in order to present them as being *a commentary upon* victimisation, rather than simply (as could be argued) *an instance of* victimisation.

The suggestion that Starling is not just a victim but a heroic female character is used to establish the film's distinction from the popular. Schubers's article quotes Foster: 'What's great about this character is that her lot in life, as the hero, is to save the underdog, because she's lucky enough not to be the underdog anymore. I feel like there's never been a female hero who uses femininity as a warrior thing, and not like Rambo – Rambette – in underwear. This is not some male version of a female hero'.[40] In saying this, Foster was trying to distinguish the film from a range of female action heroes, of whom the most famous is Ripley in the *Alien* films. Indeed, after the release of *Alien,* there were several references which associated Ripley with Rambo, most obviously in the word 'Fembo'.[41] As a result, Foster as an actor was perhaps legitimated through an association with masculinity and realism, as opposed to the popular, the fantastic and the generic.

The title of Schubers's article – 'A Kind of Redemption' – emphasises the idea of Foster's performance as an act of feminist struggle. It derives from Foster's comment that

> I realise that I play certain characters to redeem them. I think in some ways what my makeup is, and my lot in life, is that I've used fiction to save women who otherwise would have been spat upon or passed off, not paid attention to. To reverse a certain negative history. That's why I've always played those people, to make them human. It has reverberations in my life, how I feel about my family and how I feel about the literature I studied and the things that I do.[42]

Schubers draws attention to Foster's education: her 'Yale major was literature (with a concentration on African-American works), Toni Morrison her thesis subject'.[43] Suggesting that Foster 'seems to see her work in *Silence* as the actor's equivalent of a slim, pithy novel', the article constructs another link between the film and legitimate culture.[44]

Foster's observations on redemption establish a series of connections between her own status as serious artist and the character of Clarice Starling. The idea of redemption is linked to the religious association of the film's title: *The Silence of the Lambs* refers to the slaughter of the innocents and to the figure of the saviour, identified with Starling. References to her 'make-up' or her 'lot in life', however, also draw attention to the fated or psychologically compulsive aspects of her character. Starling's psychological 'make-up' and her narrative 'lot in life' are directed towards saving the women who are compulsively dehumanised by killers such as Gumb.

Foster's comments also refer to her own life and particularly the way in which 'I feel about my family'. Schubers stresses that Foster's family lacked a father and revolved around a strong maternal figure, while Foster herself supported the family financially throughout her childhood. This discussion of her family background presents Foster as the strong daughter: the brilliant young actress whose talent, intelligence and hard work rendered a male bread-winner unnecessary, combining ideas of female strength and independence with the image of Foster as a serious artist. For example, the supposedly semi-autobiographical features of her directorial début, *Little Man Tate,* serve to establish her not only as a serious actress, but also as an auteur director through the supposedly personal nature of the material as well as through the 'sensitivity' of its handling.

Schubers's article presents the film as having all the pleasures of a horror film without threatening the self-image of those audience members who distinguish themselves from 'the horror fan'. Most significantly, it seeks to detach the film from the horror genre's associations with voyeurism, misogyny and formulaic simplicity. At the time of the film's initial release, the quality press, much of the promotional material, and even the film's own *mise-en-scène* all sought to evoke an association with the terms 'Gothic' and 'terror', rather than horror.[45] These terms engage a familiar set of distinctions by which 'the Gothic novel' and 'the tale of terror' are not constructed as the other to legitimate culture (as they have been in other contexts) but rather are associated with legitimate culture through a series of distinctions in which 'horror' is constructed as their own other.

The mediation of *The Silence of the Lambs* illustrates the ways in which genre distinctions operate not to designate or describe a fixed class of texts, but as terms that are constantly and inevitably in a process of contestation. Imbricated in that contest are questions of cultural value, privilege and the authority to determine cultural legitimacy through the act of genre definition. Rather than horror having a single meaning, different social groups construct it in different, competing ways as they seek to identify with or distance themselves from the term, and associate different texts with these constructions of horror. In such circumstances, the definition of genre becomes, like the definition of the literary canon, both the site and the stake of contention as these groups compete for the legitimacy of their definition in order to demonstrate the legitimacy of their claim to cultural authority. As Randal Johnson comments, Bourdieu's analysis suggests that 'such struggles in fact constitute the dynamic of change in the cultural field', for what is always at stake in such struggles is the cultural authority to promulgate legitimate definitions of classification and cultural hierarchies.[46] From such a critical perspective, the reductive project of trying to define whether *The Silence of the Lambs* is a horror film or something else is replaced by the much more interesting tasks of interrogating how such a definition is constructed and contested, and examining what forms of cultural authority are at stake in the process of generic definition.

Notes

1   James Naremore, 'American *Film Noir*: The History of an Idea', *Film Quarterly*, vol. 49, no. 2 (winter 1995–6), p. 14. Naremore enlarges on his discussion in Chapter 1 of his book, *More than Night: Film Noir in Its Contexts* (Berkeley, CA: University of California Press, 1998), pp. 9–39.

2   Ibid.

3   Ibid.

4   Ibid., p. 14.

5   See, for example, Andrew Tudor, 'Genre', in Barry K. Grant (ed.), *The Film Genre Reader* (Austin: University of Texas Press, 1986), pp. 3–10; and Andrew Tudor, *Monsters and Mad Scientists: A Cultural History of the Horror Movie* (Oxford: Blackwells, 1989).

6   Ien Ang, 'Wanted: Audiences. On the Politics of Empirical Audience Studies', in Ellen Seiter *et al.* (eds), *Remote Control: Television Audiences and Cultural Power* (London: Routledge, 1989), p. 107.

7   Pierre Bourdieu, *Distinction: A Social Critique of the Judgement of Taste*, trans. Richard Nice (Cambridge, MA: Harvard University Press, 1984), p. 6.

8   Ibid. p. 56.

9   Andrew Ross, *No Respect: Intellectuals and Popular Culture* (New York: Routledge, 1989), p. 61.

10 Bourdieu, *Distinction,* p. 60.

11 For a corroboration of this view, see Brigid Cherry, 'Refusing to Refuse to Look: Female Viewers of the Horror Film', in Melvyn Stokes and Richard Maltby (eds), *Identifying Hollywood's Audiences: Cultural Identity and the Movies* (London: BFI, 1999), pp. 190–205.

12 Ibid.

13 Jonathan Lake Crane, *Terror and Everyday Life: Singular Moments in the History of the Horror Film* (Thousand Oaks, CA: Sage, 1994); and Carol Clover, *Men, Women and Chain Saws: Gender in the Modern Horror Film* (London: BFI, 1992).

14 Fred Schubers, 'A Kind of Redemption', *Premiere,* US edition (March 1991), p. 52.

15 Janet Staiger, 'Taboo and Totem: Cultural Meanings of *The Silence of the Lambs*', in Jim Collins *et al.* (eds), *Film Theory Goes to the Movies* (New York: Routledge, 1993), p. 143.

16 Pierre Bourdieu, 'The Field of Cultural Production, or: The Economic World Reversed', in Pierre Bourdieu, *The Field of Cultural Production: Essays on Art and Literature,* ed. Randal Johnson (Oxford: Polity Press, 1993), p. 37.

17 Barbara Klinger, *Melodrama and Meaning: History, Culture and the Films of Douglas Sirk* (Bloomington: Indiana University Press, 1994), p. xvii.

18 Robert C. Allen and Douglas Gomery, *Film History: Theory and Practice* (New York: Knopf, 1985), p. 90. This point is also discussed by Thomas Poe in Chapter 7 of this volume.

19 Bourdieu, 'The Field of Cultural Production', pp. 35–6.

20 See Ien Ang, *Watching 'Dallas': Soap Opera and the Melodramatic Imagination* (London: Methuen, 1985).

21 Klinger, *Melodrama and Meaning,* p. 70.

22 Ibid., p. 71.

23 Charlotte Brunsdon, *Screen Tastes: Soap Opera to Satellite Dishes* (London: Routledge, 1997).

24 Staiger, 'Taboo and Totem', p. 142.

25 Clover, *Men, Women and Chain Saws,* p. 20.

26 'Review', *Premiere* (February 1991), p. 12; Schubers, 'A Kind of Redemption', p. 52; 'Review', *Playboy* (April 1991), p. 24; 'Review', *Radio Times* (12–18 October 1996).

27 'Review', *Playboy* (April 1991), p. 24.

28 Ibid.

29 'Review', *Premiere,* February 1991, p. 12. Compare this to the review of *Dr X* by James E. Mitchell in the *Los Angeles Examiner* in 1932: 'Take the girl friend and by the middle of the first reel she'll have both arms around your neck and holding on for dear life'. Cited in Rhona J. Berenstein, *Attack of the Leading Ladies: Gender, Sexuality, and Spectatorship in Classic Horror Cinema* (New York: Columbia University Press, 1996), p. 60.

30 Schubers, 'A Kind of Redemption', p. 52.

31 'Review', *Playboy* (April 1991), p. 24.

32 Schubers, 'A Kind of Redemption', p. 52.

33 Ibid.

34 Amy Taubin, 'Killing Men', *Sight and Sound,* vol. 1:issue 1 (1991), pp. 14–18; Clover, *Men, Women and Chain Saws,* esp. pp. 35–42.

35 *Time Out Film Guide* (Harmondsworth: Penguin, 1989), p. 666.

36 Schubers, 'A Kind of Redemption', p. 53.

37 Ibid.

38 Richard Dyer, *Stars* (London: BFI, 1979) and *Heavenly Bodies* (London: BFI, 1987).

39 'Contents', *Premiere* (March 1991), p. 7.

40 Schubers, 'A Kind of Redemption', p. 52.

41 Harvey R. Greenberg, 'Fembo: *Aliens* Intention', *Journal of Popular Film and Television*, vol 15, no. 4, (winter 1988), pp. 165–71.

42 Ibid., p. 53.

43 Ibid.

44 Ibid.

45 Compare, for example, the 'Gothic' dungeon in which Clarice encounters Lector in Demme's film with Michael Mann's presentation of the modernist/postmodernist asylum in which Will Graham confronts Lecktor [sic] in *Manhunter,* a film based on *Red Dragon,* the Thomas Harris novel which immediately precedes *The Silence of the Lambs.*

46 Randal Johnson, 'Editor's Introduction' to Pierre Bourdieu, *The Field of Cultural Production*, pp. 19–20.

3
Interpreting *All About Eve*: A Study in Historical Reception

Martin Shingler

During the 1940s, Bette Davis's particular brand of female strength, independence, professionalism, ambition and power appealed to millions of women in the United States and Britain, making her one of Hollywood's most successful stars. At the beginning of the next decade, however, in the film *All About Eve* (1950), the actress appeared to sacrifice all of these qualities in favour of housewifery. This chapter considers how this film has been received by audiences in Britain and the United States since the early 1950s. For this purpose, I am using the historical-materialist approach to film reception proposed by Janet Staiger as an alternative to both psychoanalytical theories of film spectatorship and to a much earlier stage of sociological audience research conducted, for example, by J. P. Mayer and Leo Handel, together with the work of Mass Observation.[1] This does not involve any aspect of ethnographic research, audience interviews, polls, discussion groups, etc., but entails analysis of extra-cinematic discourses including film reviews, publicity and film journalism, institutional practices such as casting and cultural, social and ideological discourses circulating at the time of the film's release or re-releases.

In her article 'The Handmaiden of Villainy: Methods and Problems in Studying the Historical Reception of a Film', Staiger states that the central purpose of her work is to determine not the 'correct' reading of a particular film but 'the range of possible readings and reading processes at historical moments and their relation to groups of historical spectators'.[2] Making a strong case against a generalised and idealised notion of the film spectator, 'devoid of networks of sexual, cultural, political, racial, cognitive and historical differences', she also argues against the use of traditional sociological or empirical analyses of individuals 'which only tell investigators what spectators thought they saw or felt or believed'.[3] In *Interpreting Films* (1992), she observes:

> reception studies research cannot claim to say as much about an actual reading or
> viewing experience by empirical readers or spectators as it might like. Several factors
> intervene between the event and any possible sense data available for its study. As any
> cognitive psychologist would point out, verbalized manifestations by a subject are not
> equal to the original experience or its memory. Reporting, whether through a crafted
> enthnographic interview or a published review, is always subject to the problem of
> retrieval, as well as to language, schemata, or representations of the subject that mediate
> perception, comprehension, and interpretation.[4]

Applying her own methodology to the analysis of the film *Foolish Wives* (1922), Staiger relied heavily upon contemporary reviews from newspapers and periodicals such as the *New York Times, Motion Picture Classic, Moving Picture World, Variety* and *Photoplay* in order to gauge the reaction of original viewers to this Hollywood film. She then located such reactions within a historical context of political and social events, movements and existing legislation. Finally, Staiger attempted to account for the harsh criticism which she discovered the film to have received on its initial release by speculating upon the way in which it conflated a number of fundamental binary oppositions (for example, American/European, masculine/feminine, hero/villain). She hypothesised that the film's conflation of conventional polarities would have been received as threatening by mass audiences in America in the early 1920s, thus accounting for the hostile reaction in the popular press. What emerged from Staiger's attempt to employ her methodology of historical reception to the 1922 film was that, despite the importance of data and evidence, the researcher must necessarily retain conjecture and supposition as primary tools of analysis and explanation. As she wrote in her article, 'a constant dialogue between theory and "evidence" is necessary'.[5]

Since the development of Staiger's approach to historical film reception, this methodology has found increasing acceptance within film studies, informing Barbara Klinger's proposal of a 'total film history'.[6] It forms the basis of my approach to *All About Eve*, which aims to relate the events portrayed in the film, and the comments of reviewers, to wider cultural concerns at the time of its initial release, and particularly to public debate in the late 1940s and early 1950s on gender, sex roles and the 'woman problem'. I shall also examine the changing meanings and uses of this film from one historical moment to another, in particular the ways in which the determinants of meaning circulating around the film changed after 1960 when it began to be used and understood by gay audiences in alternative ways.

Written and directed by Joseph L. Mankiewicz, *All About Eve* is a stylish melodramatic comedy, a highly verbose film about the theatre and its people. The plot is built around a volatile and vulnerable ageing actress, Margo Channing (played by Bette Davis), whose status as the theatre's greatest star is threatened and usurped by an ambitious and devious *ingénue*, Eve Harrington (Anne Baxter). In the course of the movie, Eve plots and schemes her way to the top of the New York theatrical world, transforming herself from 'just another tongue-tied fan' into Broadway's newest and brightest star. By the end of the film, she has won the coveted Sarah Siddons award for her achievements in the theatre. Margo, on the other hand, has given up the theatre to become, in her own words, a 'four-square, upright, downright, forthright married lady'. During the final scenes, the film is seen to resolve itself happily for Margo and unhappily for Eve, who (despite her success) is bitter, cynical and unloved. The original publicity for the film highlighted the fact that the narrative centres upon women and, more particularly, female relationships with men. Posters for the film declared that it was 'all about women – and their men'. The title itself was highly suggestive, not only naming one of the main characters but also evoking biblical references to the first woman, who was also, of course, the first problematic woman.

Despite such publicity, virtually none of the initial reviews in the major New York press nor the film magazines made any direct reference to the film's engagement with the 'woman problem'. Rather, the majority noted that the film was about the Broadway theatre and that it featured some 'magnificent' performances from the principal actors, most notably, Bette Davis. Reviews also tended to stress the film's wit, maturity, sophistication and literacy or, less flatteringly, its verbosity.

On the film's American release in October 1950, Bosley Crowther's review in the *New York Times* applauded the film's wit, maturity, and its 'truly sterling cast'. He reserved his highest praise for Bette Davis, a 'brilliant screen actress' whose performance, in his opinion, merited an Academy award.[7] Many British critics and reviewers would echo these sentiments when the film was released in Britain in December of the same year. Caroline Lejeune wrote in the *Observer* that

> There are few actresses on the screen to-day who can beat Miss Davis at her best, and she is at her flaming best in this one. As a hard-working, impulsive, nerve-ridden theatre star of forty, who looks every year of her age and knows it, she uses no false aids to persuasion, nor pretends to youthful beauty she has lost if she ever had it. By sheer integrity of performance, by thinking deeply about the woman she is playing, by using all the technical tricks she has learnt in her long career as a public entertainer, she magnificently suggests an actress who must inevitably dominate any stage, and still, with all her tantrums, inspire loyalty and affection off it. When Miss Davis disappears from the screen, a reel or so before the end of the film, the fire seems to go out and the embers die, although they flare up again at last with a teasing little splutter.[8]

Lejeune's words convey a strong sense of her delight in Davis's early appearances in the film, suggesting that she found the actress both compulsive viewing and hugely entertaining. For her, Davis dominated the film, commanding her full attention and sympathy and creating a strong identificatory relationship.

Similarly, in her review of the movie for *Films in Review* in December 1950, Ann Griffith declared that

> It is wonderful to find oneself on Bette Davis's side at last. To cry when she cries, to long to have her laugh and be happy, to sympathize with her troubles and tantrums, *and to rejoice when she gets her man*, is certainly a novel experience.[9] [My italics]

Griffith's comment indicates that she found Davis's ultimate act of self-sacrifice in giving up her acting career a cause for rejoicing. On the evidence of these reviews, the film's depiction of a woman's marriage–career conflict, in which true satisfaction was achieved through housewifery and domestication rather than a highly successful career (involving fame, wealth and independence), appears to have appealed to some members of its original audience. If we consider this film within the context of American and British society in 1950 we can understand why such a reaction to the film might be the case. By 1950, many millions of women in America and Britain had left jobs and given up independent lifestyles to embrace marriage and motherhood. Many of these women might have been gratified to witness one of Hollywood's greatest female movie stars taking a similar step in *All About Eve*, accepting the assurance the film offered them that, in swapping the office or the factory floor for the kitchen or the nursery, they had done the right thing.

There is, however, evidence to suggest that this was not the only way in which women responded to Davis's actions at the end of *All About Eve*. Writing in the popular British journal *Picture Post* on 9 December 1950, Catherine de la Roche described the film's ending as 'dangerously romantic'.[10] Her choice of words not only suggests that the film's conclusion (and its message to women) might be regarded as both unrealistic and idealistic, but also implies that such a solution could be both damaging and destructive. The sense that, for some women, the ending of the movie was more troubling than reassuring was also implicit in Lejeune's review, in which she recorded a sudden and serious loss of attention and pleasure when Davis herself disappeared from the screen, having supposedly withdrawn into the seclusion of married life. Having announced her character's decision to marry, Davis only appears once more in the film for a brief moment to deliver one line (presumably Lejeune's 'teasing little splutter') in which she tells Eve to put her award where her heart should be.

All About Eve (1950): having renounced her successful stage career in favour of marriage, Margo Channing (Bette Davis) tells Eve Harrington (Anne Baxter) not to worry about her heart as she can always put her award where her heart should be

In my research I have only come across one review from the time of *All About Eve*'s original release which makes any overt reference to the film's sexual politics. This was published in a relatively minor – and certainly marginal – journal with a small and discerning readership. *Film Sense* described itself as 'A progressive journal of film news and opinion, published by the Film Division of the New York State Council of Arts, Sciences and Professions', and promoted itself as 'A hard-hitting antidote for Hollywood pap'. At one point, it was endorsed by the *National Guardian* as 'America's outstanding film magazine'. As well as publishing reviews of 'serious' film books such as Hortense

Powdermaker's *Hollywood: The Dream Factory*,[11] the magazine featured articles primarily concerned with issues such as the representation of race, violence, religion, war (including atomic warfare), minority groups and male supremacy. It regularly reviewed European as well as contemporary American films (independent productions on 16 mm as well as major Hollywood releases) and was clearly aimed at a left-wing intelligentsia rather than a mass readership. Consequently, it was very different in style and content to the vast majority of commercial mainstream film publications. So far as its review of *All About Eve* is concerned, the magazine certainly responded differently to the film than any of the major film journals or newspapers.

Entitled 'Nothing About Eve' and written jointly by Vanna and Jay Starr, *Film Sense*'s review debated the merits of the movie, with Vanna on the attack and Jay in defence. At one point in their exchange, Jay told Vanna, 'Be glad they didn't have the career woman ending up over a hot stove, or telephoning diaper service'.[12] Vanna responded:

> You think there was no male supremacy? Find me one career woman in the film who didn't have either an alcohol or neurotic jag. Bette Davis, the ageing actress, was over-ripe for Dr Franzblau's couch. And Eve was biting everyone else's nails besides her own. Only Celeste Holm, the playwright's wife, was a happy woman. That's because she was content to remain domesticated and bask in her husband's success. I didn't see her darning his socks or broiling his lamb chops, but I'm sure she handled the maid and the butler with the true instincts of the professional man's spouse.[13]

Vanna reinforced her charge of inherent sexism at the very end of the article:

> VANNA: Maybe you won't think I'm being petty or too female-conscious, if I mention one other example of discrimination. You remember how, in the end that pretty little monster begins the cycle all over again by winning her way into the now-successful Eve's home. Again it's a female who's the conniver. Never do any of the male theatrical professionals hit below the belt.
>
> JAY: OK. But will you admit that if we know nothing about Eve, we do know …
>
> VANNA: I've changed my mind. We do know a little about Eve, but we know too much about Hollywood.[14]

In the process of airing their different opinions of *All About Eve*, Vanna and Jay Starr established an alternative reading of the movie, very different from those that had appeared in the popular press. At the same time, they articulated a crucial tension between what might be thought of as 'sophisticated' or 'innocent' readings of the film. That *All About Eve* should simultaneously elicit both sophisticated and innocent readings is not a unique feature of this movie but rather, as Richard Maltby has suggested, a fairly typical aspect of the classical Hollywood film.[15] In his essay ' "A Brief Romantic Interlude": Dick and Jane Go to Three and a Half Seconds of the Classical Hollywood Cinema', Maltby has demonstrated how Hollywood movies 'presuppose multiple viewpoints, at multiple textual levels, for their consuming audience'.[16] He analyses a brief scene from *Casablanca* (1942), and describes the reactions of two hypothetical historical American viewers, Dick and Jane, who disagree over the significance of the scene. In this account, the male viewer performs a 'sophisticated' reading – reading into

Casablanca elements that are not explicit in the movie – while the female viewer defends an 'innocent' reading of the film which accepts the scene at face value and no more. Nevertheless, while Jane might be regarded as an 'innocent' reader of the film, Maltby notes that not only does she have her own reasons for defending her reading of the film (involving a vested interest) but that her reading has its own degree of sophistication, drawing as it does on her knowledge of Ingrid Bergman's star persona. Dick's 'sophisticated' reading, on the other hand, draws upon his knowledge of the Production Code and censorship, which he uses to argue in favour of a meaning that must remain hidden or discrete. Maltby argues that *Casablanca* 'quite deliberately constructs itself in such a way as to offer distinct and alternative sources of pleasure to two people sitting next to each other in the same cinema'.[17] This process would ensure the greatest economic returns for a film on the grounds that it could appeal equally (but differently) to very different types of people. One consequence of this would be, as Maltby points out, that the ideological coherence of the film would be reduced. In short, the greater the scope for audiences to derive their own meanings from a particular film, the less scope for that movie to present a cogent message. However, as Maltby writes:

> To some extent this contradiction between textual construction and ideological project, between economic efficiency and ideological affect, is contained by the way in which alternative possibilities are subsumed within relatively crude binary categories, of which my division of audiences by gender would be a case in point.[18]

The creation of specifically defined gendered reading positions, that is one set of meanings for female spectators and another for male spectators, presupposes a certain degree of ideological coherence. Maltby's thesis would suggest that not only does *All About Eve* articulate distinct male and female meanings, but also that its failure to sustain a coherent ideological position on, for instance, the 'woman problem', is partially disguised by what is assumed to be different gender reactions to the issues played out on the screen.[19]

Vanna and Jay Starr's disagreement over the meaning of *All About Eve* is not, however, identical to that articulated in Maltby's account of Dick and Jane's argument over the meaning of *Casablanca*. In the Starrs' dispute, the female adopts the 'sophisticated' reading position. More crucially, the Starrs are eventually reconciled on an agreed assessment of the film. In fact, it would seem that their disagreement was primarily rhetorical and was mainly staged in order to provide support for the views articulated by Vanna. After exchanging their interpretations of *All About Eve*, Jay allowed himself to be persuaded by Vanna's suggestion that the film was inherently sexist in the way it presented its female characters, while Vanna backed down from saying that the film told its audience nothing about Eve. In the process of settling this dispute between the two, an interpretation of the film that would now be called feminist was articulated. Although such an interpretation was subsequently widely adopted by critics and historians, in 1950 it constituted a marginal view – in Stuart Hall's terminology, a 'resistant reading'. Hence, perhaps, the cautious tactic of revealing such insights by way of an argument, charting the gradual transformation of a sceptical male critic who is eventually persuaded to accept the inherent sexual discrimination of a Hollywood movie.

Thirteen years later, at a formative stage of the post-war women's liberation movement, Betty Friedan, in her groundbreaking book *The Feminine Mystique* (1963), described the ways in which American women had been lured back to the home after World War II. In particular, she noted how the heroines of women's magazine fiction were transformed from the 'New Woman' of 1939 (happy in, and proud of, her career) to the professional woman who, in 1949, decided to give up her career to become a housewife.[20] Clearly, Margo's renunciation of her career in *All About Eve* echoed the scenarios of magazine fiction at that time, while it shared its basic plot situation with several contemporaneous films starring actresses who had, like Davis, achieved stardom in the early 1930s.[21] By the 1980s, indeed, the film was regarded by film historians as a classic example of the reactionary and anti-feminist tendencies of 1950s Hollywood cinema. In *American Film Since 1945* (1984), Leonard Quart and Albert Auster discuss the film in terms of its 'typically' reactionary approach to the subject of female emancipation, understanding it not only to be representative of Hollywood's treatment of the 'woman problem' but also symptomatic of post-war American society itself.[22] In their account, the film demonstrates the patriarchal tendencies both of Hollywood cinema of the 1950s and American post-war society in general. My own concern in this chapter, however, is to understand the ways in which it corresponded or connected with social and cultural discourses in America and Britain from the time of its release in 1950. Alongside trends in film, popular literature, journalism and broadcast radio and television, *All About Eve* circulated within a particular set of social and ideological discourses. At the time of its release, such discourses included quasi-scientific theories of femininity, for example Marynia Farnham and Ferdinand Lundberg's influential book *Modern Woman: The Lost Sex* (1947), which provided the rationale for so many Americans to base their attack upon feminists and career women in the late 1940s and early 1950s.[23]

The main theme of this book was that women constituted one of the main unsolved social problems in America during the late 1940s. In the foreword, Lundberg wrote that

> The central thesis of this book is that contemporary women in very large numbers are psychologically disordered and that their disorder is having terrible social and personal effects involving men in all departments of their lives as well as women. It is by no means an a priori thesis, which the authors have set out to prove, but is a conclusion arrived at and resting on clinical work in psychiatry carried on over a long period by Dr Marynia F. Farnham of New York. Many involved case histories, of men as well as of women, underlie the broad prospect unfolded in this book, although it is not a collection of case histories but a general psychosocial study of women and the recent historical changes that have affected their personal lives, materially for the better but psychologically for the worse.[24]

Drawing upon Freudian psychoanalysis, particularly that of Helene Deutsch,[25] Farnham and Lundberg attempted to prove that women were by nature passive, dependent, maternal and home-loving and that only motherhood and marriage could ever make a woman's life meaningful and satisfying. A woman's career, they argued, was directly at odds with her femininity (that is, her true nature) and invariably resulted in her development of masculine characteristics, leading to unhappiness, frustration and, ultimately, illness. Thus, after the end of World War II, Farnham and Lundberg informed women of the dangers of work outside the home, providing government officials, educators, religious leaders, employers and others with what appeared to be a scientific basis for anti-feminism and, more specifically, for the removal of women from the workplace at a time of rising levels of unemployment. At the same time, Farnham and Lundberg helped to demonise the 'modern woman' – a stereotype of the working woman created particularly during World War II, when millions of women had taken over the civilian duties of the men drafted into the armed services.

Farnham and Lundberg described the modern woman as a chimera: the she-monster of Greek mythology, with a lion's head vomiting flames, and a serpent's tail. This she-devil, they argued, was man's rival (rather than companion) who, in her working life, had developed 'the characteristics of aggression, dominance, independence and power'.[26] These qualities were increasingly removing women from their 'true' state, essentially motherhood, and driving them 'steadily deeper into personal conflicts soluble only by psychotherapy'.[27] For the sake of their own well-being (if not for the good of their husbands or the nation), women were urged to give up their careers and embrace motherhood and domestication. The work of Farnham and Lundberg had a tremendous impact in the United States during the initial post-war period. William Chafe, in his book *The American Woman* (1972), observed that

> Lundberg and Farnham had clearly touched on an issue of great interest, for within a brief period of time the theme they established was echoed by others. As might have been expected, women's magazines led the list of supporters, and the joys of 'femininity' and 'togetherness' became the staple motifs of periodicals like *McCall's* and the *Ladies Home Journal*.[28]

However, while dominant discourses were extolling the virtues of femininity and domestication for women, others were highlighting its dangers and frustrations. In fact, the anti-feminism of Farnham and Lundberg only represents one side of what was actually a hotly-debated issue. Other researchers and writers sought to demonstrate the similarities between the sexes and also the social rather than biological nature of gender. For instance, Margaret Mead's anthropological study *Male and Female* (first published in 1950) highlighted the extent to which qualities such as aggression, courage, dominance, passivity and gentleness were determined by environmental conditions and child-rearing techniques rather than acquired 'naturally' by one or other of the sexes.[29] Mead in fact referred directly (and slightingly) to *Modern Woman* in her book:

> Literature in the United States at the present is raucous and angry on this whole question of the relationship between men and women. We have had a spate of books that claim women are being masculinized, to their ill, to men's ill, to everybody's ill ... When one follows the shrill insistencies of books like *Modern Woman: The Lost Sex*, which end by attacking men as well as women, one realizes that we are passing through a period of discrepancies in sex roles which are so conspicuous that efforts to disguise the price that both sexes play are increasingly unsuccessful ... As surely as we believe that the present troublesome problems of sex adjustment are due to the possibilities of women alone, we commit ourselves to a long series of false moves as we attempt to push women out of the home, into the home, out of the home, adding mounting

confusion to the difficulties born of a changing world-climate of opinion, a shifting technology, and an increasing rate of violence of cultural change.[30]

Other dissenting voices could also be heard in the field of journalism. For example, Mary McCarthy's scathing review of Farnham and Lundberg's book in *The New Yorker* rendered their arguments both disingenuous and contentious.[31] 'In the intellectual sphere', McCarthy argued, 'the Lundberg–Farnham argument remains purely contentious. No jot of evidence is brought forward to support the crucial proposition … For the disingenuousness of this kind of reasoning that uses its own hypothesis as proof, that appeals always to the authority of "facts" and allows itself at the same time the anarchy of interpretation, *Modern Woman: The Lost Sex* offers an unforgettable illustration'.[32]

Though such dissent may have been largely marginal (that is, confined to a learned and 'highbrow' readership) and almost completely drowned out by the feature writers of *Ladies Home Journal* and *Life*,[33] nevertheless, the existence of alternative discourses on the issues of womanhood and femininity within American and British culture during the late 1940s and 1950s provided a context in which *All About Eve* could be read 'against the grain' or, at the very least, represent the site of a struggle over meaning, such as that suggested by the Starrs' review in *Film Sense* – even if such alternative readings of *All About Eve* in 1950 and 1951 were really only available to a middle-class left-wing readership.

While these alternative readings were not simply determined by gender, the latter did play a crucial role in generating distinct and different readings of *All About Eve*, principally in relation to the audience's capacity to interpret Margo Channing's actions according to their knowledge of Bette Davis as a star. As Barbara Leaming wrote in her 1992 biography, Davis, 'the most potent symbol of wartime female independence and self-sufficiency appeared suddenly [in *All About Eve*] to accept and even recommend the retrograde sexual politics of the 1950s'.[34] It could be argued that Davis's star persona demonstrated the full scale of the country's U-turn on gender roles since the late 1930s and early 1940s. By refashioning a real-life actress famed (and once celebrated) for her dedication to work and for her independent, fighting spirit into the character of an actress prepared to sacrifice all for home and husband, the film might be seen as showing how even the most 'modern' of women could successfully be transformed into one of the most traditional and conservative. On the other hand, Davis's 'modern woman' persona might have been resilient enough not only to withstand the film's ending but also to render it unbelievable or ironic. Some members of the audience (namely, her staunchest fans) might well have been able to read and even enjoy the ironies of this spectacle and interpret these actions as untenable, as the stuff of myth or (Hollywood/male) fantasy.

Davis's casting in *All About Eve* would have certainly played a crucial role in determining the ways in which audiences made sense of the actions of her character, Margo Channing. Her star persona, the characteristics of 'Bette Davis' established through publicity, news, interviews, biographies and gossip, in combination with the legacy of her previous screen roles, necessarily played an integral part in the meaning system of *All About Eve*. Davis's identity as a star was associated with female independence and even feminism, two traits repeatedly reflected and celebrated in the films she made for

Warner Bros. throughout the 1930s and 1940s. This is something that has often been commented on by critics, biographers and film historians. Written in 1966, Henry Hart's comments are fairly typical:

> The part of our *Zeitgeist* which Miss Davis' screen image subserved is feminism.
> Which is not to say that Miss Davis' films have been overt feminist propaganda. What is meant is this: in her every role audiences sensed an exemplar of 'the new woman'. The result was women had a double pleasure watching her since, in addition to a good acting performance, they saw one of their own confront the male with a new independence, as well as with the immemorial web.
> Why did men like her? I am not sure they did, *really* ... Some knowing men of my acquaintance enjoyed watching the phenomenon of Bette Davis herself – a not especially good-looking girl, slightly ex-ophthalmic in fact – getting away with an arrogance that had *what* to back it up?
> The 'what' is described by Miss Davis' admirers and detractors. The latter are voluble about her ... 'masculine protest'; about, in fact, almost everything except the things Miss Davis' admirers emphasize – intelligence, self-discipline, capacity for hard work and, above all, ambition.[35]

As this appraisal of Davis's appeal by a male critic indicates, not only did men and women have very different responses to Bette Davis, but those men who professed to like her found it difficult to explain why. Some men's delight in the image of Davis contains a suggestion of masochism, since she so often either destroys men or manages perfectly well without them in her films. It is, moreover, the 'knowing men' of this critic's acquaintance who appreciate her.[36] The majority of Bette Davis's fans were, as they had been throughout the war years, female. However, whereas during the war the actress and her studio could count on high returns at the box office from her devoted following of American and British female fans, after the war circumstances altered dramatically, since the male viewers who accompanied their wives and girlfriends to the cinema may not have wished to see a 'rebellious and threatening figure like Bette Davis'.[37] Stripping the Davis persona of her power and independence at the end of *All About Eve* possibly sent reassuring signals to male viewers. The same spectacle may not, however, have received such a favourable reaction from her female fans, given that this ending so crucially undermined those aspects of her star persona which had won her such devoted favour among women during the early 1940s.

Although significant numbers of women no doubt shared with male viewers the pleasure of seeing Davis 'come to her senses' and opt for marriage over career, for large numbers of women, the ending would have been a disappointment. For some, like Catherine de la Roche, it was both unrealistic and damaging. For those like Caroline Lejeune, it dampened out the fires which had burned so brightly. Others, like Vanna Starr, found the film's treatment of female characters not only disappointing but offensive. Many women must have shared Vanna Starr's fury at the film's depiction of ambitious women as conniving little monsters who 'hit below the belt' and thus deserved their fates as lonely, embittered and sexually frustrated neurotics. If the movie suggested that career women were ripe for the couch of Dr Marynia Farnham and could only avoid such treatment by giving up everything in order simply to bask in their husband's glory as the dutiful spouses of professional men, Vanna Starr's commentary showed that, as a professional, left-wing woman, she could both see through and reject the anti-feminist message of *All About Eve*. Clearly, *All About Eve* did not provoke a coherently 'female view' (in opposition to a 'male view'), given that published opinions of female reviewers and critics were so various and contradictory. The film was too ambivalent for this, particularly for those viewers who recognise the contradictions involved in the relationship between the star persona of Bette Davis and her character Margo Channing.

The ambiguities, contradictions and ironies which emerged largely as a result of the casting of Bette Davis as Margo Channing would have lasting appeal to 'knowing' audiences in later years and, increasingly, much of the writing about this film would eventually come to highlight its duplicities and ambiguous qualities, securing it a prominent place within, for instance, gay culture. The publication in 1973 of an article by Lawrence J. Quirk entitled 'The Cult of Bette and Joan: The True Reasons Why They Drive Homosexuals Wild' clearly suggests the extent to which Davis's gay appeal had been noted by critics, commentators and regular film-goers by the early 1970s.[38] According to Quirk:

> For years now, a great deal has been made of the homosexuals' addiction to Bette Davis
> and Joan Crawford and their films. Transvestites, female impersonators and campy
> types of all descriptions and traditions ape Davis mannerisms and shout 'Peter, The
> Letter!' and 'You disgust me, you worm!'[39]

Quirk pointed out that, for some years, it had been generally believed that 'some kind of frenzied, high-camp, super-comical element was involved in this Gay preoccupation' and that, according to this theory, Bette Davis (along with several other major Hollywood actresses) 'mirrored certain frenzied, self-projective, super-compensating principles that psychologists and psychiatrists have spotted in more aggressive and flamboyant homosexuals, especially those in showbusiness'.[40]

However, Quirk proposed a 'deeper' meaning for the Davis mania among gays and his article was devoted to exploring this in more detail, concentrating on the appeal for closeted gay viewers:

> One fact of 1973 is that appearances tell nothing. Here I am not concerned with the
> iceberg-tip of 'fag prima donnas' but with the typical cross-section homosexual, in or
> out of showbusiness. Why does *he* get a bang out of old Bette–Joan movies? The answer
> is really quite simple. For in their top films of yore, Davis and Crawford were usually in
> aggressive, intent pursuit of one or all of three things: men, money and power. These
> three drives motivate the lives of most homosexuals I have known.[41]

At one point Quirk argues that

> it is not being 'Anti-Gay' to state that many homosexuals are quite sad and lost people.
> And the great Davis–Crawford movies were often about sad and lost people with whom
> they could identify. The Crawford–Davis films, besides mirroring subtle forms of
> unhappiness and restless detours from the positive life-force, often possessed a negative

intensity that reached super-masochistic heights, proving therapeutic to many a tormented Gay.[42]

So far as *All About Eve* was concerned, Quirk found the film's core to consist of

> Davis and Anne Baxter battling for men and careers; Davis at 40 hates Baxter because she's 24 (the Gay Obsession with Youth); doublecrossings, bitcheries of all descriptions, nasty verbal exchanges, putdowns, ego ripoffs – all gleefully purgative to Gays whose past, present and future are full of this kind of ego-game activity in which Power is as important a prize as Sex.[43]

Although Quirk's piece is highly individualistic and sheds very little light on the real reasons why gay men have become such devoted fans of Bette Davis and her films, his essay does foreground the subject of Davis's gay appeal. It also suggests, at least implicitly, a desire for Davis to be reclaimed by heterosexual audiences since the article itself seems rooted in Quirk's personal frustration that his own favourite films should also appeal so strongly to what he calls the 'lunatic fringe of flamboyant "queens" '.[44] This sentiment is clearest in the final paragraph of his essay, where he describes how his recent viewing of *All About Eve* at the Waverley Movie Theater in Greenwich Village, New York City, had been interrupted by the 'savage screams and whistles and stampings of a largely Gay audience'.[45] His article ends with what is little short of a plea for gay audiences to leave Bette Davis alone – to leave her, indeed, to those (like himself) who are truly capable of admiring her.

As well as suggesting that Bette Davis's gay appeal was well established by the time of the gay liberation movement of the late 1960s and early 1970s, Quirk's article also indicates that gay men had begun to construct their own readings of her films and saw their own lives and experiences expressed in the subtexts of these films. In the process, a struggle over meaning appeared to be forming between straight and gay fans over which group constituted the 'true' or 'sophisticated' audience for her films.[46] With the increasing visibility of gay people as a result of the gay liberation movement, it must have seemed that the members of this newly emergent yet still marginal social group were establishing their own cultural identity by appropriating aspects of mainstream culture and 'dragging them down to their level'. According to such a view, products of the dominant culture, such as the Hollywood films of Bette Davis, would seem to have been appropriated by the gay community, acquiring a range of new meanings in the process. But a number of gay writers have subsequently claimed that, in the case of *All About Eve*, the gay meanings were there from the start, and that this was less a matter of gay audiences choosing to read (or wilfully misread) these movies in a gay way than of them recognising these inherent meanings in spite of the fact that, until the 1970s, the majority of professional reviewers and critics had failed to acknowledge such meanings in print.

In 1981, Vito Russo described the inherent gayness of *All About Eve* in *The Celluloid Closet,* noting the ways in which two of the principal characters, Eve Harrington (Anne Baxter) and Addison de Witt (George Sanders) were implicitly homosexual. He referred to the critic Addison de Witt as not only 'suave and lethal' but also as a 'symbol of sophisticated decadence'[47] and described Eve as a 'subliminally gay character', commenting

upon her 'boyish' looks and referring to her as 'a sort of malevolent Huck Finn'.[48] Russo
even claimed that the reason for her ultimate downfall was her lesbianism:

> According to writer-director Mankiewicz, her vulnerability in the last scene to another
> conniving woman is the result of physical attraction. Eve does not have the kind of
> generosity that led Margo Channing (Bette Davis) to take a waif like her under her
> wing. To ask Phoebe (Barbara Bates) to spend the night rather than take the subway
> home to Brooklyn could only have one motive, and it spelt the beginning of the end for
> Eve Harrington.[49]

This is an example of the way in which gay writers, by the 1980s, were highlighting the
underlying homosexuality of the film, inviting gay viewers to read more into the scenarios of this and other Hollywood films.

There is, however, evidence to suggest that viewers had in reality been making such
readings since the 1960s. For instance, Ken Geist, in his biography of Joseph L.
Mankiewicz, *Pictures Will Talk* (1978), noted that the director had informed him that
from about 1968 he had begun to receive fan mail enquiring about the gay subtext of
the film. In a footnote, Geist included the following statement:

> Mankiewicz says that only within the past five years [i.e. 1968–73] has his mail reflected
> viewers comprehending the significance of Eve and her room-mate in night clothes,
> linking arms as they ascend the staircase. By revealing Eve's mannishly cropped hair
> after she removes her curled stage wig, and by having Eve suggest that Pheobe stay the
> night rather than make the long subway trip home, Mankiewicz subtly suggests Eve's
> Sapphic nature.[50]

Geist's comment suggests that Mankiewicz had encoded these meanings in details of
mise-en-scène and character action.

By the 1990s, *All About Eve* was circulating in a context where homosexuality had
attained a high media profile and with considerable literature publicly available on the
subject, designed to appeal to a (lucrative) gay market. The film not only came to feature prominently in gay textbooks[51] but also in other media texts, including three cinematic gay reworkings of the film: an avant-garde short by American gay film-maker
Jerry Tartaglia;[52] a gay pornographic video pastiche called *All About Steve*;[53] and a
Spanish art-house homage by Pedro Almodóvar called *All About My Mother*.[54] In recent
years, gay writers, film-makers and historians have both celebrated and reinscribed the
gay significance of *All About Eve*, creating a context for audiences to recognise its gay
meanings.[55]

This chapter began with a discussion of the earliest reviews of *All About Eve* in the
United States and Britain. I found that what had struck me as the most significant
aspect of the movie, namely its engagement with the 'woman problem', went largely
unspoken in these reviews. This alerted me to the existence of a structuring absence in
the way that mainstream reviews shifted the meanings of the film away from those indicated by its narrative, title and original publicity. Despite the fact that the film was promoted as being 'all about women – and their men', the majority of the reviewers in 1950
avoided such a contentious and divisive topic at a time when, as one contemporary

commentator noted, much of America was 'raucous and angry on this whole question of the relationship between men and women'.[56] Vanna and Jay Starrs' critique of the film in *Film Sense* represents an exception to the way *All About Eve* was originally reviewed and marks the early formation of 'alternative' or 'resistent' readings of the movie.

These strategies by mainstream reviewers and critics were tantamount to removing the film from its social and cultural context. What this suggests is that an examination of the dominant discourses which cluster around a film (most notably, publicity, advertising, reviews, journalistic features, star and director interviews, etc.) provide only a partial indication of a film's meaning. In other words, a historiographical approach to film reception that is dependent upon reviews and journalistic features in mainstream publications is limited to revealing the construction of dominant or 'preferred' meanings. Resistant, negotiated or alternative readings may emerge when marginal discourses are available for investigation or when a diachronic approach is used; that is, an examination of subsequent rereading and reinterpretations by commentators, writers, scholars and fans from different historical moments and from different social or cultural sections of society. Any review, of course, inevitably leaves something unsaid and, as this chapter has confirmed, what is left out of public discourse can be as fruitful for analysis as what is included. Identifying and accounting for the unspoken is thus an important part of the historian's task. This is particularly true, of course, for feminist and gay historians of film reception who seek to identify the meanings of films from a time when feminism and homosexuality were unacceptable subjects for public discourse. *All About Eve* suggests that, for all its sophisticated talk, its most critical messages went unspoken and remained so until the context available for interpretation changed.

Notes

1 J. P. Mayer, *Sociology of Film* (New York: Arno Press, 1972, first published in 1946) and *British Cinema and Their Audiences* (New York: Arno Press, 1978, first published in 1948); Leo Handel, *Hollywood Looks at its Audience* (Urbana: University of Illinois Press, 1950); Jeffrey Richards and Dorothy Sheridan, *Mass Observation at the Movies* (London: Routledge & Kegan Paul, 1987).

2 Janet Staiger, 'The Handmaiden of Villainy: Methods and Problems in Studying the Historical Reception of a Film', *Wide Angle*, vol. 8, no. 1 (1986), p. 20.

3 Ibid., pp. 21, 26.

4 Janet Staiger, *Interpreting Films: Studies in the Historical Reception of American Cinema* (Princeton, NJ: Princeton University Press, 1992), pp. 79–80.

5 Ibid., p. 22.

6 Barbara Klinger, 'Film History Terminable and Interminable: Recovering the Past in Reception Studies', *Screen*, vol. 38, no. 2 (summer 1997), pp. 107–28. Klinger writes that 'the grand view behind a *histoire totale* has several valuable functions for film history' and embraces 'a scholarly aim rather than an absolutely achievable reality' (pp. 108–9). Like Staiger, she allocates a significant role to extra-cinematic materials, such as advertising and publicity, reviews and criticism, star interviews and features in film journals, fanzines, the popular press and lifestyle magazines but acknowledges that 'questions of history must extend beyond the industry to engage in a potentially vast system of interconnections, from the film and its immediate industrial context to social and historical developments' (p. 111).

7 Bosley Crowther, *New York Times* (14 October 1950), p. 13.

8 Caroline A. Lejeune, 'A Star at Eve', *Observer* (10 December 1950), p. 6.

9 Ann Griffith, *Films in Review,* vol. 1, no. 9 (December 1950), pp. 37–8.

10 Catherine de la Roche, *Picture Post* (9 December 1950), p. 18.

11 Hortense Powdermaker, *Hollywood: The Dream Factory* (New York: Little, Brown & Co., 1950).

12 Vanna and Jay Starr, 'Nothing About Eve', *Film Sense,* vol. 1, no. 6 (October 1950), p. 8.

13 Ibid.

14 Ibid.

15 Richard Maltby, ' "A Brief Romantic Interlude": Dick and Jane Go to Three and a Half Seconds of the Classical Hollywood Cinema', in David Bordwell and Nöel Carroll (eds), *Post-Theory: Reconstructing Film Studies* (Wisconsin: University of Wisconsin Press, 1996) pp. 434–59.

16 Ibid., p. 436.

17 Ibid., p. 443.

18 Ibid., p. 444.

19 However, one could say that a film theorist's project of assigning alternative readings of a film to male and female viewpoints – as I am doing here with Vanna and Jay Starr's reading of *All About Eve* – obscures in the process the extent to which the film itself presents an ideologically incoherent or even contradictory message. Thus, while it may appear that *All About Eve* offers conflicting meanings and pleasures to male and female audiences by enabling them to interpret differently, another view might suggest that such diverse readings and pleasures emerge because the film actually expresses or represents the ambivalent or contradictory aspects of gender ideology at a specific historical moment.

20 Betty Friedan, *The Feminine Mystique* (London: Victor Gollancz, 1963), pp. 38–44.

21 Between 1946 and 1954, for example, Ginger Rogers appeared in four films playing a major stage or screen star, in professional or personal competition with a much younger woman: *Weekend at the Waldorf* (1946); *The Barkleys of Broadway* (1949); *Forever Female* (1953); *Black Widow* (1954).

22 Leonard Quart and Albert Auster, *American Film Since 1945* (London: MacMillan, 1984) p. 55.

23 Marynia F. Farnham and Ferdinand Lundberg, *Modern Woman: The Lost Sex* (New York: Harper and Brothers, 1947). Dr Marynia Farnham was a psychologist and Ferdinand Lundberg a sociologist. The book originally cited the authors as Lundberg and Farnham, lending more prominence to the name of the male scholar. This may have been intended to reflect his greater input into the actual writing of the book, which implies simultaneously that Farnham's input was primarily concerned with the provision of 'clinical evidence'. The precedence of Lundberg's name might have been due to his more well-known reputation as an author, having previously published two books. It could also have been, of course, because he was male. This would certainly have been in keeping with the general philosophy of the book. However, the common practice for citing this book now is to reverse the order of the authors' names and list them alphabetically. Most bibliographical entries now refer to the authors as Farnham and Lundberg and the book is currently catalogued by the British Library in this way.

24 Ibid., Foreword, p. v.

25 Helene Deutsch's book *The Psychology of Women: A Psychoanalytic Interpretation* (New York: Grune and Stratton) was first published in 1944. Deutsch linked female sexuality to an inherently masochistic drive and tendency which supported notions of their willing (and natural) subjugation to male supremacy or dominance.

26 Ibid., p. 236.

27 Ibid.

28 William H. Chafe, *The American Woman: Her Changing Social, Economic and Political Roles, 1920–70* (New York and London: Oxford University Press, 1972), p. 206.

29 Margaret Mead, *Male and Female: A Study of the Sexes in a Changing World* (London: Victor Gollancz, 1950).

30 Ibid., p. 300.

31 Mary McCarthy, 'The Tyranny of the Orgasm' (April 1947), reprinted in *On the Contrary: Articles of Belief 1946–61* (London: Heinemann, 1962), pp. 167–73.

32 Ibid., pp. 171–3.

33 Not until the publication of Betty Friedan's *The Feminine Mystique* (1963) would such dissension reach a wider and more popular audience in the United States and Britain.

34 Barbara Leaming, *Bette Davis: A Biography* (London: Weidenfield & Nicolson, 1992), p. 202.

35 Henry Hart, foreword to Gene Ringgold, *The Films of Bette Davis* (Secaucus, NJ: Citadel Press, 2nd edn, 1973), pp. 7–8.

36 Henry Hart gives no indication of what he actually means by the phrase 'some knowing men of my acquaintance'. It could well be an innocent remark which implies nothing more than a discerning minority of male viewers acquainted with the critic (possibly fellow critics). At the time of publication, however, this remark could be more knowing than this, and refer covertly to the growing band of gay male fans who had begun to worship Bette Davis, making their presence known at public screenings of her films and at her stage appearances. See Lawrence J. Quirk, 'The Cult of Bette and Joan: The True Reasons Why They Drive Homosexuals Wild', *Quirk's Reviews*, no. 9, March 1973, pp. 1–5, and Lawrence J. Quirk, *Fasten Your Seatbelts: The Passionate Life of Bette Davis* (New York: William Morrow and Co., 1990), pp. 411–12.

37 Leaming, *Bette Davis : A Biography*, p. 191.

38 Quirk, 'The Cult of Bette and Joan', pp. 1–5. Quirk (nephew of James R. Quirk, editor and publisher of *Photoplay* in the 1920s and 1930s) was the editor and chief reviewer of his own independent film journal in New York City.

39 Ibid., p. 1.

40 Ibid., pp. 1–2.

41 Ibid.

42 Ibid., p. 3.

43 Ibid.

44 Ibid.

45 Ibid.

46 Quirk wrote that 'it should be noted that like all true artists, Bette Davis and Joan Crawford strike universal chords, and can evoke positive and cathartic responses from all kinds of people – women, old folks, sensitive adolescents, thoughtful cineastes, film scholars who admire the more intelligent and depthful and tasteful aspects of their work. Here, of course, lie the bulk of their admirers and they are mostly heterosexual in orientation'. Ibid., p. 2.

47 Ibid., p. 95.

48 Vito Russo, *The Celluloid Closet* (New York: Harpers & Row, 1981), p. 94.

49 Ibid., p. 101.

50 Ken Geist, *Pictures Will Talk* (New York: Charles Scribner & Sons, 1978), p. 167, n. 20.

51 For example, Keith Howes, in his encyclopaedia of homosexuality on film, radio and television, *Broadcasting It* (1993), establishes the inherent homosexuality of Eve and de Witt, writing that 'Eve Harrington, with her ambiguous clothes, hairstyle and body language, has an uneasy intimacy with the acerbic theatre critic and we witness a seduction of a young fan at her apartment' (p. 21). He describes George Sanders's heterosexual smoke-screen tactic of being seen with 'a starlet (Marilyn MONROE) on his arm' making him appear to be a 'womanizer', but that his dressing-room scene with Eve reveals that they share the same unspeakable sexuality. Keith Howes, *Broadcasting It: An Encyclopaedia of Homosexuality on Film, Radio and Television in the UK 1923–63* (London and New York: Cassell, 1993), p. 21.

52 *Remembrance* (Jerry Tartaglia, 1990), a five-minute short film mixing repeated scenes from *All About Eve* with home movies, in order to explore the director's life-long fascination with Bette Davis and her films.

53 *All About Steve* (Chi Chi La Rue, 1993). This gay pornographic video features a pastiche of the opening scene which replaces the original Sarah Siddons award ceremony with the Gay Video Awards. In this version Margo becomes Marco (Derek Cruise), ageing gay porn star, and Eve becomes Steve Carrington (Mark West), an aspiring porn star who sleeps his way to the top, his rise chronicled in intimate detail.

54 *Todo sobre mi madre/All About My Mother* (Pedro Almodóvar, 1999). This movie includes scenes from *All About Eve* being watched on Spanish television (dubbed into Spanish) by a young man (gay by implication of the fact that he reads Truman Capote and is fascinated by an ageing actress performing the role of Blanche in Tennessee Williams's *A Streetcar Named Desire*) and his mother. The film also includes a number of scenes which closely resemble moments from *All About Eve*.

55 In the process, of course, the significance of the film's ambivalent engagement with the 'woman problem' issue has once more been obscured.

56 Mead, *Male and Female*, p. 300.

4
The Fall and Rise of *Fantasia*

Amy M. Davis

Some films are received by audiences in a positive way, and immediately become critical and/or commercial successes. Others are disregarded by both audiences and critics
and survive only as footnotes in cinema reference books and on late-night television. A
third type of film is poorly received when it first appears, but becomes a success with
later audiences. This chapter analyses the circumstances surrounding the 'fall and rise'
of one such film: Walt Disney's *Fantasia*, first released in 1940. It examines the reasons
for the film's initial commercial failure, and the manner in which its popular reception
changed over time.

The makers of *Fantasia* saw it as a new kind of animated film, as did some enthusiastic film critics. Otis Ferguson, for instance, declared *Fantasia* to be 'strange and beautiful … the only excuse I have ever seen for having eyes and ears at the same time',[1] while
Peyton Boswell, editor of *Art Digest,* called it 'an aesthetic experience never to be forgotten'.[2] The movie-going public, however, appeared considerably less enthusiastic and
the film initially failed at the box office. This disappointing début was followed by a slow
climb towards profitability and public esteem over the next three decades. By the time
of its fiftieth anniversary rerelease in 1990, *Fantasia* had proved sufficiently durable to
be included on the list of the top 200 highest-grossing films ever made. Released on
video in 1991, it rapidly became the largest-selling video marketed to that date.

In 1934, Walt Disney Studios had begun work on its first animated feature film, *Snow
White and the Seven Dwarfs.* As production costs soared to what was then a shocking
$2 million, movie industry insiders, doubting that Disney could ever make back his
production costs on such an expensive 'cartoon', dubbed *Snow White* 'Disney's Folly'. In
1937, however, it was released to great critical acclaim and staggering popular success,
making over $8 million at the box office in 1937–8 and saving the studio from bank-
ruptcy.[3] This success gave Disney the confidence to expand the studio, and although he
rapidly abandoned his original goal of releasing an animated feature every year, he
invested heavily in researching and developing new technologies for the medium, and
in educating his artists through classes taught by artists from the Chouinard Art
Institute.[4] Throughout his career, in an effort to 'expand the boundaries of animation'
(to paraphrase his own often-expressed ambition), Disney repeatedly put his studio in
debt, gambling on both his own reputation as an entertainer and on what he saw as the
ability of cinema audiences to recognise and appreciate well-produced animated films.
Such risks had turned out to be great successes in terms of both Disney's own reputation as an innovative film-maker and his studio's finances. Thus, when *Fantasia* premièred at the Broadway Theatre in New York City on 13 November 1940, the fact that

its production costs had reached $2,250,000, exceeding those of *Snow White,* did not seem to concern him. However, if *Snow White and the Seven Dwarfs* showed that this strategy could pay off handsomely, *Fantasia* demonstrated that it was none the less still a gamble.

The various accounts of why Disney embarked on the project of *Fantasia* all converge on an encounter between Disney and the conductor Leopold Stokowski, during which Disney divulged that he had been working on a *Silly Symphony* featuring Mickey Mouse (the cartoon which would later become the 'Sorcerer's Apprentice' segment of *Fantasia*). Stokowski allegedly offered to conduct the recording of the score without a fee, and extended Disney's idea by suggesting that they join forces to create a film that would combine various classical works with animation.[5] This last idea, of expanding the project from a single short to a feature-length film, appealed to the studio for both creative and financial reasons.

According to John Culhane, *Fantasia* was 'a new concept, a group of separate numbers, regardless of their running time, put together in a single presentation. Instead of calling it a vaudeville show, it turned out to be a concert – something novel and of high quality.'[6] Disney himself later stressed the film's innovative approach, arguing that it

> was made at a time when we had the feeling that we had to open doors here. This medium was something we felt a responsibility for, and we just felt that we could go beyond the comic strip, that we could do some very exciting, entertaining, and beautiful things with music and pictures and color.[7]

Disney had sought to 'expand his medium' throughout his career. *Steamboat Willie* (1928), the first Mickey Mouse cartoon, was also the first sound cartoon and the resources of the tiny Disney Brothers Studio had been set at risk in Disney's campaign to get the film released. *Flowers and Trees* (1932) began production as a black and white cartoon in the *Silly Symphony* series but, taking a financial risk the major companies were unwilling to attempt, the studio changed its animation procedures to make the film as the first cartoon in Technicolor's three-strip colour process. As Richard Neupert has argued, Disney's schematic use of colour as an instrument of narrative and character motivation was widely praised, particularly in comparison to the early uses of colour in feature films, and Disney's colour aesthetic became the prototype for how colour should be used in Hollywood's live-action cinema by the late 1930s.[8]

Disney continually presented himself as being less interested in financial considerations than in artistic ones. 'Money – or rather the lack of it to carry out my ideas – may worry me,' he declared, 'but it does not excite me. Ideas excite me.'[9] He saw each of the studio's cartoons as an arena for experimentation with new techniques, tools, story ideas and character types. The *Silly Symphony* series, in particular, was a testing ground for innovations which would develop the artistic and technological resources necessary for the studio to create a feature-length 'cartoon'.[10] Once *Snow White* succeeded and Disney's belief that audiences could accept and appreciate feature-length animation had been proved correct, he continued to apply his studio's entire resources to improving the quality of animation. While there is no doubt that some of this constant striving for improvement was inspired by his artists' devotion to their work and their pride in being associated with the quality linked with the Disney name, Disney's own ambitions were probably the most crucial motivating force.

Disney was concerned both with the status of his product and with his own status in comparison to that of other studio heads.[11] He was intensely aware that, even within cinema, cartoons were seen as being less important than feature films, at best serving only as an extra entertainment between showings of the principal attraction and rarely advertised or presented as an attraction themselves.[12] Despite their critical acclaim, his studio's films rarely received the promotion Disney believed they merited. In an inter-office memo in July 1937, he commented that the studio had 'hammered and done everything we could – conducted campaigns, etc. In certain spots we were fairly successful, but in others it is impossible to impress a theatre man that a short subject is worth advertising'.[13] Even more importantly, the cartoons' share of box-office income undervalued their contribution to a theatre's whole bill of attractions. These concerns encouraged the studio's move into feature production. In 1937, the studio released a compilation of its most celebrated shorts as *Walt Disney's Academy Award Revue,* promoting the film with an extensive newspaper advertising campaign, a series of radio broadcasts and tie-ups with more than a hundred Disney product licensees. *The Academy Award Revue*'s promotion was a model for the even more extensive campaign marketing *Snow White* the following year, while the compilation-type structure of the film itself served as a prototype for the structure of *Fantasia.*[14]

The conscious construction of Disney's public persona was as much a part of the studio's attempt to address the status and earning power of its products as was the move to features. The success of Disney's technical and aesthetic experimentation in the 1930s was widely recognised and celebrated by a series of Academy awards, and by the inclusion of several Disney films in the permanent collection of the Chicago Art Institute and the sale to both private collectors and the New York Metropolitan Museum of Art of cels from *Snow White*. In late 1930s popular journalistic discourse, Disney defined animation, and very little was published on the subject that did not refer to the studio as personified by Disney himself. A plethora of enthusiastic newspaper and magazine articles equated Disney with Chaplin as creators of universally popular entertainment. In 1938, Yale University awarded him an honorary degree, describing him as the 'creator of a new language of art' and 'an ambassador of international good-will'.[15] This apparently unanimous opinion of Disney was encapsulated in an article by Paul Hollister entitled 'Genius at Work: Walt Disney', published in the December 1940 issue of *Atlantic Monthly* as part of the publicity campaign for *Fantasia*. The new Disney film, declared Hollister, was 'a revolution': 'a pictorial fantasy on the screen contrived to interpret, animate, enrich, expand, and vitalize the music as music has never before come to life'.[16]

This discourse enthusiastically celebrated Disney's universal appeal. As one Nebraska theatre manager declared, the studio's output managed to appeal 'to every living person from the ages of 2 to 102', and this success promoted his presentation as 'the consummate artist, the perfect combination of the corporate and the creative'.[17] Mickey, Donald, Goofy and the rest had established the Disney studio as 'the children's storyteller *par excellence*', and certainly the child audience was central to the commercial, aesthetic and moral appeal of its product.[18] But Disney himself always claimed that he was trying to appeal to adults as well as children, although in a manner that addressed the child in the adult:

I go right straight out for the adult. As I say, for the honest adult. Not the sophisticates. Not these characters that think they know everything and you can't thrill them anymore. I go for those people that retain that something, you know, no matter how old they are; that little spirit of adventure, that appreciation of the world of fantasy and things like that, I go for them. I play to them. There's a lot of them, you know.[19]

In the late 1930s, Disney cartoons were seen as 'the most appropriate first-run supplement to films marketed as important and adult' such as *Dodsworth* (1936), *These Three* (1936) or *The Good Earth* (1937).[20] But as Leon Schlesinger, head of cartoon production at Warner Bros., commented in 1939, 'while the cartoon today is excellent entertainment for young and old, it is primarily the favorite motion picture fare of children'.[21] Richard deCordova has usefully distinguished between the two different registers that attached children to the cinema, and to cartoons in particular: childrens' consumption of films themselves; and their broader consumption of the products displayed in films or marketed through movie tie-ins. DeCordova argues that Disney's merchandising and promotion system created 'elaborate networks of mutual reference between these two registers of consumption'.[22] From the early 1930s, according to deCordova, American children were addressed as consumers through the merchandising of Mickey Mouse.[23] As early as 1932, Mickey Mouse had become a 'star of the toy department', while Mickey Mouse Clubs developed to incorporate the cultural activities of children within a community oriented around their consumption not just of movies but also of toys.[24]

Before *Snow White*'s release, Disney and RKO launched a huge campaign promoting the film in movie theatres, newspapers, magazines, grocery stores and shop windows, and also through merchandising and licensing tie-ups. There were dolls modelled after Snow White and the seven dwarfs (produced by a number of different companies and made from a wide variety of materials), wind-up tin toys, marionettes, lamps and nightlights, bookends, glasses and dishes, tins, soaps, games, blocks, banks, handbags, radios and a host of other items.[25] *Variety* noted the 'very unusual' extent to which 'merchants, newspapers, etc. want to tie-in with the film'.[26]

Advertising for *Snow White* was everywhere, and there can be no doubt that its box-office success was at least partially the result of the media saturation it received. According to Richard Neupert, *Snow White*'s popularity with children had been such that 'several cities complained that Disney's film was draining children's piggy banks' so they would be less likely to go to 'other "kids' pics", like *Tom Sawyer*, in the near future'.[27] The number of children attending it was so great that RKO's distribution wing tried hard to persuade local theatre owners to stop charging children lower admission prices. In cities where children's prices were suspended, *Snow White* broke box-office records, whereas cities which kept children's prices saw new records only in audience attendance, not revenue.[28] In 1939, MGM encountered the problem of children's pricing even more acutely, when *The Wizard of Oz* failed to turn a profit on its $2,777,000 production budget, in large part because it attracted an audience made up largely of children.[29] The exhibition strategies devised for *Fantasia* may well have been influenced by concerns about the profitability of high-budget films appealing predominantly to children.

The success of the company's merchandising activities was also not without its attendant difficulties for the studio's product, since the merchandising was far more explicitly aimed at the child market than the films themselves. *Fantasia* represented the studio's attempt to address another audience segment: those who had, with Sergei Eisenstein, recognised in the *Silly Symphonies* Disney's 'astounding sensitivity to melody in his graphic line'.[30] Richard Schickel argues that, as well as presenting the studio with the technical challenge provided by complex music, the production of *Fantasia* represented 'a commercially intelligent decision to differentiate his work from that of competitors who showed neither the ability nor the ambition to move beyond their low origins'.[31]

Disney's move into animated feature films coincided with a wider trend toward 'quality' or 'prestige' films in Hollywood, and his desire to have his studio seen as a maker of quality cinema – and as something more than merely 'children's entertainment' – may have been encouraged by his personal desire to be viewed by other studio heads and film-makers as being a member of the Hollywood 'élite'.[32] His socio-artistic aspirations, however, sat awkwardly with his constant self-identification with 'ordinary folks', and this contradiction was nowhere more evident than in the studio's construction of the audience it expected to attract with *Fantasia*. In an inter-office memo on 24 November 1941, dealing with the cuts to be made to the picture for its RKO distribution, Disney told his brother Roy that: 'We must remember that there are a lot of people who have seen it and who will now come back to see *Fantasia* again, and we do not want to spoil it for those who appreciate the finer things just to sell a few highschool [sic] tickets'.[33]

It is, however, unlikely that Disney meant to exclude the child audience. Much of *Fantasia*'s imagery – Mickey Mouse in 'The Sorcerer's Apprentice' sequence and the ostrich and hippopotamus ballerinas in the 'Dance of the Hours' sequence, for example – would appeal easily to children. The studio, indeed, decided not to end the picture on the 'Night on Bald Mountain' sequence, but instead on the more uplifting, tranquil 'Ave Maria' sequence, because the images in 'Night on Bald Mountain' were too terrifying for children to be left as the end of the film.[34] But if, in terms of its production, *Fantasia* was designed for 'everyone', adults and children alike, it was marketed, unlike Disney's other animated films, primarily at adults. Newspaper advertisements for the film were sophisticated, discreet and without any significant illustration. When compared to the advertisements that appeared alongside such items, *Fantasia*'s 5 December 1940 ad in the *New York Times* was unusually sedate.[35] Moreover, the *New York Times Book Review* on 8 December 1940 included an advertisement for a book on *Fantasia* by the film's narrator, musicologist Deems Taylor, who was a familiar public figure through his commentary on the New York Philharmonic Orchestra's radio broadcasts. This advertisement – much larger and more heavily illustrated with characters from the film than was the earlier advertisement for the film itself – described Taylor's work as being 'The First Disney Book Designed for Adults!'.[36]

Through its association with Leopold Stokowski (not to mention Bach, Beethoven, Stravinsky and the other featured composers), *Fantasia* was Disney's attempt to appeal to both 'ordinary folks like ourselves'[37] and 'those who appreciate the finer things'. With his trademark mane of flowing white hair and his habit of conducting without a baton, Stokowski had become one of the best-known conductors of his day. Through his appearance in the 1937 Deanna Durbin film, *One Hundred Men and a Girl*, and also through the widespread press reports of his romantic involvement with Greta Garbo,

Stokowski additionally symbolised the increasingly close relationship between music and the movies. In the programme accompanying *Fantasia*'s initial release, he argued that mass audiences were only uncomfortable with 'highbrow' music because they were unused to it: 'The beauty and inspiration of music must not be restricted to a privileged few but made available to every man, woman and child. That is why great music associated with motion pictures is so important, because motion pictures reach millions all over the world'.[38] Disney also asserted that *Fantasia* was intended to make classical music more accessible to the masses. The studio's in-house 'bulletin' editorialised that, after seeing *Fantasia,* 'barbers, bankers, and taxi drivers throughout the nation will whistle while they work, random themes from Tchaikovsky, Beethoven, and Bach'.[39] As a medium for popularising classical music in this way, of course, *Fantasia* failed.

One reason for that failure could have been the role played by cultural gate-keepers. In her essay on the film's difficult climb to popular success, Moya Luckett emphasises the widespread condemnation *Fantasia* received from music critics at the time of its first release. As she notes, most objected to the combination of music with screen pictures, rather than to the fact 'that the music itself was chopped up and rearranged'.[40] In particular, Luckett stresses these critics' concern with 'the effects that the film would have on "lowbrow" audiences'. For instance, Edward Barry commented in the *Chicago Daily Tribune* that: 'it may be said that *Fantasia* will give the unwary the idea that the core of musical experience may be approached by the Disney route and that the ecstasy and exaltation which the art offers have something to do with visual images. This danger is especially serious since the picture bears, by implication at least, the seal of approval of such respected musicians as Stravinsky, Stokowski, and Taylor'.[41] Luckett usefully compares these critics' response to the initial criticisms made of the Book-of-the-Month Club for its standardisation and popularisation of classical literature. Like Harry Scherman's project, Disney's movie represented an attempt to disseminate high culture through the mechanisms of the mass cultural market, and, in seeking to do so, it also represented a challenge to established concepts of cultural authority and the separation of cultural spheres. The unsympathetic responses of some music critics decried the lowbrow reactions of the film's audiences – who applauded 'exactly where it would have applauded if the score had been composed by a Hollywood musician' or laughed during the centaur sequence, drowning out the segment of Beethoven's 'Pastoral' symphony accompanying it – with almost as much venom as they brought to their denunciation of the film itself.[42]

These élite critical opinions were, however, no more than a single factor (and perhaps a marginal one) in *Fantasia*'s initial failure, which came as a considerable surprise to Disney. When viewed in the context of the studio's use of music between 1929 and 1940 and Hollywood's broader connections with music, it is easy to see why he might have expected a more favourable response. The *Silly Symphony* series had consistently been both popular and profitable, and several had won Academy awards. Other Disney cartoons, including Mickey Mouse's colour début *The Band Concert* (1935), featured orchestral music performed in the classical style. More generally, classical music had been used as accompaniment to silent cinema, and during the 1930s the classical symphonic scores of composers such as Erich Wolfgang Korngold and Max Steiner became the Hollywood norm.[43] Throughout the decade, too, the major studios adapted the conventions of operetta not only to films starring Nelson Eddy and Jeannette MacDonald, but also to others featuring opera stars such as Grace Moore and Lawrence Tibbett.

Fantasia was an obvious outgrowth of earlier trends in the Disney studio and Hollywood generally. Why, then, was it such a failure on its first release? Ben Sharpsteen, the picture's production supervisor, believed that the general American public in the late 1930s was not comfortable with what he called 'highbrow' music written for the concert hall.[44] Many of the hostile reviews by music critics similarly implied that the majority of Americans were largely unfamiliar with classical music, and needed to be educated in its appreciation. During the 1930s, however, the orchestras of the New Deal's Works Projects Administration Federal Music Project had given symphony concerts attended by more than one hundred million people. Free music classes were also offered, attracting over half a million pupils every month. Classical music was regularly played on commercial radio: CBS formed its own symphony orchestra in 1928, NBC followed suit in 1933, and sponsored broadcasts by various city orchestras were common.[45] In 1940, there were fifteen season-long radio programmes playing classical music, each broadcasting for between thirty and ninety minutes. As John Dunning notes in his encyclopaedia of American radio programming, the classical music broadcast on the four principal radio broadcasting chains had both variety and depth: 'People in Wisconsin and rural Kansas could now hear the symphony orchestras of Rochester, Cleveland, or Indianapolis on a weekly basis, and the names of Toscanini, Walter, Ormandy, and others – long famous in their fields – became known in the heartland'.[46]

Disney and Stokowski were not being unrealistic in their view of the general public's possible appreciation of classical music. All around them was evidence that a film featuring selections of well-known classical music would be well within the reach of the public at large. Stokowski had devoted many hours to the idea of making classical music available to popular audiences, and even the renowned solo violinist Jascha Heifetz eventually realised the potential of radio to create much larger audiences for classical music and began broadcasting more of his concerts.[47] *Fantasia*'s box-office failure cannot be accounted for mainly by its musical content. Indeed, all the music used in the film was fairly familiar by 1940. Even Stravinsky's 'The Rite of Spring' was no longer seen by many Americans as particularly avant-garde. The only controversy this piece ever created in relation to its use in *Fantasia* was Stravinsky's own well-publicised criticism, some years after *Fantasia*'s initial release, of Stokowski's arrangement and re-orchestration of the work.

The commitment made by Disney and Stokowski to bring classical music to the masses, however, was undermined and contradicted by the manner in which *Fantasia* was marketed and exhibited. According to John Culhane, 'Disney wanted the theaters to showcase *Fantasia* as they had showcased *Gone With the Wind* ... with reserved seats and matinee and evening performances, so that word of mouth could gradually build the movie's reputation as a new and revolutionary kind of film entertainment'. RKO agreed to relax Disney's distribution contract with them so that the Disney Studio could set up its own distribution unit headed by Irving Ludwig, a young film salesman who would later create the Disney Studio's Buena Vista distribution company. Ludwig decided to use the important theatres in major cities, and installed the specially designed 'Fantasound' sound system, intended to enhance the overall experience of the film, at a cost of $30,000 in cinemas which ran *Fantasia*.[48] He also ordered curtain con-

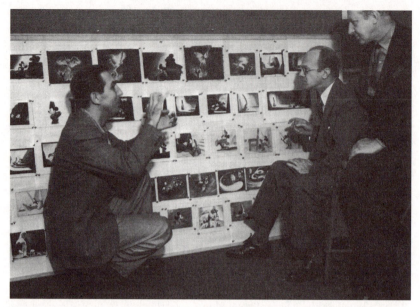

Walt Disney, Deems Taylor and Leopold Stokowski consulting on the storyboards for *Fantasia* (1940)

trols and special lighting to set off each of *Fantasia*'s various sequences, and hired and trained the staffs of each theatre to treat audiences with particular consideration.[49] The initial distribution plan was that the film would never go into general release, but would instead travel the country as a roadshow, with the order of its sequences being constantly changed and updated, and with new sequences added from time to time so as to give it more of the feeling of a classical music concert.

Fantasia originally played in just twelve theatres in the US and one (the Royal Alexandria Theater of Toronto) in Canada.[50] The idea was to portray it not just as a movie, but as a major cultural event. According to Leonard Maltin, Disney wanted *Fantasia* marketed as more of a concert than a film and there was even some studio talk of releasing it in concert halls rather than in cinemas. Since Fantasound equipment was expensive and the movie theatre concerned was obliged to close for a week during its installation, the studio also saw the idea of releasing *Fantasia* to only a small number of theatres at any one time as a way of keeping its costs down. Eventually, the film would make a circuit of larger theatres, always as a reserved-seat attraction, and possibly never playing in the smaller neighbourhood cinemas.[51]

The problem with marketing *Fantasia* in this way, however, was that in order to be treated like clients at a theatre, the audience were obliged to pay roadshow prices, which were between three and ten times the 25-cent average price of a movie ticket.[52] Evening prices at the Broadway Theater in New York (where *Fantasia* premièred) were 75 cents, $1.10, $1.65, and $2.20; at the Carthay Circle Theater in Los Angeles, tickets were 75 cents, $1, and $1.50.[53] Although these prices were not out of line with other roadshow prices of the time, they would have restricted child attendance. In other respects, too, *Fantasia* did not conform to the conventions of a prestige picture for roadshow exhibition. It lacked the 'pre-sold' ingredients of a roadshow success such as *Gone With the Wind*. It was not a long-anticipated film based on a best-selling book, but an unfamiliar work with no distinct storyline. Its only 'star', apart from the Disney name, was Mickey Mouse, and Mickey's own film career had recently been in something of a slump compared with those of Donald Duck and Goofy.[54] Because of the Disney name, Fantasia was widely perceived as being more 'family' entertainment than most prestige pictures, which were targeted primarily at adult audiences.

Fantasia's limited availability and the expense of its roadshow exhibition denied most of the 'average' people, for whom Disney and Stokowski claimed it was intended, the opportunity to see it. The style of its advertising may have discouraged those sections of the audience uninterested in seeing a Disney 'experiment'. Another of *Fantasia*'s initial problems was its limited promotion by the studio, particularly when compared to the amount of advertisement invested in films such as *Snow White*. *Fantasia* was much less heavily advertised and, apart from the Deems Taylor book, little publicity or merchandising accompanied its release in 1940. Such a strategy might have been appropriate to the limited number of exhibition venues and the film's marketing at adults, but it also meant that *Fantasia* did not benefit from the widespread, all-encompassing promotion *Snow White* had received. Its limited distribution meant that the potential audience from which it could draw was reduced even further. World War II effectively prevented any further expansion of the roadshow programme since, as Luckett points out, RCA switched resources from producing Fantasound installations into manufacturing radio apparatus for defence uses.[55]

By April 1941, five months after being released, *Fantasia* had earned only $1.3 million as a result of its first eleven engagements. On top of production expenses, the cost of the Fantasound installation meant that the film had made a loss on its first release.[56] After it became clear that the roadshow strategy had failed to return a profit, Disney's bankers brought pressure on him to cut the film from 130 minutes (including the intermission) to 81 minutes, and RKO put it into general release, where it often played on double bills with a western.[57] What its commercial success would have been had it been put into general release in its original form and on its own can only be surmised, but its chances could hardly have been worse than they were in a chopped-up form and attached to a movie with which it could have had no possible connection.

It is possible that the full-length *Fantasia*'s difficulties were also connected with its lack of what Disney called 'heart': the feelings of warmth, emotional attachment, interest and empathy on the part of the audience for the characters on the screen. The scene in *Dumbo* (1941) in which Mrs Jumbo caresses and cradles her son through the bars of her cage as the song 'Baby Mine' plays on the soundtrack exemplifies this quality. Disney once declared that

> Until a character becomes a personality it cannot be believed. Without personality, the characters may do funny or interesting things, but unless people are able to identify themselves with the character, its actions will seem unreal. And without personality, a story cannot ring true to its audience.[58]

Much of the animation in *Fantasia* is spectacular, but it does not achieve its effects by pulling at the heart strings or charming its audience. Disney seems to have expected pure technical animation skill and musical artistry to have carried *Fantasia*. In the film, many of the characters can indeed be seen as doing 'funny or interesting things'. Here and there, a character emerges who particularly catches the audience's attention, such as Hop Lo, the smallest dancing mushroom in the 'Chinese Dance' segment of the 'Nutcracker' sequence. But these characters are only briefly on the screen and, once gone, do not reappear. In 1940, it was not possible for most people to view *Fantasia* more than once, and thereby develop their appreciation for its technical innovations. There were few characters for audiences to love and remember, and only superior technical achievement for them to talk about to others for that 'word of mouth' endorsement upon which Disney was counting to bring in the audiences.

Despite its commercial failure, *Fantasia* contributed significantly to what Eric Smoodin has called 'Disney Discourse'. Its ambition, cost, and technical experimentation confirmed the public image of Disney as a risk-taking, artistic innovator. Not until three years later, in a review of *The Three Caballeros*, would *The Saturday Review* declare that Disney was 'having audience trouble; that he could not make up his mind whether he was appealing to the young or the old; and that he was trying both to have his cake and eat it'.[59]

In 1946, the *New York Times* reported that after 'tests' in ten cities, *Fantasia* was being re-released: 'The film has not been ballyhooed in ads … but has been sedately presented "as a typical concert announcement"'.[60] The marketing strategy for the film – that of limiting its availability and keeping its advertisement to a minimum – was unchanged from its original exhibition, and this second release was also not a commercial success. By the time of *Fantasia*'s second reissue in 1956, however, audiences had become more familiar with it. The 'Rite of Spring' sequence had been distributed on 16 mm to schools as a geology film[61] and, more importantly, Disney's 1955 television anthology series on ABC, *The Disneyland Story*, broadcast prior to the park's opening, interspersed segments of *Fantasia* with scenes describing the construction of the various 'lands' in Disneyland. By the time *Fantasia* was re-released in 1956, many of its spectators would have seen some of its segments on television, and seeing them in black and white may have made some viewers curious enough about what they looked like in colour to encourage them to see the film, restored to almost its original length, in the cinema.[62] On its third reissue in 1963, *Fantasia* finally broke even on its production costs, and by 1965, its domestic gross was $4,800,000,[63] its general popularity was definitely on the rise and it was grossing an average of $2 million annually.[64]

By this time, it had come to be regarded in many ways as a 'classic'. One 1963 review, for example, asserted that: 'Walt Disney's film "Fantasia" is, of course, a classic and one of the finest films Disney has ever produced'.[65] In his 1965 discussion of *Fantasia*'s 'Silver Anniversary', Jimmie Hicks declared that '*Fantasia* seems destined to be a one-time thing'.[66] This uniqueness, he implied, was simultaneously a loss to the cinema and a proof of *Fantasia*'s greatness. It achieved 'classic' status in part through the company's promotion, but while the Disney Studio has not shirked in its efforts to promote *Fantasia*'s status as a classic, it regularly accords this status to its animated films, even in the first phases of their initial release. In part this status came from the fact of the film's commercial survival despite its initial failure, in part from the fact that it remained original and unimitated. Its status as a unique object allowed it to garner much of the appreciation the film has received, but this in turn has led to a constant exploitation by the Disney company of such appreciation. Ironically, *Fantasia*'s achievement of 'classic' status, as a high cultural object, at least within the Disney canon, finally rendered the film's original advertising strategy, adhered to in all its subsequent reissues, successful. In the more successful second half of its commercial life, the conflicts between high- and low-cultural authority that the film engendered on its original release were dissipated, as *Fantasia* rose to both financial profitability and cultural recognition.

Since 1969, *Fantasia* has remained in almost continual release, thanks largely to its popularity with the baby-boom generation and their children and grandchildren. In the early 1970s, the film was appreciated for its 'psychedelic' aspects, viewed by some sections of American culture at this time as an accompaniment to drug-taking. In reading reviews of *Fantasia* from 1970, one cannot help but conclude that the baby-boom generation watching it saw in the film concepts which seem never to have entered the minds of either its original audiences or the film's creators. In 1970, Tom Ramage asked if Disney, 'that icon of the silent majority, father figure of Middle America', was 'secretly a flower child?'. Describing Disney as 'as a kind of square Lewis Carroll', he suggested that 'In our psychedelic time the temptation to see modern analogies in Disney's 30-year-old full-length cartoon film are strong ... The fascinating thing about *Fantasia* ... is its juxtaposition of sexual innocence (almost naivete) and ripe sensuality'.[67] William Zinsser, writing for *Life* magazine at the same time, agreed:

> The other day I went to the movie again and saw just what the young have instead discovered – that Disney was zonked out of his mind while making the movie and so was his entire studio. Safely hidden behind the chaste pillars of classical music, behind the impeccable tails of Leopold Stokowski, he was a hippie 30 years ahead of his time, producing a psychedelic light-and-sound show that was his only flop because nobody was freaked out enough to dig it.[68]

Although this reading of *Fantasia* seems to have disappeared along with the rest of the psychedelic era, the appeal of the interpretation itself seems to have survived as a fond memory and quirk of the film's history. At the time of *Fantasia*'s 1990 re-release, a cartoon in the *Los Angeles Times* mimicked the television advertisement for the film by suggesting that the two best things about the re-release of *Fantasia* were that 'a whole generation will be seeing it for the first time' and 'a whole generation will be seeing it for the first time without drugs'.[69]

While the film's popularity had improved throughout the first four decades of its history, the general condition of its existing prints had not. In 1981, Disney Studio executives hired conductor Irwin Kostal to re-score and conduct a new version of *Fantasia*'s entire soundtrack. On the release of this version in 1982, the new soundtrack was heralded as a technological masterpiece, but audience reaction to Kostal's reworking of Stokowski's original score was distinctly unfavourable.[70] There were also objections to the removal of Deems Taylor's narration as an essential component of the 'classic' *Fantasia*. Considering the controversy which once surrounded Stokowski's re-orchestrations of the 'Rite of Spring' and other pieces, there was more than a touch of irony in this criticism, which had now turned Stokowski's score, unusual in its day, into a sacred object in its own right. Fans of *Fantasia*, in criticising this new version, signalled both a clear proprietorial relationship to the film itself and a determination to protect its integrity as a text.

In 1988, with this criticism in mind, the studio embarked on a multi-million dollar effort to restore the original soundtrack, complete with Fantasound, in time for the film's 1990 fiftieth anniversary re-release. In a repetition of the original limited release, *Fantasia* was now released on video and laser disc as a one-time-only, limited-availability collector's piece. This meant that, for the first time since 1940, all of *Fantasia* could be viewed, complete with the scenes cut from earlier re-releases (such as the avant-garde animation which accompanies the Bach 'Toccata and Fugue' beginning the film), the Deems Taylor narration and the Stokowski/Philadelphia Symphony Orchestra recordings for the soundtrack. Baby-boomers, who had either already established or were beginning to establish families and video libraries of their own, seized the opportunity to purchase a copy of this Disney classic both for their own and their children's enjoyment.

What has shifted in the sixty years of *Fantasia*'s circulation is not the film's relation with its audience so much as the audience's relationship to the film. Over time, audiences have come to accept the studio's interpretation and positioning of the movie, as a movie primarily appealing to adults. The film and the various attempts to sell it have remained remarkably constant. So, too, have its claims to a unique cultural position. Its audience of recent decades, and perhaps specifically its baby-boom spectators, who might first have viewed it in segments on *The Disneyland Story*, came eventually to accept a marketing strategy for *Fantasia* that their predecessors – both real and potential – had once rejected.

On 1 January 2000, sixty years after *Fantasia* was released, Walt Disney Pictures released *Fantasia 2000*, intended to be both a sequel to the original and a fulfilment of Disney's original intention constantly to update and rearrange the sequences in *Fantasia*. Publicity for the film emphasised that it was a blend of the old and the new. One old favourite to remain from the original, for example, was 'The Sorcerer's Apprentice' segment. The film itself, however, was marketed in ways that closely followed the strategy behind the original *Fantasia*. On its release, *Fantasia 2000* was billed as being the first feature-length production to be released exclusively as an IMAX film. In a direct parallel with *Fantasia*'s Fantasound, this promotional strategy claimed that the film was using cutting-edge technology to create a new experience in the cinematic art. Like the original *Fantasia*, *Fantasia 2000* is characterised by limited availability (since IMAX cinemas are still relatively rare) and high admission prices (IMAX theatres normally have higher prices of admission than ordinary cinemas). Again, like *Fantasia*, Disney – at the end of its initial run – will withdraw *Fantasia 2000*, reformat it and put it into general release.[71]

The main difference between *Fantasia* and *Fantasia 2000*, however, is the extensive promotional campaign for the new film launched on television. With at least one lesson learned from 1940 (the need for energetic advertising), *Fantasia 2000* seems likely to become a commercial success far more quickly than its predecessor. In early April 2000, according to *Screen International*, it was the thirteenth highest-earning film in the US and the third-highest grossing (after *Mission to Mars* and *The Tigger Movie*) for the Disney Studio.[72] According to *Variety*, *Fantasia 2000* (while having only fifty-four engagements in all) had total box-office takings of $1,295,458 for the week of 7 to 13

April. By that point, it had already earned a worldwide box-office total of $52,358,188.[73] Less than four months after its release, the film was generating the kind of respectable income it had taken the original *Fantasia* years to achieve.

Notes

1 Cited in Jimmie Hicks, '*Fantasia*'s Silver Anniversary', *Films*, vol. XVI, no. 9 (November 1965), p. 534.

2 Quoted in Marc Eliot, *Walt Disney: Hollywood's Dark Prince* (London: André Deutsch, 1999), p. 136.

3 Ibid., p. 532.

4 The Chouinard Art Institute later merged with the Disney art 'school' to form the California Institute of the Arts, or Cal Arts (as it is more colloquially known).

5 Hicks, '*Fantasia*'s Silver Anniversary', pp. 15–16.

6 Ibid., p. 18.

7 Ibid., p. 12.

8 Richard Neupert, 'Painting a Plausible World: Disney's Color Prototypes', in Eric Smoodin (ed.), *Disney Discourse: Producing the Magic Kingdom,* (London: Routledge, 1994), p. 107.

9 From John Canemaker's essay 'Walt as Boss', found via the 'Library' section under 'Expert Essays' on the CD-ROM *Walt Disney: An Intimate History of the Man and His Magic* (Santa Monica, CA: Pantheon Productions Inc, 1998).

10 Bob Thomas, *Walt Disney: an American Original,* (New York: Hyperion, 1994) p. 99.

11 On Disney's attempts to join Hollywood's social élite, see ibid., p. 119; Bob Thomas, *Building a Company: Roy O. Disney and the Creation of an Entertainment Empire* (New York: Hyperion, 1998), p. 161.

12 This subject is discussed at greater length by Thomas Doherty in 'This Is Where We Came In: The Audible Screen and the Voluble Audience of Early Sound Cinema', in Melvyn Stokes and Richard Maltby (eds), *American Movie Audiences: From the Turn of the Century to the Early Sound Era* (London: BFI, 1999), pp. 149–59, 152–6. See also Steven Watts, *The Magic Kingdom: Walt Disney and the American Way of Life* (New York: Houghton Mifflin Company, 1997), pp. 120–31.

13 Inter-Office Memo from Walt Disney to Chester Cobb, dated 12 July 1937. Found under 'Walt, Criticism' via the 'Library' section of the CD-ROM *Walt Disney: An Intimate History of the Man and His Magic.*

14 Neupert, 'Painting a Plausible World', p. 114.

15 Quoted in Margaret Thorp, *America at the Movies* (London: Faber & Faber, 1946), p. 16.

16 Paul Hollister, 'Genius at Work: Walt Disney', *Atlantic Monthly,* vol. 166 (December 1940). Reprinted in *Disney Discourse,* p. 26.

17 Quoted in Thorp, *America at the Movies* p. 16; Eric Smoodin, 'Introduction: How to Read Walt Disney', in *Disney Discourse,* p. 6.

18 Eric Smoodin, *Animating Culture: Hollywood Cartoons from the Sound Era* (New Brunswick, NJ: Rutgers University Press, 1993), p. 15.

19 'Walt Talks About Appeal to Adults', the CD-ROM *Walt Disney: An Intimate History of the Man and His Magic,* 'Library' section.

20 Smoodin, *Animating Culture,* pp. 66–7.

21 Leon Schlesinger, quoted in 'Hollywood Censors Its Animated Cartoons', *Look*, 17 January 1939, pp. 17–20.

22 Richard deCordova, 'The Mickey in Macy's Window: Childhood, Consumerism and Disney Animation', in *Disney Discourse*, p. 204.

23 Ibid., p. 209.

24 Ibid., p. 206.

25 Margaret Thorp reported that, in total, Disney licensed 147 concerns to manufacture 2,183 different novelty products based on the *Snow White* characters. Thorp, *America at the Movies* p. 77. While many such items may be seen in flea markets, junk shops, antique stores and private collections, an easy way to see photos of these items is in speciality collectors' books, such as David Longest and Michael Stern's T*he Collector's Encyclopedia of Disneyana: A Value and Identification Guide* (Paducah, KY: Collector Books, 1992), plates 522–626 (pp. 133–54).

26 *Variety* (16 February 1938), p. 11.

27 Neupert, 'Painting a Plausible World' p. 115.

28 Ibid., note 30, p. 241.

29 Patricia King Hanson and Alan Gevinson (eds), *The American Film Institute Catalog, Feature Films, 1931–40* (Berkeley CA: University of California Press), p. 2449.

30 Sergei Eisenstein, 'On Colour', in Michael Glenny and Richard Taylor (eds) *Eisenstein, Volume 2: Towards a Theory of Montage* (London: BFI, 1991), p. 255.

31 Richard Schickel, *The Disney Version* (New York: Avon, 1968), pp. 103–4.

32 Thomas, *Walt Disney*, p. 119.

33 Memo reproduced on the CD-ROM *Walt Disney: An Intimate History of the Man and His Magic*. Found via the library section under 'Fantasia (Memo about Fantasia)'.

34 Charles Solomon, *Enchanted Drawings: A History of Animation* (New York: Knopf, 1989), pp. 69–70.

35 Advertisement for *Fantasia, New York Times,* Thursday, 5 December 1940, p. L33.

36 Advertisement from the *New York Times Book Review,* 8 December 1940, p. 39.

37 John Culhane, *Walt Disney's* Fantasia (New York: Harry N. Abrams, Inc., 1987), p. 10. The full quote is 'We say that the public – that is, the audience – would always recognize and appreciate quality. It was this faith in the discrimination of the average person that led us to make such a radically different type of entertainment as *Fantasia*. We simply figured that if ordinary folk like ourselves could find entertainment in these visualizations of so-called classical music, so would the average audience'.

38 Moya Luckett, '*Fantasia*: Cultural Constructions of Disney's "Masterpiece"', in *Disney Discourse*, p. 225.

39 Richard Holliss, 'The Creative Explosion', CD-ROM *Walt Disney: An Intimate History of the Man and His Magic*.

40 Luckett, '*Fantasia*', p. 224.

41 Ibid., p. 222.

42 Franz Hoellering, '*Fantasia*', *The Nation*, 23 November 1940, reprinted in Stanley Kauffman with Bruce Henstell, *American Film Criticism: From the Beginnings to* 'Citizen Kane' (New York: Liveright, 1972), p. 391; Edward Barry, '*Fantasia*: Great Music Buried in Orgy of Color and Sound, Movie and Music Critics Find', *Chicago Daily Tribune*, 20 February 1941, cited in Luckett, '*Fantasia*', p. 220.

43 Royal S. Brown, *Overtones and Undertones: Reading Film Music* (Berkeley CA: University of California Press, 1994), pp. 50–66.

44 Ibid., p. 13.

45 Maldwyn Jones, *The Limits of Liberty: American History 1607–1992* (Oxford: Oxford University Press, 2nd edn, 1995), pp. 463, 70.

46 John Dunning, *On the Air: The Encyclopedia of Old-Time Radio* (New York: Oxford University Press, 1998), p. 174.

47 One music critic, reviewing *Fantasia* in 1940, accused Stokowski of acting in a 'phony' way by presenting himself as a pioneer in this campaign, since Toscanini had been the first to attempt to bring classical music to the masses by means of his regular Sunday radio broadcasts with the New York Philharmonic. B. H. Haggin, '*Fantasia*', *The Nation*, 11 January 1941, reprinted in Kauffman with Henstell, *American Film Criticism*, p. 395.

48 Culhane, *Walt Disney's* Fantasia, p. 9.

49 Ibid., pp. 10–11.

50 Ibid.

51 Leonard Maltin, *The Disney Films* (New York: Hyperion Press, 3rd edn, 1995), p. 44.

52 Cobbett Steinberg, *Reel Facts: The Movie Book of Records* (New York: Vintage Books, updated edn, 1981), p. 44.

53 Personal correspondence between the author and Dave Smith, Chief Archivist, Walt Disney Studio Archives, via e-mail, Smith's reply dated Monday, 1 December 1997.

54 As can be seen from a filmography of the Disney Studio's cartoon shorts, the number of Mickey Mouse cartoons, as opposed to the number of Donald Duck, Goofy and Pluto cartoons, declined throughout the 1930s. According to Bob Thomas, Disney only came up with the idea of doing 'The Sorcerer's Apprentice' segment of *Fantasia* out of concern for Mickey's 'career'. This section of the film was regarded by the studio as Mickey's 'comeback' vehicle. Thomas, *Walt Disney*, pp. 151–2.

55 Luckett, '*Fantasia*', p. 227.

56 Ibid., p. 229.

57 Culhane, *Walt Disney's* Fantasia, p. 11.

58 Dave Smith, *Walt Disney's Famous Quotes* (Buena Vista, FL: The Walt Disney Company, Disney's Kingdom Editions, 1994), p. 16.

59 'Mr Disney's Caballeros', *The Saturday Review*, 24 February 1945, p. 22, quoted in Smoodin, *Animating Culture*, p. 102.

60 '*Fantasia* Forever', *New York Times*, 29 September 1946.

61 Maltin, *The Disney Films*, p. 45.

62 Hicks, '*Fantasia*'s Silver Anniversary', p. 535.

63 Ibid.

64 Ibid.

65 Gerald Faris, 'Revival of Classic: Disney's "Fantasia", Beautiful Film', *Citizen News*, 22 February 1963.

66 Hicks, '*Fantasia*'s Silver Anniversary', p. 535.

67 Tom Ramage, 'Sexual Fantasies and LSD Colors Mark "Fantasia"', *BAD*, 25 February 1970.

68 William Zinsser, 'Walt Disney's Secret Freakout: Another, and Surprising, Look at "Fantasia"', *Life*, vol. 68 (3 April 1970), p. 15.

69 Silent Pictures Maratta, *Los Angeles Times*, 21 October 1990.

70 Solomon, *History of Animation,* p. 70.

71 While it is not yet clear precisely how such reformatting will change the film, the transfer from IMAX format to 35 mm is likely to feature considerably cropped images.

72 'North America, Weekend April 7–9, 2000: Top 30', *Screen International,* no. 1254 (14–20 April 2000), p. 30.

73 'Variety Box Office', *Variety* (17–23 April 2000), p. 12.

5
Changing Perceptions of the Movies: American Catholics Debate Film Censorship

Gregory D. Black

In the summer of 1956, prominent Catholic theologian John Courtney Murray published an article questioning the authority of the Catholic Church to censor movies by means of its Legion of Decency. Since 1936, the Legion had been classifying movies for Catholics, forbidding them from attending films that it considered immoral. The Legion's authority to dictate what movies American Catholics could and could not see was the foundation on which it built its power to influence what subjects Hollywood could screen as entertainment. Murray's article, however, questioned whether Catholic adults had any obligation to follow restrictions imposed on their consumption of mass media by the Catholic hierarchy, arguing that in a pluralistic society no minority group 'has the right to impose its own religious or moral views on any other group, through … force, coercion, or violence'.[1]

The Legion of Decency grew out of protests by the Catholic Church in the early 1930s over what it saw as increasingly immoral movies. In 1930 the industry had adopted a code of production partially drafted by a Catholic priest, Daniel Lord. Subsequently, however, Lord and other Catholics became convinced that the code was being ignored in movies loaded with sex and violence such as *She Done Him Wrong* (1932), *Baby Face* (1933), and *Scarface* (1932). In 1933/34 the Catholic Church created a Legion of Decency and threatened that its twenty million members would boycott all movies unless the industry agreed to enforce the Production Code more vigorously. In response, Will Hays, head of the Motion Picture Producers and Distributors Association (MPPDA), appointed Catholic Joseph I. Breen as director of the Production Code Administration (PCA).[2]

Officially christened in 1936, and headquartered in the New York archdiocese, the National Legion of Decency reviewed all films released and rated them according to content. Films were classified in four categories: A-I (unobjectionable for general audiences); A-II (unobjectionable for adults); B (objectionable in part for all); and C (condemned). A condemned rating was forbidden viewing for all Catholics in each of the 103 American dioceses and Hollywood regularly edited out whatever the Legion demanded in order to avoid a condemned classification. Breen and the Legion worked closely together for the next two decades. Indeed, at times, Breen used the possibility of a Legion condemnation to force producers to remove scenes and dialogue he found offensive. Equally, the Legion, preferring to appear an independent reviewing board, occasionally objected to films that Breen's PCA had approved. In 1941, for example, when MGM produced *Two-Faced Woman,* a comedy starring Greta Garbo and Melvyn Douglas, the Legion condemned it for 'its un-Christian attitude toward marriage'. The film was quickly withdrawn, re-edited, and new scenes inserted to eliminate the impression that Douglas was knowingly having an affair with Garbo's twin sister. The revamped film was given a B rating.[3]

To the extent that the Legion's influence was based on its capacity to control Catholic audience behaviour, however, it relied on a largely false premise. Soon after the original furore which had led to its creation died down, most Catholic bishops paid little more than lip service to the Legion. At their annual meeting in Washington, DC, funding for Legion expenses was often a contentious issue. Even more tellingly, there was clear evidence that the Legion could not prevent large numbers of Catholics from attending movies it had condemned. In only a few of the more than 100 archdioceses did it have much influence (Chicago, New York, Boston, Buffalo, Philadelphia, St Louis and Los Angeles) and, even in those areas, Catholics attended condemned movies with little heed to Legion opinion. A Legion complaint about a film typically produced a vastly expanded audience intent on seeing what all the fuss was about. In 1934, the movie critic for the *Baltimore Sun* complained 'he had scarcely been able to get into a theater during the past three weeks' because of Catholic protests.[4] In Chicago, a hotbed of Legion activity, investigators for Hays reported that the Legion 'exercises virtually no audience control'.[5]

When, in 1946, the Legion threatened to condemn *Duel in the Sun,* producer David O. Selznick considered releasing the film without a PCA seal or a Legion rating. To investigate the box-office implications of such a move, he commissioned the Gallup organisation to survey regular film-goers over how many would refuse to attend a Legion-condemned film. The answer suggested by the poll was a meagre 5 per cent. When the MPPDA refused to support him, however, Selznick himself surrendered and made the cuts demanded by the Legion.[6]

This response was typical. Before the 1950s, only Howard Hughes openly defied the Legion. He refused to alter *The Outlaw* (1943) and, while critics savaged the film and the Legion condemned it, it proved a box-office smash wherever it played. In 1953, Otto Preminger followed Hughes's lead when he and RKO refused to alter *The Moon is Blue,* a bedroom comedy supporting virginity as a strategy for women who hoped to hook a good man. It was condemned by the Legion for offending 'traditional standards of morality' and for its 'suggestiveness'.[7] The PCA denied a code, but the movie was a moderate success – especially, indeed, in urban areas with large Catholic populations. Martin Quigley, the influential conservative Catholic publisher of *Motion Picture Herald* and a major force in the founding and continuing operations of the Legion of Decency, informed Bishop William Scully with considerable dismay that 'the Catholic people have not cooperated'.[8]

A year before the release of Preminger's film, the forces of censorship had been dealt a major blow when the United States Supreme Court reversed its 1915 decision in the *Mutual Film Corp. v. Ohio* case that the movies were not entitled to the free speech protections of the Constitution because they were a 'business, pure and simple'. In *Burstyn v. Wilson,* which began with the Legion's condemnation of a short Italian film, *The Miracle* (1948), the court extended First Amendment protection to the movies. It would take more than a decade for a series of court decisions to strike down state and local censorship boards, but the future was now clear. Even so enthusiastic a supporter of censoring movies as Quigley saw the writing on the wall when he told New York's Cardinal Spellman that 'the Legion of Decency ... is able no longer to exert its influence'.[9]

It was against this background, later in the 1950s, that two debates about censorship broke out within the Catholic Church itself. One focused on whether, and by what right, Catholics should be forbidden from attending certain films. The second, more revealing perhaps in terms of attitudes to films themselves, exposed an increasingly complex range of opinions among clerical and lay Catholics over the reception of a number of films that themselves expanded the boundaries of what was permissible in film entertainment.

John Courtney Murray's article, 'Literature and Censorship', appeared in the July 1956 issue of *Books on Trial*, a journal devoted to reviewing contemporary literature from a Catholic perspective. Murray, a leading Jesuit intellectual and editor of the highly respected *Theological Studies*, argued that censorship in a democratic society was a dangerous infringement on freedom of expression and should be done only within a rigidly defined legal structure to prevent or restrict pornography. In what sounded like a direct attack on the Legion of Decency, he wrote that no censor should ever be allowed to 'display moral indignation', 'fussiness' or to use personal judgement in evaluating a creative work. There was simply no room, in his opinion, for the 'personal, the arbitrary, the passionate' among censors, especially in a pluralistic society like America. Murray made his views on the Legion clear when he concluded that, instead of carrying placards in front of movie theatres, which made the Church look 'ridiculous', Catholics had 'to stand before the world as men and women of faith, and ... of reason too'.[10]

Murray also argued that intelligent men and women did not need any help in determining what was obscene. They have, he wrote, 'a fairly clear notion of what obscenity' is and, he continued, 'can make, for themselves, a pretty good judgement on whether a particular work is obscene'. With the publication of his article, Murray made public a debate that had been raging within Catholic theological circles for several years. What was the ecclesiastical authority to prohibit Catholics from attending certain films? Was it a mortal sin, as some American bishops had maintained, to attend a condemned film? Or, as others argued, could well-informed, intelligent Catholic adults make up their own minds on whether or not a film might lead them into 'an occasion of sin'? According to Murray, 'the Code of Canon Law' allowed ordinary Catholics to make their own decisions.[11] His article, published 'with ecclesiastical approval', signalled an internal shift developing within the Catholic Church over the role of movies.

The issue of whether or not Legion ratings were binding on all Catholics was central to the internal debate within the Church that developed over the movies. Father John C. Ford, a professor of moral theology at Weston College in Massachusetts, agreed with Murray. When the Catholic bishops asked him to determine whether or not there was foundation within Canon Law for strictly enforcing Legion classifications, Ford asserted that there was no 'ecclesiastical law which makes the classifications of the Legion binding on the consciences of all United States Catholics'. And, he added, it was common knowledge that Catholics 'pay little attention to the classifications of the Legion'.[12] A year later, he published a longer and more detailed version of his views (co-authored by Father Gerald Kelly) in *Theological Studies*, which made it clear to any interested

Catholic that there was a serious disagreement among clerics over the authority of the Legion.[13] The American bishops, indeed, sent a letter of appreciation to Kelly and Ford stating that the article represented their own views.[14]

On the other side of the debate stood some of the most powerful members of the Catholic hierarchy: Cardinal Francis Spellman of New York, Cardinal James McIntyre of Los Angeles and Msgr. Thomas Little, director of the Legion were determined to sustain Legion control of Hollywood. So, too, was Martin Quigley. When Quigley saw Murray's article, he was outraged, firing off a letter to Bishop William A. Scully, Archbishop of Albany and Chairman of the Episcopal Committee for Motion Pictures. Quigley told Scully that Murray's position 'reflects the whole chain of arguments we have been hearing from the Left' including, he added, 'the Supreme Court'. If Murray was correct in his assessment that individuals can make their own determination, then, Quigley concluded, 'all the agencies and all the persons who have been seeking to deal with the movie problem are in a straitjacket'.[15]

It was clear that, by the late summer of 1956, there was strong disagreement within the Catholic Church over the authority of the Legion to dictate to lay Catholics. Catholics, in fact, may have been well ahead of the moral theologians. They were not especially shocked to learn they did not have to obey the Legion because, as noted above, there is little compelling evidence to suggest that they ever did. In the 1940s and 1950s, box-office records clearly suggest, for example, that highly controversial films like Otto Preminger's *The Moon is Blue* and *The Man With the Golden Arm* (1956), Howard Hughes's productions of *The Outlaw* and *The French Line* (1953), Elia Kazan's *Baby Doll* (1956), *Splendor in the Grass* (1961) and the filmed version of Robert Anderson's *Tea and Sympathy* (1956) did exceedingly well in urban areas with large Catholic populations. Father Ford was right: Catholics paid little attention to the Legion.

In September 1957, reflecting growing pressure on the worldwide Catholic Church to liberalise its view of what constituted legitimate entertainment, a new papal encyclical, *Miranda Prorsus,* was issued. Pope Pius XII told the faithful in his letter that the motion picture was one of the 'most important discoveries of our times'. The cinema, he stated, had the potential to be 'a worthy instrument by which men can be guided toward salvation'. It was, therefore, 'essential that the minds and inclinations of the spectators be rightly trained and educated' to understand the art form used by film-makers. The Pope consequently urged Catholics to 'devote ... deep and prolonged study' to the cinema in Catholic schools and universities.[16]

The encyclical itself was by no means a rejection of the Legion of Decency. But it was unmistakable that the tone of *Miranda Prorsus* was radically different from Pope Pius XI's 1936 encyclical, *Vigilanti Cura,* which called for a ban on improper movies. Given this clear signal from Rome, the Catholic bishops vowed to change the direction of the Legion of Decency. They directed Msgr. Little and Father Patrick Sullivan, assistant director of the Legion, to find ways for Catholic adults to view films with adult themes without committing a mortal sin. Little reported to the Bishops that, in his view, the A-I (Morally Unobjectionable for General Audiences) and C (Condemned) were working as intended, but that the A-II and B classifications were not. The A-II classification (Morally Unobjectionable for Adults and Adolescents) had become increasingly restrictive over the years as Hollywood moved toward more adult themes. As Little explained it, films like *The Hunchback of Notre Dame* (1956), science fiction favourites such as *Lost*

Continent (1951), cowboy yarns such as *3:10 to Yuma* (1957) and comedies like *My Man Godfrey* (1957) had been restricted to adults because of a scene or two that reviewers believed harmful to teenagers. By the same token, adults had been asked not to attend such B films as *Don't Go Near the Water* (1957), *Gunfight at OK Corral* (1957), *The Rainmaker* (1956) and *Will Success Spoil Rock Hunter?* (1957). To allow more flexibility, the bishops accepted a new series of classifications. A-II films could now be seen 'by the young' and A-III could be seen 'by adults'.[17]

Even more crucial, however, than the addition of new classifications was the addition of a new group of reviewers. When the National Legion of Decency was created in 1936, the movie division of the International Federation of Catholic Alumnae (IFCA) had been appointed as the Legion reviewing staff. Based in New York, the IFCA reviewers were some twenty to forty volunteers who judged movie morality. This conservative group often came under fire for their parochial interpretation of films. *The Motion Picture Exhibitor,* for example, labelled the IFCA 'a group of unskilled and untrained amateur "Critics" who could not be relied upon to separate technical details from personal entertainment preferences'.[18] Even Legion authorities questioned the competence of the IFCA. Bishop Scully, for example, told Jack Vizzard not to be too hard on Msgr. Little because he was surrounded by 'old ladies, most of whom should be retired'.[19]

The movement toward a more positive and enlightened Legion required new reviewers. The Legion reduced the IFCA's influence in 1957 by appointing a Board of Consultors, which included teachers at Catholic schools and colleges, priests from the New York Archdiocese and Catholics involved in the film and theatre business as well as leading Catholic lawyers, doctors and professionals. The Board, which often numbered as many as one hundred, was much more sophisticated and worldly than the women of the IFCA and played a major role in the new Legion. Board members were quite willing to engage Legion authorities in spirited debate over what was and what was not moral entertainment. A series of films, many of them of European origin, released in the 1960s provoked serious debates among Board members over the nature of harmful entertainment.

Splendor in the Grass (1961) is the story of two young high-school students in Independence, Kansas. The two are very much in love but are unable to consummate their passion because of societal pressures and parental interference. The young girl, Deanie Loomis (Natalie Wood), desperately wants her boyfriend, Bud Stamper (Warren Beatty), to make love to her. She is literally driven insane by his refusal to take her virginity and spends several years in a local asylum. He, in turn, is driven into the arms of one of the 'fast girls' in town, but soon leaves Kansas for Yale, where eventually he flunks out. When the Depression sweeps through Kansas, his family is driven into bankruptcy. In the end, Deanie marries a young doctor from the hospital and Bud returns to Kansas, where he scratches out a living as a farmer.

When the script for the film arrived at PCA headquarters in April 1960, its then head, Geoffrey Shurlock, objected to a scene in which Deanie begs Bud: 'Take me, Bud. Take me. Here. Right here' (though Bud does not). Shurlock also objected to scenes of heavy necking, Ginney (Barbara Loden) openly making love to several men in the parking lot of a bar and a love scene between Bud and a town girl, Juanita (Jan Norris). But the director of the film, Elia Kazan, paid little attention to Shurlock. He made the movie with the scenes intact and included a nude scene with Deanie taking a bath and then

Natalie Wood (Wilma Dean Loomis) and Warren Beatty (Bud Stamper) in *Splendor in the Grass* (1961)

running down the hallway, her bare bottom in full view of the camera. When the finished film was screened for Shurlock, he refused the PCA's seal of approval because of 'an overly vivid portrayal of sex' and Wood's bare rear.[20] Kazan, however, remained unresponsive. His earlier battles with the PCA and the Legion over *A Streetcar Named Desire* (1951) and *Baby Doll* had convinced him that giving in to censors ruined his films. Kazan's contract with Warner Bros. gave him final cut authority and he refused, in February 1960, to make any of the cuts demanded by Shurlock.[21]

While negotiations between the PCA and Warner Bros. continued, the film was sent to New York for preview by the Legion. When Legion consultants viewed the film in early May 1961, they saw essentially the same version that Shurlock had rejected several months earlier. The reaction of the Legion consultors is most revealing, indeed, since they were far from shocked. A Catholic priest from Xavier High School in New York City could not find 'anything immoral' in the film. A local parish priest stressed that the sexual realism was 'called for by the plot'. The overall impression, he informed Fathers Little and Sullivan, was that the film 'can be harmonized with moral principles'. He recommended an A-III rating. A Dominican priest agreed with both of his colleagues on a A-III although he disliked the suggestion that 'being good and preserving virginity [was] followed by [commitment to a] mental institution'. A lay Catholic woman also worried that the film was 'dangerous' for adolescents because the theme seemed to be 'that chastity would lead to insanity'. She favoured a more restrictive B rating 'objectionable in part for all'. However, another lay reviewer judged the film 'unobjectionable' and told the Legion it should be required viewing 'by both parents and adolescents alike'. This reviewer recommended an A-II classification that would open the film to all ages.[22]

Some Board members did, however, argue for condemnation. A male lay Catholic was especially adamant. He judged the film 'a confused, salacious and morally unwholesome motion picture' which promoted 'free love'. This man demanded that the Legion issue a strong condemnation. Father Little, director of the Legion, also agreed with the view that the film carried a 'free love' theme and should be condemned.[23]

Just a few years earlier, there is little doubt that Little and the Legion would, in fact, have condemned the film. But the newly expanded body of Legion reviewers complicated the Legion's operations. Quigley was not invited and there was no consensus among the diverse body of reviewers. Further complicating matters was the fact that the most liberal of the new group were the priests. While they found some scenes offensive, they did not believe that they were necessarily immoral or harmful. Most, like Father Murray, took a more worldly view of what Catholics could reasonably see on the screen.

Little, however, personally favoured a condemnation and decided to try to force Warner Bros. to edit some of the material that he found objectionable out of the film by implying that the Legion was considering condemning the film. When word of Little's threat reached Los Angeles, the PCA's Legion expert, Jack Vizzard, was quickly dispatched to New York to negotiate a compromise. Vizzard rapidly learned what scenes troubled Little most: Deanie begging Bud to 'take her' and a discussion by Bud's father in which he stated that it was perfectly acceptable to have sex with 'fast girls' but not with respectable ones. The parking-lot scene also troubled the priest because it clearly indicated that Ginny willingly and eagerly had sex with several different men. He was also disturbed by the nude scene and the shot in which Bud grabbed his genitals in frustration after turning down Deanie's plea to take her.[24]

After some discussion, Vizzard convinced Kazan to trim all the offending scenes and to replace dialogue in the scene where Deanie begs her lover to 'take her'. When Warner Bros. accepted the condition that the film would be restricted to those 16 years and older and that no scenes would be reinserted in the picture for foreign release, the Legion issued a B rating. But, in passing the film, the Legion warned Catholic viewers that 'The visual eroticism of this film is excessive and without dramatic justification; moreover its theme presents a confused pattern of moral behavior to young adults'.

The division within the Legion was reflected in Catholic reviews of the film. *The Sign* blasted the film as 'verging on the pornographic'. While the Legion had not finally condemned the film, *The Sign* warned readers 'it cannot be recommended for any audience'. *America,* a Jesuit publication, was less troubled by the film. It told readers the film was confusing but made no mention of morality. *The Commonweal* labelled *Splendor in the Grass* a 'curious mixture of realism, sensationalism and fancy'. It merited 'consideration' even if it was controversial.[25] So, just like the Legion, some professional Catholic reviewers found the film objectionable and some found it worthwhile.

As usual, moreover, Catholics paid little heed to either Legion warnings or negative reviews from Catholic publications. When the film opened a few blocks from Legion headquarters in New York City, it did 'a great $60,000' at the box office during its first week.[26] It was still running strong seven weeks later. In Philadelphia, with its huge Catholic population, *Splendor* did equally well, generating $31,000 in its first two weeks. It played to good audiences in Pittsburgh, Cleveland, Detroit, Toronto, Seattle, Los Angeles and even smaller cities like Omaha, Kansas City and Indianapolis reported solid box-office returns throughout the autumn and early winter of 1961. While *Splendor in the Grass* was not a smash hit, it finished a respectable twelfth in *Variety*'s box-office hits for 1961, just behind a sensational Italian import that was condemned by the Vatican and assaulted many Legion sensibilities.

Federico Fellini certainly challenged the boundaries of what was acceptable adult drama in the early 1960s when he released his personal essay on the decadence and spiritual vacuum of modern society, *La Dolce Vita* (1960 in Europe, but 1961 in the United States). Set in Rome, the fast crowd that Fellini portrayed exchanged sex partners as casually as they might bridge partners, with little regard for any traditional notions of sexual morality. That Fellini himself disapproved of this new lifestyle was only too clear, of course, to those who looked past the sex, sin and flesh that dominated the screen. The Vatican quickly banned Italian Catholics from seeing this scathing portrayal of modern Italy. It was, however, a smash hit in Rome and in cinemas throughout the rest of the country, and it was awarded the Grand Prix at Cannes. The film had no trouble winning a Production Seal from the PCA and the New York Film Critics gave it their 'Best Picture' award for 1961.

The Legion, however, was deeply troubled. Could a film banned by the Pope be acceptable entertainment for American Catholics? Did the movement towards a more realistic, adult cinema mean that the vivid bacchanal of Fellini could be seen without moral corruption by Catholics? These questions certainly caused Father Little great concern when he assembled a large group of reviewers to watch *La Dolce Vita* in May 1961.

Little sketched out the options available to the 120 consultors he brought in to evaluate Fellini's film. There was no way, he told them, that the Legion could keep the film out of American theatres by condemning it as they had in the past. Nor, he added, was it likely that a condemnation would 'be supported by the public'.[27] When he and Father Sullivan tabulated the reports from ninety-five clerics and lay Catholics who submitted written evaluations to the Legion, it was again clear that there was little consensus among the consultors on what constituted moral entertainment. Twenty-three (twelve of whom were priests) favoured an A-III rating. One told Little that, in his view, the 'theme of the movie is certainly a moral one'. There *were* shocking scenes in the film, he admitted, but they 'were never exploited for sensual delight'. A representative from *The Catholic World* pronounced it a 'dull documentary on corruption' that 'would not harm "the average adult"'. Another priest judged it 'a morality play' for adult viewers.[28]

There was almost equal support for a condemnation. Twenty-two consultors, including thirteen members of the IFCA, voted to condemn the film. One priest who voted for a 'C' was offended by the 'suggestiveness' of the film. Another found its treatment of religion 'scandalous' and 'irreverent'. One advocate of a C rating summed up the objections for his group: 'The complete lack of all moral standards, the inclusion of male homosexuals and lesbians and transvestites together with all kinds of illicit intercourse and degeneracy can do no good whatever for the cause of decent entertainment'. It was, he concluded, 'first-rate Communist propaganda'.[29]

Twenty-two of the consultors, however, favoured a B rating and another twenty-eight thought the film fitted into a 'Special Classification' category, used by the Legion when it could not fit a controversial film into its regular rating system. All of the consultors who favoured a B believed the overall theme of the film was 'moral' but were squeamish about the flesh and sex in the movie. When Little and his staff read the various reports, they were struck by the fact that so many of the consultors were convinced that Fellini was condemning the lifestyle he was illustrating. Everyone except those who recommended outright condemnation believed Fellini's overall theme was moral. 'In a word', Little wrote in his report to Bishop James McNulty, 'the majority [76.8 per cent] of our reviewers and consultants judged *La Dolce Vita* to be moral in theme and decent in treatment at least for mature audiences.'[30]

McNulty understood that a condemnation of the film would only serve to make the Catholic Church – as Father Murray had suggested in 1956 – look ridiculous. He supported Little's recommendation that the Legion demand that Astor Pictures, the distributor, exhibit the film in a subtitled 'Italian only' version limited to audiences over the age of 18. In return for these conditions, the Legion would place *La Dolce Vita* in a 'Separate Classification' which implied neither approval or disapproval. The distributor jumped at the offer and the film opened to curious audiences nationwide.

Martin Quigley, several bishops and Cardinal McIntyre of Los Angeles were outraged by the Legion's decision. Quigley challenged the Legion view that, by restricting the film to Italian with English subtitles, only mature adults would attend. He told Bishop McNulty and Father Little that the typical movie fan would not see 'sardonic commentary' on modern society but rather 'vivid images of … adultery, fornication, prostitution' and striptease. The images were so strong, Quigley predicted, that movie-goers would not even notice that the film was in Italian.[31]

But Quigley's opinion no longer counted for much at the Legion itself or in Catholic circles outside New York. For the most part, the Legion decision enjoyed the support of the Catholic press. *Ave Maria* editorialised that 'the Legion should have our support for its adult response to a difficult task'. *The Commonweal* congratulated the Legion for its 'intelligent comment and evaluation'. Moria Walsh, writing in *America,* described Fellini's film as a 'salutary moral warning' and supported the Legion's decision. And Edward Fisher, reviewer for *Ave Maria,* reminded his readers of a basic fact about movies. After praising *La Dolce Vita,* he pointed out that 'The only thing I can say definitely is that if anyone goes and finds this is too strong for him he can always get up and leave'.[32] This was a sensible bit of advice that, at times, too few were willing to accept – especially when it came to filming the story of a love affair between a young girl and an ageing man.

How would the Legion, indeed, classify a filmed version of Vladimir Nabokov's infamous novel about a middle-aged college professor's lust for a 12-year-old nymphet, Lolita? Would the Legion agree with Fisher that those who were offended could just walk out or not go? In one of the great ironies of this whole debate, Stanley Kubrick, the director of *Lolita* (1962), hired Martin Quigley as a consultant to help him to secure Legion approval for a film on paedophilia. Quigley managed to eliminate or soften some of the scenes, but it still remained very controversial. *Lolita* was screened for fifty-two Legion consultants who were again divided on the merits of the film. Nine, including four priests, saw Lolita as an A-III film which would do no harm to adults. A larger number, fourteen, including eight priests, were concerned enough to place the film in the B category. An even larger group, twenty-six, including eight priests, were shocked and voted for outright condemnation. A parish priest from Manhattan, who favoured a condemnation, told Little the film had 'no reason for existence'. It was, he added, 'stupid, dull and consistently boring'. Another C vote came from a professor from the Fordham Law School who called Lolita 'a disgusting chronicle of perversion' which was 'objectionable in its entirety'. He did not believe Catholics would want to see either of the seduction sequences. Four consultants voted to give *Lolita* a 'Separate Classification'.[33]

The Legion staff voted separately and were also equally divided. Little was, 'without qualification', in favour of condemnation. Sullivan opted for a 'Separate Classification' and Mary Looram, long-serving chair of the IFCA, judged it a B. Again, there was no clear consensus: twenty-seven total votes for a condemnation and twenty-six total votes placing the film in some other classification. Msgr. Little was in the last category. He did not like any part of *Lolita* and was determined to condemn the film. He arranged a second screening on 10 October 1961 for the man who would cast the determining vote. Bishop McNulty, chair of the Episcopal Committee, would decide whether or not Martin Quigley had succeeded in purifying the morals of the notorious film he had heard so much about. While Quigley was convinced that McNulty did not understand the moral dangers inherent in Fellini's work, McNulty was certain that *Lolita* was immoral. He dismissed the opinion of reviewers who saw morality in the film and ordered Little to condemn it out of hand.[34]

As in the past, negotiations between the film-makers and the Legion resulted in another 'Separate Classification' rating for *Lolita,* which was restricted to adults. Catholics were urged to use 'caution' when deciding whether or not to see the film. Not many seem to have followed this advice. The film played extremely well in large urban areas, but not so well in smaller cities and rural areas. It finished sixteenth in *Variety*'s annual box-office chart with $4.5 million in rentals.

By the mid-1960s it was increasingly clear, even to the staff of the Legion, that personal opinion was the determining factor in whether or not individuals saw films as moral or immoral, rather than a rigid, doctrinal morality dictated by the Legion. Catholic priests from various religious orders disagreed over what was moral entertainment. They were not shocked to sit in movie theatres and watch films like *La Dolce Vita.* Well educated, and faced with the realities of the modern world in their parishes, they found the restrictive views of the Legion to be out of step with the modern direction of the Catholic Church. Over the next few years, the Catholic Church and the Legion would pressure the movie industry into scrapping the censorship system of the Production Code and move toward some type of ratings system that would restrict adult movies to adults.

In the 1960s, the winds of change reflected in the Vatican II council swept through the Catholic Church. Father John Courtney Murray, author of the 1956 article questioning the Legion's authority, wrote the most important document of Vatican II, the 'Official Declaration of Religion' that marked the radical changes the Catholic Church was about to undergo. In general terms, Vatican II gave lay Catholics a much greater role in governing their local parish and in determining issues of personal morality. According to one scholar of religion, the impact of Vatican II was that 'Catholics were less likely to attend Sunday mass, more likely to use birth control, more willing to accept divorce and sexual relations outside marriage'.[35] Catholics increasingly questioned episcopal authority on issues of personal morality. If lay Catholics were less concerned about attending mass and using birth control, they certainly were not going to allow the bishops and the Legion of Decency to determine which movies they attended.

That the Catholic Church had changed its opinion on what was moral entertainment was strikingly illustrated by its reaction to *Darling*, a 1965 British release directed by John Schlesinger. The film starred Julie Christie, playing a beautiful, completely amoral young woman who leaves her husband, consorts with a wide variety of men, participates in an orgy, appears in the nude, gets pregnant, has an abortion, divorces her husband and marries a man she does not love. The film was a litany of offences against Catholic doctrine and would have been immediately condemned by the Legion a decade earlier. But by 1965 the Legion was no longer the Legion. It was the National Catholic Office for Motion Pictures (NCOMP) and it granted *Darling* its Best Picture of 1965 award. Moria Walsh, film critic for the Jesuit publication, *America,* supported the decision in the face of a flood of Catholic protests. She told her readers: 'I question the premises of those who translate their personal distaste into a general principle that finds the movie harmful for other people'.[36]

Most Catholics, lay and clerical, agreed with Walsh that going to the movies was a personal choice. Msgr. Little came to much the same conclusion when he admitted that moral issues that had once seemed so clear were, in his later years, filled with shades of grey. Father Sullivan preached the same message. The decision to see any movie, he said, was an 'exercise of individual responsibility in conscience'.[37] As even Martin Quigley admitted, lay Catholics had in practice always believed that movie-going was an individual choice. From the very beginnings of the Legion, they had exhibited an independence that frustrated Legion officials. Vatican II simply made this independence official.

Notes

1 John Courtney Murray, 'Literature and Censorship', *Books on Trial* (July, 1956), pp. 393–5, 444–6. See also John Courtney Murray, 'The Bad Arguments Intelligent Men Make', *America,* no. 96 (3 November 1956), pp. 120–3.

2 Gregory D. Black, *Hollywood Censored: Morality Codes, Catholics and the Movies* (Cambridge: Cambridge University Press, 1994), p. 181.

3 Ibid., pp. 298–9.

4 Ibid., pp. 187–8.

5 Lupton Wilkinson to J. J. McCarthy, 4 August 1934, Martin Quigley Papers, Box 1, Georgetown University [hereafter MQP].

6 David O. Selznick to Paul MacNamara, 11 August 1947, Box 3368, Selznick Papers, University of Texas-Austin. For an extended discussion of *Duel in the Sun,* see Gregory D. Black, *The Catholic Crusade Against the Movies, 1945–75* (New York and Cambridge: Cambridge University Press, 1998), Chap. 2.

7 Black, *The Catholic Crusade Against the Movies,* p. 125.

8 See Martin Quigley to Thomas Little, 9 April 1954, Box 2, MPQ.

9 Richard S. Randall, 'Censorship: From *The Miracle* to *Deep Throat*', in Tino Balio (ed.), *The American Film Industry* (Madison: University of Wisconsin Press, 2nd edn, 1985), p. 433; Quigley to Spellman, 7 July 1956, Box 1, MPQ.

10 Murray, 'Literature and Censorship', pp. 393–5, 444–6.

11 Ibid., p. 445.

12 John C. Ford. 'Moral Evaluations of Films by the Legion of Decency', n. d., Box 56, Archives of Los Angeles Archdiocese, Mission Hills, California.

13 Gerald Kelly and John C. Ford, 'The Legion of Decency', *Theological Studies,* vol. 18 (September 1957), pp. 387–93.

14 'Bishops' Minutes', 12 November 1957, National Catholic Conference [of Bishops] Archives, Catholic University, Washington, DC.

15 Quigley to William A. Scully, 25 June 1956, Box 1, MPQ.
16 For a discussion, see William A. Scully, 'The Movies: a Positive Plan', *America,* vol. 96 (30 March 1957), pp. 726–7.
17 Minutes, Episcopal Committee on Motion Pictures, 12 November 1957, Box 56, Archives, Archdiocese of Los Angeles, Mission Hills, California.
18 Quoted in James Skinner, *The Cross and the Cinema: The Legion of Decency and the National Catholic Office for Motion Pictures, 1933–70* (Westport, CT: Praeger, 1993), p. 133.
19 Joseph Breen to Martin Quigley, 21 February 1957, Box 1, MPQ.
20 Geoffrey Shurlock to Elia Kazan, 13 February 1961, *Splendor in the Grass,* Production Code Administration Files, Academy of Motion Picture Arts and Sciences Library, Beverly Hills, California [hereafter PCAF].
21 See Sullivan to Little, 11 July 1961; Sullivan to Files, 23 May 1961 and Little to Files, June 1961, *Splendor in the Grass,* Legion of Decency Files, Archdiocese of New York [hereafter NYLOD].
22. Ibid. While the files of the Legion are open for scholarly research, a condition of their use requested by Mr Henry Herx, director of the Catholic Office for Film and Broadcasting, is that none of the names of the consultors be used.
23 *Splendor in the Grass,* NYLOD.
24 Father Patrick Sullivan to the Files, 23 May 1961, ibid.
25 *The Sign,* 41 (November 1961), p. 50; *America,* 106 (14 October 1961), p. 60; *The Commonweal,* 75 (27 October 1961), p. 121.
26 *Variety,* 18 October 1961, p. 9.
27 Little to Bishop McNulty, 24 May 1961, *La Dolce Vita,* NYLOD.
28 See consultors' reviews, *La Dolce Vita,* ibid.
29 Ibid.
30 'Memorandum to Bishop McNulty', 24 May 1961, ibid.
31 Quigley to McNulty, 17 May 1961, Box 2, MPQ.
32 *Ave Maria,* 93 (17 June 1961), p. 17; *The Commonweal,* 74 (26 May 1961), p. 221; *America,* 105 (3 June 1961), p. 411; *Ave Maria,* 94 (26 August 1961), p. 15.
33 Memo to Cardinal Spellman, 20 October 1961, NYLOD.
34 Little to Cardinal Spellman, 11 October 1961, ibid.
35 Catherine L. Albanese, *America: Religions and Religion* (Belmont, CA: Wadsworth Press, 1981), p. 80.
36 *America,* vol. 113 (21 August 1965), p. 190.
37 Frank Walsh, *Sin and Censorship: The Catholic Church and the Motion Picture Industry* (New Haven: Yale University Press, 1996), p. 323.

6
Historical Spectatorship Around and About Stanley Kramer's *On the Beach*

G. Tom Poe

In early 1959, United Artists released *On the Beach,* Stanley Kramer's film version of Nevil Shute's bestselling novel depicting the human race in the death throes of nuclear annihilation. Despite an impressive cast including Gregory Peck, Ava Gardner, Fred Astaire and Tony Perkins, *Variety,* Hollywood's chief prophet of profitability, predicted that the film's depressing story – 'heavy as a leaden shroud' – would severely limit its audience appeal. According to the trade paper, the film's success would have to depend on its star power and on how well it could attract 'the non-movie-going moviegoer' by being promoted as 'a status symbol'. *Variety* went on to define a 'status symbol': that is, 'something to be seen despite its grim nature'.[1]

In any event, Kramer's film did surprisingly well at the box office. By the end of 1959, *On the Beach* had generated $6.2 million in domestic rentals, making it the eighth highest-earning film of the year, outgrossing such inspirational fare as *The Big Fisherman* and *The Story of Ruth* by more than $3 million. Robert Hatch, film critic of *The Nation,* admitted to being perplexed by audiences' positive reaction to Kramer's dark and pessimistic film. 'As the last flicker of life disappeared off the face of the earth', he wrote, 'the audience applauded. That is unusual movie-house behavior and I wondered what they were applauding. Had they "enjoyed" the picture or were they glad to be alive?'.[2] This essay explores the cultural logics employed by various spectators not only to make sense of *On the Beach,* but also to find it entertaining or, in some cases, dangerous to the public welfare. As well as provoking a range of audience responses, Kramer's film also occasioned a public debate that served contradictory political and social ends.

In arguing for a 'historically materialist' approach to film spectatorship, Janet Staiger rightly insists that talk as a 'social event' occasions contradictory effects. The talk that gathers around and about a particular film can both limit the interpretative possibilities available to historically situated spectators, and at the same time, as Staiger suggests, 'create a dispersion of discourses that work toward a disintegration and reconfiguration of meanings and institutions'.[3] In the case of *On the Beach,* powerful political and cultural institutions did indeed try to contain the 'loose talk' generated by Kramer's anti-nuclear melodrama. This attempt was, however, hardly new. As recent historical studies have documented, for over two decades culturally conservative special-interest groups actively sought to empty the screen of controversial political content as well as violence and sexual indiscretions.[4] The Production Code Administration (PCA) had always held the position that it was 'against industry policy' to produce films that would invite political controversy, while special-interest groups such as the Legion of Decency (LOD) had proved successful in using the threat of the boycott to discourage film-makers from pursuing projects that might generate debate around subjects the Catholic Church considered 'closed' questions, such as abortion, suicide, sex outside of marriage and – in the early years of the cold war – anything deemed pro-Communist. By the late 1950s, however, the decline in the power of the PCA and the LOD, coupled with what seemed the growing threat of television, allowed Hollywood studios to exploit politically explosive topics more safely. Nevertheless, *On the Beach* still had to be marketed as a 'status event' that would generate what both audiences and political and cultural opinion leaders would regard as 'serious' talk. Beyond the usual confines of fan magazines and film reviews, the film did indeed become the subject of columns by political columnists, newspaper editorials, and speeches on the floor of Congress. Discussion of its political impact even found its way onto the agenda of several White House Cabinet meetings.

Like the political thrillers of the early 1960s (*Advice and Consent,* 1962; *Fail Safe,* 1963; and *Seven Days in May,* 1964), *On the Beach* marketed political controversy, and in attempting to assess the cultural exchange value of these films, we should consider their social utility as generators of political discourse. In 1963, Sidney Lumet defended *Fail Safe*'s melodramatic enactment of the risks of nuclear war, declaring, 'I don't care if it's on a sensational level ... Any discussion is good.'[5] This essay will examine Lumet's rhetorical claim. Is the generation of discourse in and of itself progressive, as some readings of Bakhtin might suggest? Is any and all talk equal in its social significance, or in its power? In thinking about the talk generated by such political films, I want also to consider the extent to which institutional spectators continued to wield over the public reception of political films. The official or professional talk generated by institutional spectators (agents of the state, the church and the press) largely shaped the interpretive schemata that audiences employed in viewing the picture. As Barbara Klinger insists, 'textual meanings are negotiated by external agencies'. Thus, we must consider the 'contributions that contextual factors, as opposed to textual devices or viewer subjectivities, make to an understanding of how texts mean'.[6]

Although all spectators may have had an equal ability to produce personal, even idiosyncratic meanings, they were not all equal in their power to affect cultural discourse. Some talk had institutional status, and thus the power to be heard beyond the limits of the kitchen table or the factory floor. Before proceeding to an examination of the talk generated around *On the Beach,* I want first to reconsider the usual limits of our understanding of spectatorship.

First, let us consider a film's production history as itself one act of spectatorship. In linear transmission models of communication, the producers of a text are generally figured as the binary opposite of the spectator. Before any film has a material existence, however, it is seen in the mind's eye of its creators. In most Hollywood films, the material text is the product of a number of creative and institutional points of view. In the case of *On the Beach,* the producer, the writers, the director, the PCA and the LOD all saw the film in different ways. These various ways of seeing the film worked to shape and reshape the text before it was viewed by other professional or institutional spectators (film reviewers, political columnists and government officials) who in turn influenced the interpretative strategies available to the film's theatrical spectators.

PCA officials, representatives of the LOD and government officials can be described as 'administrative' spectators in that they watched the movie with the intention of administering the potential meanings available to the public. In seeking to influence how the general audience would view the film, these administrative spectators had at their disposal political or cultural institutional structures, in the form of legislation, 'industry policy', or institutionally sponsored boycotts. Other professional spectators – film critics, entertainment reporters and political columnists – watched *On the Beach* knowing that they would be paid to have something interesting to say about it. It was the job of such professional spectators to speak both to and for more or less specific constituencies. Unlike the filmmaker as spectator, administrative and professional audiences spoke not only to the audience who chose to go to the film, but also to a collateral audience of people who heard things about the film without themselves seeing it. These non-spectators were also an audience of sorts, taking part in the film's release as a political event, an occasion for talk and sometimes for direct action. In large part, this official, administrative talk is all that remains for historians of film spectatorship to study. While many Americans spent a good bit of time talking about films, most of that talk evaporated into thin air.

What we are left with is the 'professional' talk around and about a specific film, that is, the talk of film critics, or columnists, or reporters, or industry employees, or politicians, or preachers, or officials of censorship boards or officers of social, religious, political and other special-interest organisations. To what extent does this official discourse tell us anything about what individual spectators really thought? Is culling through film reviews and PCA archives really doing historical audience reception study?

This discourse does not necessarily reflect either the variety or complexity of what individual viewers made of Hollywood films, but official talk does tell us a lot about film audiences. Most of it is talk about audiences and what they should or should not be thinking about a particular film. While official discourses around a film do not reflect every possible meaning constructed by every historical film-goer, they do nevertheless document the operational schemes made available to historically situated audiences. Official and professional spectators taught audiences how and often what to think about the films they saw.

The surfeit of authority attributed to official talk does not, however, make it all powerful. Official talk was necessitated by institutional opinion leaders' recognition that sometimes they had to talk fast and furiously if they were to limit public perceptions. To many institutions, loose talk around and about a film was deemed dangerous. The following case study of *On the Beach* offers us a chance to catch this complex process of ideological containment in the rhetorical act.

On 9 September 1957, Kramer announced his intention to film *On the Beach*, proclaiming that his film version of Shute's bestseller would be 'a concept of hope on celluloid ... to reach out to the hearts of people everywhere that they might feel compassion – for themselves'.[7] Following Kramer's dramatic announcement, a year would pass before he sent a copy of the script to the PCA. The agency's director, Geoffrey Shurlock, received the script on 20 October 1958, nine days before Kramer was scheduled to leave for Australia to begin filming. Shurlock was especially dismayed by the script's handling of scenes in which the government handed out suicide pills to the radiation-stricken public. The PCA director asked his assistant, Jack Vizzard, to address his concerns.

After two negotiations with Vizzard in the same week, Kramer agreed to add a few additional lines of dialogue which would serve as a voice of morality against mercy killing. For example, in the scene where Mary, a young wife and mother, accepts a suicide pill from her devoted husband, she was now to turn to the camera and say, 'May God forgive us for what we are about to do'. Another scene was added in which a Salvation Army-type street preacher voices a similar plea for forgiveness. On 28 October, Vizzard told Shurlock that Kramer had revised enough of the original screenplay to 'somewhat counter-balance the manner in which the suggestion of euthanasia is proposed in this script', but 'we told him frankly that there was still doubt in our minds whether it would be sufficient to satisfy the Legion of Decency'.[8] With that word of warning, the PCA approved the script and Kramer left the next morning to begin filming in Australia.

When the officials of the Legion of Decency saw a rough cut of the film, they were unsure what to make of it, much less how to fit it into the Legion's rating system. On 23 September 1959, nearly three months before the film's public première, Legion Director Msgr. Thomas F. Little and his assistant, Father Patrick J. Sullivan, met with the film's co-producer George Schaefer to discuss the Legion's continuing objections to the PCA-approved content of the film. During the meeting, Little told Schaefer that the Legion had interpreted the script as a 'condonation of race suicide'. More surprisingly, he attacked the PCA's added 'voice of morality', complaining that the lines added to give moral balance intellectually compounded the moral problem 'precisely because these speeches, while admitting that suicide is wrong, intend to say that under these circumstances God will understand'.[9]

Schaefer suggested to Kramer that he agree to the Legion's request to cut the scene showing survivors taking suicide pills. Kramer, who was still in Australia, replied that he was 'stunned' by the Legion's reaction, and further that 'as a good Catholic', he 'prayed' that the Legion would 'look beyond the trees of partial objection to the forest of potential good'. In Kramer's view, the added lines asked forgiveness for the 'sin of having permitted the world to reach the state in which it finds itself'. This, he thought, 'far transcends the idea of a sin to come ... This is – and make no mistake about it – the sin with which youth today charges us, namely our total inability to have implemented God's will for peace on earth'.[10]

Kramer's passionate defence worked. Msgr. Little was persuaded, against the advice of many of his own reviewers, to revise his interpretation, declaring the film to be 'morally unobjectionable for adults'. Concerned that criticism from conservative priests could prove embarrassing, however, he tried to lessen their objections by adding a special note to the published rating:

> There are certain moral issues in the development of this story which superficially seem
> to involve a condonation of race suicide. These dramatic elements, however, are
> intended to be a challenging symbol to argue the central theme of the film, namely, that
> nuclear warfare *is* race suicide.[11]

Despite this attempt to justify the Legion's position, its revised interpretation of the film did not square with that of many Church leaders. Cardinal McIntyre of Los Angeles, as well as New York's Cardinal Spellman, contacted the Legion demanding an explanation of its action. Little assured McIntyre that no film in recent years had received more serious consideration. It had been reviewed by 'a large number of our qualified male and female lay and clergy viewers'. While 'the controversial nature of the film elicited various types of receptivity from a moral point of view', Little maintained that after 'prolonged discussions', the Legion had decided that Kramer's film offered 'a very potent and moral argument against nuclear warfare', one that 'truly reflects the sentiments of our own Holy Father John XXIII that nuclear warfare is race suicide'.[12]

McIntyre was not convinced. He continued to fight the film, going so far as to contact the FBI to request an 'investigation of the personnel and circumstances concerning the preparation and the production of *On the Beach*'. The FBI co-operated, and sent a confidential memorandum to the CIA asking for its help.[13] Both agencies reported, however, that they could find no 'information to support [the contention] that *On the Beach* is a communistic vehicle of propaganda'. This did little to calm McIntyre's fears. He wrote to Bishop McNulty that he 'well understand that this information is not traceable by the FBI', but that in his opinion, 'this would not diminish its likelihood. We are living in strange days, and communist propaganda finds expression in unexpected channels'.[14]

Other government agencies, including key members of the Eisenhower Administration, shared the Cardinal's concerns, if not his paranoia. Throughout November and early December 1959, discussions of Kramer's film found their way on to the agenda of several White House Cabinet meetings. The potential problem presented by the film came to the attention of the President on 6 November, when the director of the Office of Civil Defence Management, Karl Harr, was asked to report on his agency's progress in developing prototypes for fallout shelters. During the discussion, Secretary of State Christian Herter noted that the American Red Cross had been asked to sponsor the première of *On the Beach*. This bothered Herter because, as he saw it, the film was 'extremist, ban-the-bomb propaganda'. He informed Cabinet members that, 'given the unprecedented publicity given this film, the President has asked me to add a discussion of the film to the next Cabinet meeting'.

In Herter's view, a positive reception of Kramer's *On the Beach* would constitute a 'serious obstacle' to national security. If audiences embraced the film's 'extremist' message, it could have 'tremendous impact', undermining public support for the government's civil defence programme and military expenditure. Karl Harr agreed, decrying the film for making his fallout shelter programme appear 'utterly hopeless'.[15]

At the end of 1958, an opinion poll sponsored by the Office of Civil Defense Management (OCDM) indicated that 78 per cent of Americans who had 'heard of fallout' believed that the H-Bomb would be used against the United States in a world war. The OCDM was discouraged to find that despite an optimistic publicity campaign promising that only minimal precautions were necessary to protect from the dangers of fallout (the now infamous 'duck and cover' ads), only 18 per cent of the American population believed that their chances for survival were very good, even if they were housed in a fully equipped bomb shelter. By 1959, moreover, for all the government's attempts to encourage the building of family fallout shelters, only 2 per cent of the American population had constructed such a shelter. Most respondents said they simply did not want to spend the money.[16]

The government psychologists who analysed these opinion polls concluded that what appeared to be mere apathy was in reality a sign that the public was psychologically unable to 'think about the unthinkable' without falling into total despair. This, they argued, was the greatest danger to civil defence. The government thus faced the challenging predicament that not thinking about the dangers of nuclear war led to apathy, while thinking about it led to despair. The government soon found that for all its power and prestige, its ability to affect spectator reaction to a Hollywood film was limited. As Secretary of Defense, Robert Anderson would come to conclude, 'Given the film's undeniable emotional power, it's a tricky problem'. The best they could do, Christian Herter concluded, was 'to turn this emotional response into support of our own quest' for increased military spending and civil defence.[17]

White House concerns were heightened by the announcement that, on 17 December, Kramer's film was to have simultaneous world premières in eighteen major world capitals, from Berlin to New Delhi, including Moscow. Kramer declared the simultaneous world premières to be 'an invitation to the world's leaders to share a collective moment of reflection on the dangers of nuclear war'.[18] Indeed, the press co-operated in making the première of the film appear to be a major news event. *Variety* claimed that the premières, attended by some 33,000 people, aroused comment from Moscow to Melbourne and reported that, in Tokyo, 'many of the 1,500 persons in the first-night audience wept openly'. The *New York Times* compared political reactions in Washington and Moscow, while Los Angeles *Mirror News* editor Dick Williams wrote that 'various Capitol Hill solons have been blasting or boosting the picture, with the result that the film may wind up with as many clippings from the Congressional Record as from the daily papers'.[19]

Eisenhower was not pleased, telling Herter that 'given the unprecedented publicity being given this film', the matter of *On the Beach* should be placed on the agenda for more discussion at the 2 and 11 December Cabinet meetings. A pre-meeting memo sent to all Cabinet members suggested that, in view of attempts to get Cabinet members to attend the Washington première, it would be helpful to 'develop guidance for members of the government, as well as for USIA and our missions overseas'.[20] Cabinet members were also asked to attend a private White House screening of the film prior to the 7 December meeting. (Hollywood studios routinely provided the White House with pre-release prints of their latest product.)

In the meeting that followed the special screening, Karl Harr reiterated his earlier view that the film was extremely dangerous. Admitting that it presented a difficult problem for the government, the OCDM director noted that 'we cannot try to suppress or even criticize the film, because it is undeniably an emotionally moving film'. Secretary McCane suggested that Secretary of Defense Anderson might go on national television to deliver a statement that would discredit both the novel and the film, in particular using his connections with religious leaders to exploit Catholic concern over the film's depiction of mass suicide. Herter expressed his doubts about these plans, fearing that they would give the film more publicity. Secretary of Labor James P. Mitchell, agreed, commenting, 'I sure hope it doesn't get advertised as "discussed at Cabinet!" '. The Cabinet finally concurred with Information Director Abbot Washburn's conclusion that 'while we can show no signs of approval, it is a tricky situation and we're stuck with it. We must not give the appearance of an American government boycott of an anti-war film'.[21]

Given that the government's options were limited, it was agreed that White House staff should prepare a classified report on the film to be distributed to all State Department and Pentagon personnel, directing them how to answer questions from the press or public about what they thought of the film. The directive recommended that 'comment be refused on the picture. However, we hardly can refuse comment on the question of whether or not the situation portrayed in the picture has scientific validity'. It included a six-page question and answer sheet with scripted questions and answers such as:

> Q. Do you have any comment on the film, *On the Beach*?
> A. I am not a movie critic, and am not particularly qualified to discuss the film's dramatic qualities or the performance of the actors.
> Q. But do you think that the film portrays a situation which could actually occur?
> A. No. I don't think this could happen. Let's assume a hypothetical nuclear war involving the detonation of somewhat more than 1400 megatons in the US and another 2500 megatons elsewhere in the Northern Hemisphere. Under these conditions, it is estimated that about 30 per cent of the US population would be killed. This would be terrible but not anywhere near total destruction ... After all, unprecedented destruction is not the same as unlimited destruction.[22]

This paper was quoted in numerous public statements made by key military and civil defence officials who fanned out across the country, presenting their arguments against the film to religious and social clubs and the press. When reviewing the movie, most American newspapers published a side-bar story reporting local civil defence officials' objections to the film. Quotations from the government document often found their way into negative reviews of the film, and it was also sent to political office holders as a way to answer constituent concerns.

The recommended strategy for members of Congress was to give a non-committal answer to questions and then to offer a specially prepared OCDM information sheet. Congressional and White House files contain numerous letters from citizens asking for the government's reaction to the film. For example, a Millburn, New Jersey dentist wrote to Congressman George Wallhauser, saying, 'It may be within your power to help prevent world wide destruction such as is shown in the motion picture *On the Beach*. If you have not seen the motion picture, I beg you to do so'.[23] Following White House guidelines, Congressman Wallhauser replied, 'I have not seen the motion picture, but I sincerely hope that the possibility of world peace is not as dismal as you indicate'.[24] The White House followed up letters from concerned citizens by sending an equally polite, if even more terse response: 'The President is always glad to have the views of all citizens. I suggest you read the enclosed releases concerning *On the Beach* that I believe will be helpful in clarifying our position in the matter'.[25]

In addition to the question and answer guide, the US Information Agency sent classified information guides to *On the Beach*, with a cover letter signed by the Secretary of State, to all embassy posts. Herter's letter began by warning that the film's strong emotional appeal for banning nuclear weapons could lead audiences 'to think in terms of radical solutions to the problem', but added that 'to a limited extent, it may offer opportunities to turn this emotional response into intellectual support for our quest for safeguarded disarmament'. The letter noted that

Our attitude should be one of matter-of-fact interest, showing no special concern. We
should refrain from public criticism of the film, which would be counter-productive.
We should, however, be ready to discuss the film in private conversation with opinion
leaders. In this connection … special points should be noted.

…The greatest impact of the film for thinking people should be to underline … the
vital importance for the US and its allies to maintain armed strength to deter
aggression and for self-protection.

… War itself is the real evil, not any particular weapon. Conventional weapons kill just
as effectively as nuclear weapons; morally there is no distinction. It will be unfortunate
if the scientific inaccuracies of the film mislead and drive them to pressure for ban-the-
bomb-type solutions.[26]

While the Administration's behind-the-scenes machinations did not result in movie
ads proclaiming 'discussed at Cabinet', they might as well have. Within days of the confidential release of Herter's directive, the document had been leaked to reporters. The
next week *Newsweek* reported that, 'In a secret six-page cable, American military VIPs
around the world were ordered to stay away from premières of the movie *On the
Beach*'.[27] The only exception to this rule was for the première held in Moscow. Here, at
least as reported in *Variety*, the contradictory values of capitalism and cold war rhetoric
came into bold relief. The Hollywood film industry was eager to open up the rich market represented by the Eastern Bloc and was more than willing to let Moscow make
some political points against the West if it served the purpose of free trade. The Moscow
première was thus a trade-off. The Soviets used their endorsement of the film as proof
to the world that the USSR was as 'peace-loving' as the United States; while the
American film industry got its foot into the film market behind the Iron Curtain. To
sweeten the deal, United Artists offered the Soviet Ministry the appearance of Gregory
Peck at the Moscow première. After some lobbying, United Artists was given permission
by the State Department to 'unofficially' première the film in Moscow as long as it was
clear that it was not part of any government-sponsored cultural exchange programme.[28]
    Peck's unofficial visit to the Soviet Union also generated publicity for the film at
home, suggesting that Hollywood was doing what governments could not do – saving
the world from nuclear disaster. Kramer and United Artists capitalised on the statement
by distinguished American scientist Linus Pauling that 'It may be that some years from
now we can look back and say that *On the Beach* is the movie that saved the world'.[29]
With a forced smile, the American Ambassador to the USSR, Llewellyn Thompson, was
forced to save face by accompanying Peck and his wife to the Moscow première,
attended by some two thousand invited guests.
    In actual fact, the Moscow première did little to open up the Soviet film market.
Despite Hollywood's hopes that the film would be granted a public Moscow run, the
Soviet Minister of Culture, Alexander Charkovskii, told *Pravda* immediately after the
première that the film would not be shown to the public, since it was 'obviously objectionable and unacceptable to Soviet audiences'. Like the government of the United
States, Soviet officials reportedly found the film far too hopeless and depressing for
public viewing. The Soviets, however, interpreted the hopelessness of the film as yet

another symptom of the exhaustion of the West. Charkovskii told the Soviet press that the film pointed out 'the atomic psychosis ... being kept up recently in ... the United States'.[30]

Meanwhile, the White House and Pentagon proved ill-equipped to compete with the favourable publicity that the studio was generating around the film. The *Los Angeles Times* appeared to have been correct in its report that government actions served little purpose, since 'these scattered criticisms are but a small volley amid a generally favorable reaction to an excellent and moving film'. Indeed, one *Los Angeles Mirror* columnist concluded that while he did not personally 'read into the film's content any subtle attempt to persuade America or the West to abandon the weapons upon which it depends for its safety,' still, 'those who pan it, ironically enough, point up the very implications of the film, that mankind, by interminable hassling and deceptive wishful thinking about the destructiveness of new H-bombs can shockingly stumble unintentionally along the path to nuclear war'.[31]

On the Beach garnered only mixed reviews. It did, however, prove a box-office draw. During its first five weeks, the film played in limited release in only six American cities. In spite of this limited distribution, *Variety* reported that the film had grossed well over a million dollars in this period. Newspapers likewise reported that the film was a great box-office hit. In reality, however, beyond the largest urban markets, the film foundered commercially, particularly in areas of the country such as the Midwest and South where polls indicated that apathy and ignorance of nuclear issues were still surprisingly strong. A government-sponsored public opinion poll taken in April 1958 showed that, in these two regions, 35 per cent of respondents had never heard of the word 'fallout'.[32] The apathy and sense of hopelessness that the government feared would be engendered by the film appears instead to have discouraged 'regular movie-goers' – primarily teens and working-class adults – from attending it in the first place. Despite the film's apparent success in attracting the 'nonmovie-going movie-goer', which boosted it into the lower half of the year's top-ten money-makers, Kramer considered it a financial disappointment. Years later he told biographer Donald Spoto that he took 'full responsibility for the film's disappointing box office', blaming it on his failure to make the film's sober subject 'exciting' enough to attract a mass audience.[33]

The film had an unexpected impact, however. The public discourse it generated resulted in its having a secondary audience beyond its actual spectators. This secondary audience, who viewed the film as a cultural event rather than a text, was made up of the countless numbers of people who read news reports, columns and letters to the editor arguing its merits. Attendance is only one indicator of a film's social impact, and this form of spectatorship has to be considered as a broader activity than film-going.

As an 'event', a film may have more impact on the production of culture than as a 'text'. In that regard, *On the Beach* seems to have been successful in winning the rhetorical debate that surrounded it. News reports of government actions against it appear to have enhanced rather than damaged its credibility. Despite the 'official' civil defence press statements opposing the film, letters to the editor ran highly in its favour and questioned the government's intentions. Ironically, public opinion polls of the time suggested that most Americans found the film realistic and accurate in its depiction of the real threat of nuclear war, and that is why they stayed away from watching it.

Several aspects of this seem to bear on the historical nature of spectatorship. Kramer,

The closing shot from *On the Beach* (1959)

The Legion of Decency, Cardinal McIntyre and White House officials may have viewed the same movie, but clearly they did not 'see' the same object. Spectatorship is as complex and negotiated inside an institutional setting as it is in a small-town theatre. Even so, Kramer was able to win the consent of the Legion to his construction of the film's meaning by offering Msgr. Little a convenient interpretation that would allow him to see the film as 'a statement against global suicide', rather than a 'condonation' of euthanasia. The same argument, however, did not work with Cardinal McIntyre.

The State Department's attempt to use the film for its own purposes had some limited success. The film did provide an opportunity for government officials to disseminate further their contrary assessment of the nuclear crisis. As the *LA Mirror* columnist noted, however, to many Americans such 'official' efforts to discredit the film only served as further evidence of the correctness of the film's condemnation of the government's inability to take the imminent nuclear threat seriously. The film made no difference to the average American's commitment to civil defence preparedness. *Science* magazine was probably correct to observe that 'the viewer leaves the theatre ... moved more by what he has brought to the film than by what the performance itself accomplished'.[34]

This study of the spectatorship around and about *On the Beach* suggests how some Americans, including a number of powerful voices, thought and talked about nuclear war, civil defence and mega-death. One of the ways they talked about these subjects was by talking about Kramer's film. As with many controversial political films, more people talked about *On the Beach* than actually watched it. The rhetorical impact of a film cannot always be judged in terms of box-office receipts, and the question of spectatorship requires us to look beyond the ticket-buying audience.

In terms of the political impact of *On the Beach,* most Americans remained either too scared or not scared enough of nuclear holocaust to spend their money on a bomb shelter. Equally, they did not choose to spend money watching Kramer's film, even though it was greeted by Pauling as the film that might 'save the world'. Many were probably buffeted by the competing discourses surrounding the film. Given the choices offered to spectators of either believing Kramer's fictional film or the official fictions offered by the Office of Civil Defence, the difference between fact and fiction indeed proved, as the President himself was well aware, 'a tricky problem'.

Likewise, a historical-materialist study of the diverse discourses generated around and about *On the Beach* exposes an equally 'tricky problem' for film scholars attempting to determine the power of political and cultural agencies to effect the meanings and pleasures of the classical Hollywood film. Clearly, *On the Beach* proved to be a social and discursive event that taxed powerful political and cultural institutions in their attempt to affect how spectators made sense of Kramer's film. No doubt, the ideological manoeuvres of government and church did effectively shape some spectators' reception of the film. At the same time, however, these powerful institutions found themselves having to contain, rather than predetermine the talk the film occasioned. As a discursive event, rather than a self-contained 'text', *On the Beach* proved a site of ideological contention, in a way that suggests that hegemony is never as stable as institutional spectators hope, or some critical theorists fear.

Notes

1 *Variety,* 2 December 1959, p. 6.
2 Robert Hatch, *The Nation,* 21 December 1959.
3 Janet Staiger, *Bad Women: Regulating Sexuality in Early American Cinema* (Minneapolis: University of Minnesota Press, 1995) p. xv. See also Staiger, *Interpreting Films: Studies in the Historical Reception of American Cinema* (Princeton: Princeton University Press, 1992), p. 81.
4 See Gregory D. Black, *Hollywood Censored: Morality Codes, Catholics, and the Movies* (Cambridge: Cambridge University Press, 1994), pp. 107–45, and Ruth Vasey, *The World According to Hollywood, 1918–39* (Exeter: Exeter University Press, 1997).
5 'Coming, The End of the World', *Newsweek,* 3 March 1963, p. 84.
6 Barbara Klinger, *Melodrama and Meaning: History, Culture and the Films of Douglas Sirk* (Bloomington: Indiana University Press, 1994), p. xvi.
7 *Los Angeles Times,* 9 September 1959, file clippings, *On the Beach* file [hereafter *OTB*], Margaret Herrick Library, Academy of Motion Picture Arts and Sciences, Beverly Hills, California [hereafter MHL].
8 Vizzard to Shurlock, 28 October 1959, *OTB* file, Production Code Administration files, MHL.
9 Little to File, 23 September 1959, *OTB* file, National Legion of Decency files, The Chancery of Washington, DC [hereafter LOD].
10 Kramer to Schaefer, 1 October 1959, LOD files.
11 National Legion of Decency rating (press release), 12 November 1959, LOD.
12 Little to McIntyre, with copies to Francis Cardinal Spellman, 4 November 1959, LOD.

13 Letter from FBI to Little, 1 November 1959, with copy to Francis Cardinal Spellman, 1 November 1959, LOD.

14 McIntyre to McNulty, 19 January 1960, Chancery Archives of the Archdiocese of Los Angeles.

15 Presidential Cabinet Agenda, 11 December 1959, The Dwight David Eisenhower Presidential Library, Abilene, Kansas [hereafter EPL].

16 Eugene Joseph Rosi, 'Public Opinion and Foreign Policy', Ph.D. dissertation, Columbia University, 1964, Appendix II.

17 Cabinet Minutes, 11 December 1959, EPL.

18 *Variety*, weekly edn, New York City, 10 October 1959, p. 7.

19 Ibid., 21 December 1959, p. 7; *New York Times*, 18 December 1959, p. 34; ibid., 19 December 1959, p. 30; ibid., 20 December 1959, II–3; *Los Angeles Mirror News*, 18 December 1959, file clipping MHL.

20 Cabinet Meeting Agenda, 7 December 1959, EPL.

21 Cabinet Meeting (hand-written notes), 11 December 1959, EPL.

22 Cabinet Paper CI–59–64, 7 December 1959, EPL.

23 Cornell Grossman, DDS to the Hon. George Wallhauser, 14 March 1960, *OTB* correspondence file, EPL.

24 Wallhauser to Grossman, EPL.

25 Jack Z. Anderson, Administrative Assistant to the President, to Hon. George Wallhauser, 22 March 1960, EPL.

26 *Infoguide* 60–24, 4 December 1959, US Information Agency, EPL.

27 *Los Angeles Mirror News*, 24 December 1959, file clipping, *OTB* files, MHL.

28 Larry Glenn, 'Russ OK on "Beach" Preem in Moscow May be Sign of Thaw', *Variety*, 30 November 1959, file clipping, MHL.

29 Quoted in Jack G. Shaheen, *Nuclear War Films* (Carbondale, Ill: Southern Illinois University Press, 1978), p. 31.

30 *New York Times*, 22 December 1959, file clipping, *OTB* files, MHL.

31 Dick Williams, '*On the Beach* Stirs Disputes', *Los Angeles Mirror*, 24 December 1959, file clipping, MHL.

32 'The American Institute of Public Opinion', reprinted in Rosi, *Public Opinion and Foreign Policy*, Table 4, Appendix I.

33 For other letters indicating viewer approval of Kramer's film, see *New York Times*, 17 January 1960, file clippings, *OTB* file, MHL.

34 'A Thinking Man's Movie?', *Science*, 18 December 1959, vol. 130, p. 1679.

PART TWO

The Spectator Reviewed

7
'Green Like Me'

Jane M. Gaines

There is no better account of the African-American child's measurement of his likeness against the luminous screen image than James Baldwin's recollection of his own childhood in *The Devil Finds Work* (1976). In these autobiographical essays, the child's racial identity is drafted and redrafted between the ages of 7 and 17, a process involving formative trips to two local theatres – a black motion-picture house, the Lincoln, and a black dramatic house, the Lafayette. At the Lincoln, he sees MGM and Warner Bros. all-white cast films from the 1920s and 1930s, and later, at the Lafayette, he sees all-black cast productions of *Macbeth* and *Native Son* directed by Orson Welles. Early on, it is clear to the boy that he does not see himself when he looks at the white screen, but he claims for himself images that the cinema mirrors back.

'Chain of many mirrors,' wrote film theorist Christian Metz, 'the cinema is at once a weak and a robust mechanism: like the human body, like a precision tool, like a social institution. Which is to say that it is really all of these at the same time.'[1] Perhaps more than any other essay, Metz's 'The Imaginary Signifier', the definitive text on mirrors and mirroring as metaphor for cinema spectatorship, bears the responsibility for introducing Lacan's reworking of Freud into contemporary film theory. Epitomising the theoretical obtuseness as well as the baroque stylistics of French film theory of the 1970s, 'The Imaginary Signifier' seems a text at odds with the question of African-American spectatorship. The fact that Metz never considered the black spectator should be taken seriously, since it alerts us to look for ways in which his theory might serve the interests of entrenched power as opposed to serving a broader knowledge of spectatorship in all its variety. To look elsewhere for a pre-existing theory of identification, incorporation and representation that anticipates the theory of black spectatorship we now need – a theory that fits the text perfectly, hand in glove – is, however, to look for the impossible. Rather, we need to concentrate on how to make existing theories say what we need to have them say, to grapple with high theory until it finally, reluctantly, yields its insights.[2] The question of blacks in cinema, like the nearly parallel question of women in film, is often a problem in what I will call the 'politics of mirroring', which asks why the bodies of blacks and women are missing from the screen, or why, if they are not missing, they are unrecognisable to the people they are supposed to represent. To this crucial question, which has occupied so many African-American and feminist critics, Metz has one answer: although one's own body is always reflected in the mirror, the spectator's own body is never reflected on the screen.

Of all the metaphors employed in attempts to describe the new phenomenon of moving pictures, the 'window' and the 'mirror' have perhaps been the most overused, to a point of exhaustion where they appear to have little left to tell us. One of Metz's projects was simultaneously to exhaust further and to revive the problem of the mirror, telling us that the screen *is* and *is not* like the empirical mirror, which he seems at times to confuse with Lacan's mirror-stage mirror (as though that symbolic process somehow involved an actual mirror).[3] The film screen is like a mirror, Metz says, but 'it differs from the primordial mirror in one essential point: although, as in the latter, everything may come to be projected, there is one thing, and one thing only that is never reflected in it'.[4] Is it because we are so accustomed to seeing ourselves in the empirical mirror that we have this expectation of the mirror-like screen? In his discussion of the semiotics of mirrors, Umberto Eco stresses the self-centredness of the empirical-mirror experience and reminds us that we are adept at using mirrors in relation to our own bodies, but unable to use them in relation to the bodies of others.[5] Eco's empirical observation only confirms the idea that the mirror contributes to the expectation that what we should be seeing on screen is our own image. Lacan's psychoanalytical account further confirms the developmental importance of symbolic mirroring, which demonstrates to the child that the image he sees is his own.[6]

What is generally taken from 'The Imaginary Signifier', however, is not the idea that the body of the viewer is missing from the mirror-like screen. It is, rather, the idea that because the viewer has had the cultural prerequisite (the lesson of the mirror), the sight of his or her own body on screen is no longer necessary, or else the idea that, because the spectator has already had experiences with mirrors (or known the mirror phase), he or she no longer needs to use his or her own body as a reference point in order to make sense of the screen image. To summarise Metz, 'what makes possible the spectator's absence from the screen – or rather the intelligible unfolding of the film despite that absence – is the fact that the spectator has already known the experience of the mirror (the true mirror), and is thus able to constitute a world of objects without first having to recognize himself within it'.[7] His observation reminds us that cultural initiation and linguistic knowledge were foremost over the years during which film theory would establish its respectability – a respectability that absolutely depended upon comparisons with language.

I want to take the rich suggestions of 'The Imaginary Signifier' in a different direction, however, and ask why there are so many complaints from women and other minorities if the cinema spectator, advanced far beyond the simple mirror, no longer needs to see himself or herself 'mirrored back' in the theatre? Why the 'politics of mirroring' when no spectator can ever expect to see his or her own body anyway? Although cinema spectators cannot expect the phenomenal mirror-image experience they have had with the looking glass (even though they might wish it), their experience of looking at others on the screen is relatively similar to looking at others in the mirror. In neither situation does the viewer have control over the bodies of others. The child, however, takes an even more important lesson from the empirical as well as from the symbolic mirror: the others imaged appear like and not like himself. In fact, it is not so much that the child cannot move on to comprehend more complex cultural phenomena without first recognising himself, but that he cannot enter society at all without the mirroring lessons that illustrate the semiotics of 'like' and 'other'.

In Metz's variation on Lacan, the mother from whom the child is early distinguished becomes the first 'other' and consequently all others, in what is a near parody of the centrality of the mother in psychoanalysis. Here, 'the child sees itself as an other, and beside an other. This other other is its guarantee that the first is really it'. The other other is of course the mother. 'Thus the child's ego is formed by identification with its like', Metz observes. But identification is with its 'like' in two senses – both metonymically and metaphorically. First, the child identifies with the 'other human being who is in the glass', and second it identifies with itself, 'the own reflection which is and is not the body, which is like it'.[8] So the child requires not one but two others (itself and its mother), both of whom are 'likes'.

The psychoanalytical understanding of identification, summarised by Anne Friedberg as 'denying the difference between the self and the other', would seem to set up a maze of mirrors within which the child finds as many selves as others, even turning itself into an other.[9] Shifting the emphasis from the mother to the ingenuity of the child in the formative stages may productively reduce the emphasis of so many accounts in which the mother of the mirror stage emerges as a doting mum with a much-petted only son. Who, other than a white middle-class mother who does not work outside the home, would have the time to accompany her child patiently through the confusing stages of the mirror? Responding to the privilege implied in the theory that sees the mirror stage as a prerequisite to language, Kobena Mercer asks: 'What if some subjects do not have access to the initial moment of recognition?'[10] Certainly, non-traditional mothering would upset the intricate process which, as so often formulated, requires *the* mother, but it is not only that too many subjects are left in the cold, outside psychoanalysis as we know it.[11] It is also that the focus on one symbolic moment, no matter how definitive, means that we miss other important formative moments. In the developmental years, there may be hundreds of mirroring experiences and thousands of fascinating experiences of similitude and repetition, striking experiences that could dramatise for the child the patternings of self and other. To look closely at the childhood spent in the motion picture theatre, then, is to de-emphasise the importance of the psychoanalytic mirror.

Viewing figures on a screen in a darkened theatre is one of the most fascinating experiences of similitude and repetition. For the black child growing up in a mixed-race society, however, the patterning of like and unlike bodies on the screen would teach special lessons. In the US, particularly during the first half of this century, the young African-American child's initiation into segregation would have involved searching for and not finding his or her likeness on the screen, looking for the 'one thing, and only one thing that is never reflected in it'. This child must know early on that the screen is in no way like a mirror and would learn quite quickly to relate his body to it accordingly. The screen that is not a true mirror teaches the calculus of black and white in the mixed-race society, a lesson in like and unlike into which his or her own body must fit. The child must supply the black half of the mixed-race society equation, the half missing from the screen. Furthermore, the child must construct an identity based on what it is that she or he sees and does not see.

Like and Not-Like Me

Is there a contemporary question more fraught than the question of raced identity? It is, of course, deceptively simple: 'You *are* who you *are*. You are who your people are'. But what if the racial group to which you think you belong, which carries the same name as the identity you think is yours, is just an abstraction – or worse, nothing more than a functional fiction? I hesitate to continue to use the term 'race' without qualification for fear of committing the error of assuming it without proving it, and of contributing to the move in recent history to see race identity as 'belonging' to all of us but to some more than others. One is backed into a corner – unable to address the issues surrounding the concept of 'race' without recourse to the terminology of race distinctions. How does one signal the trouble ahead in the category of 'race' without using the category itself, given that no other terms signify both the *identity* that is widely claimed as well as assigned throughout the world and the disputed *category,* whether cultural or natural? Simply stated, the problem as it relates to US culture is one of limitation: you are allowed only one race identity per body.[12] If you are *one* you cannot be another. Historically, you have only been able to tick one box. This problem of limitation has a corollary in the idea that identity 'comes from within' rather than from without, making it difficult to imagine how one identity could be produced in relation to others. Stuart Hall has observed that it is 'an immensely important gain when one recognises that all identity is constructed across difference'.[13] The young James Baldwin shared Hall's recognition with a particular facility, as he accumulated his identity 'across' race difference.

In part, Baldwin constructed his identity 'across' the bodies of glamorous white movie stars. In 'Congo Square', he demonstrated how he borrowed from Joan Crawford and Bette Davis, opening the essay with a description of his epiphany that the screen *moves*:

> Joan Crawford's straight, narrow, and lonely back. We are following her through the corridors of a moving train. She is looking for someone, or she is trying to escape from someone. She is eventually intercepted by, I think, Clark Gable. I am fascinated by the movement on, and of, the screen, that movement which is something like the heaving and swelling of the sea (though I have not been to the sea): and which is also something like the light which moves on, and especially beneath, the water. I am with my mother, or my aunt. The movie is *Dance, Fools, Dance*.[14]

While I will be taking Baldwin at his word in other ways, I must correct his memory here. The film he recalls is not *Dance, Fools, Dance* (1931). It is more likely that he saw *Laughing Sinners,* starring Joan Crawford and Clarke Gable.[15] Although the first scene in this film does take place on a moving train, Crawford is neither escaping nor is she alone on the train. She is not 'intercepted' by Clark Gable until much later in the film, and what he 'intercepts' is her attempt to throw herself off a bridge. Neither does Baldwin recall the redemption subplot in this film, in which ex-sinner Gable recruits Crawford into the Salvation Army. Nor was he drawn to the 'torchiness' of the film, adapted from the play *Torch Song* and featuring Crawford singing 'What Can I Do? – I Love That Man'. The young Baldwin went to see the 1931 MGM drama, but he did not see the film that everyone else saw. Instead, the black boy (quite immune to the powerful motion picture illusion) observed what no audience member ever saw – he saw that not only do shapes on the screen move, but that the screen itself moves. To the boy, the screen undulated like the sea and the illumination of the flickering projector appeared to him as light under the moving water. Not surprisingly, then, Baldwin's anti-illusionist eye also sees race categories where others would see actresses. It does not matter what the film is 'about', after all (and therefore the title is largely irrelevant). He continues with his own explanation:

> I don't remember the film. The child is far too self-centered to relate to any dilemma which does not, somehow, relate to him – to his own evolving dilemma. The child escapes into what he would like his situation to be, and I certainly did not wish to be a fleeing fugitive on a moving train; and also, with quite another part of my mind, I was aware that Joan Crawford was a white lady.
>
> (p. 4)

The young James Baldwin, who saw the swelling sea where others saw figures on a train, saw screen movement and everything else from the point of view of his 'evolving dilemma': that of who is and who is not 'black like me'. He saw Joan Crawford and thought 'white'.

No sooner had he situated Joan Crawford in the category of 'white' than he discovered the interchangeability of race categories. In the next sentence, he transformed Joan Crawford into a black woman:

> Yet, I remember being sent to the store some time later, and a colored woman, who, to me, looked exactly like Joan Crawford, was buying something. She was so incredibly beautiful – she seemed to be wearing the sunlight, rearranging it around her from time to time, with a movement of her head, and with her smile.
>
> (p. 4)

Young Baldwin started out of the store behind her. 'His Miss Crawford', as he calls her, laughed at him together with the others in the store who knew them both. Baldwin makes the point that he was in the process of learning that he was black and, considering that he was just learning, one might read this confusion between the beautiful black woman and the white Joan Crawford as the boy's 'mistake'. Actually, he got it right; society had (and has) it wrong. Baldwin both perfected the screen image and learned something about the arbitrariness of race. If he could make the black lady white, he could make Joan Crawford black. To make Joan Crawford black was also to make the screen into his mirror – a wonderful black mirror.

'It was always said among Black women that Joan Crawford was part Black,' says Michelle Wallace in her retrospective consideration of white stars of the 1940s. In her understanding of cinema spectatorship as not only bisexual but multiracial, she sees these black viewers as 'possessing' the films they loved, using them to enlarge their identities instead of rejecting white female stars outright. What Wallace thinks to herself as she views a female star such as Rita Hayworth or Lana Turner affords us an insight into the process of racial transformation: 'she is so beautiful, she looks black'.[16] This racial exchange (black for white) is a magical transvaluation with the power to colour the world. If whatever is wonderful and beautiful is and must always be black, the wonderful and beautiful white star has to be black.

Baldwin's racial transposition (black to white and white to black) is even more pronounced and successful in the lesson he had absorbed from Bette Davis, which is a transformation with even broader implications, since through it he produced race change not only in what he calls 'the cinema of my mind' (p. 10). When he looked at Bette Davis, he saw himself. To the young Baldwin, it was clear that Bette Davis looked just like he did, but it was especially her 'frog-eyes' – his eyes – that confirmed the likeness. He was aware from very early on in life that his father hated his 'frog-eyes', and that this hatred had to do with the fact that they were his mother's eyes and that he was his mother's son by a different man. 'What was he doing with these enormous eyes?' he asked himself (p. 9):

> So, here, now, was Bette Davis, on that Saturday afternoon, in close-up, over a
> champagne glass, pop-eyes popping. I was astounded. I had caught my father, not in a
> lie, but in an infirmity. For, here, before me, after all, was a movie star: white: and if she
> was white and a movie star she was rich: and she was ugly.

(p. 8)

Bette Davis/James Baldwin

All the duplicity of adult society was exposed. No, it was not as they said – that it was not possible to be rich and a movie star if you were ugly. It *was* possible to be white, rich and ugly, or, rather, white, rich and black. Watching Bette Davis and Spencer Tracy in *20,000 Years in Sing Sing* (1932), the black boy metamorphosed Davis on the screen, but this time in a more thorough and amazing way. To ward off the malevolent whiteness, he made her over as a new, more benign and familiar species, and his explanation of his motivation suggests his need for protection: 'out of bewilderment, out of loyalty to my mother, probably, and also because I sensed something menacing and unhealthy (for me, certainly) in the face on the screen' (p. 8). This loyalty to his mother, who looked just as he did, was also a kind of loyalty to his race, a loyalty that kept him from entertaining white versions of himself. Baldwin is no easy case of cross-race identification based on the assumption of a one-way process in which all blacks envy whites. Recently, Eric Lott has opened up this question for further consideration from the other side: what if whites envy blacks? In his study of blackface minstrelsy, Lott argues that whites put on 'blackface versions of themselves' at the same time that they ridiculed blacks.[17] In reference to the closely related phenomenon of Hollywood's 'nigger minstrels', Kobena Mercer asks: 'What is going on when whites assimilate and introject the degraded and devalorized signifiers of racial otherness into the cultural construction of their own identity? If imitation implies identification, in the psychoanalytic sense of the word, then what is it about whiteness that makes the white subject want to be black?'[18]

Let us also ask the companion question: if whites have wanted to be black, have blacks historically wanted to be white? The best answer to this question is probably both yes and no, depending upon the historical moment, and never, of course, in exactly the same way. Certainly, Baldwin gives the lie to the assumption that all blacks wanted to be whites, and what he describes himself doing with Davis's image suggests that his relationship to whiteness was unorthodox, if not ambivalent. What he did was quite extraordinary: making out of it something like and not like himself, something to aid identification as well as to prevent it absolutely by warding it off. 'I gave Davis's skin the dead-white greenish cast of something crawling from under a rock', he says. Think what is accomplished by producing Bette Davis as green! She inhabits the world of mixed-race society, but she is alien to it. She is a frog. She is a lizard. Even though she was 'something green crawling', Baldwin was 'held, just the same, by the tense intelligence of the forehead, the disaster of the lips: and when she moved, she moved just like a nigger' (p. 8). But she was not a black version of himself, she was a green version, neither black nor white, but in one of those 'in between' colour categories that is anomalous to white but not black society. One thinks of Kermit the Frog's lament: 'It's not easy being green.' In the child's skin fantasy, colour distinctions are imaginary, and if you 'wear' your gender, you can also imagine your own skin colour beneath, putting the one on over the other.[19]

Jimmy Baldwin had no designs on whiteness. The boy apparently constructed Bette Davis as 'ugly like me' but did not make himself into a white movie star. Instead, he met Davis in the category of 'strange', which Baldwin says he knew he belonged to because people 'treated me so strangely' (p. 9). Correspondingly, he no longer saw whiteness as transparent obviousness, but also as somewhat 'strange', a revelation that allowed him increasing latitude in his skin fantasies. By now, it should be obvious that Baldwin is not only describing the constitution of a 'raced' subject through star images, but that he is also describing the flamboyant constitution of a queer, and in his early appreciation of Joan Crawford and Bette Davis – as early as the age of 7 – there is an undeniably precocious camp sensibility at work. Undoubtedly, in his production of Davis as 'strange', we also see a fledgling critique of heterosexuality that un-sees the normal at the same time that it claims Davis for 'strangeness'.

Disidentification

Queer theory has made an end run around the 'politics of mirroring', leaving complaints about negative imaging or stereotypage in the dust. As queer theory has incontrovertibly demonstrated, selves are always concocted, never simply given and received.

Following queer theory, identification is not about 'denying the difference between the self and the other', the mirror moment that produces normalcy. It may be more about using differences, about accumulating possible selves – a process, in fact, that is more accretive than anything else and thus offers a direct challenge to the rule of one identity per body.

This historical connection between identification and normalcy – 'modelling oneself after another' – should alert us to the conservatism in identification. Queer theory has suggested that *within* identification something complicated occurs which undermines and prohibits and thus protects the identifier. Recently, José Muñoz has reworded the concept of disidentification, giving it a political edge and understanding it as a survival strategy. In effect, he makes a case for a notion of identification that is to some extent aware of the pitfalls of identity formation, and this concept has a particular relevance for understanding the black subject who comes of age in a white society. Muñoz wants to understand Kobena Mercer's famous admission of 'ambivalence' toward Robert Mapplethorpe's photographs of black nudes as a 'disidentificatory pleasure', which, even as it is relished, is all the while cognisant of the political danger for a black gay critic in loving the very images that fetishise the black male body.[20] We can take the particular mix of danger and pleasure – a pleasure that tastes like 'ambivalence' – from this concept of disidentification. We must, however, still know how the concept is significantly different from other critical moves that have helped us to deal with troublesome texts, such as reading 'against the grain', or 'distanciation', the critical stance that in Brechtian approaches to film was meant to break the spell of identification. Still, 'disidentification' could offer more, and clearly has the edge of provocation. The two crucial components of 'disidentification' seem to me to be the hissing 'dis' prefix, the echo of the street slang that puts people in their place, as though identification itself is 'dissed', and the 'crossing' that is characteristic of queer reading. Indeed, work on literary 'cross-identification' from within queer theory is foundational here.[21] In this, it is crucial to retain the closeness between 'queerness' and 'crossing', remembering, as Eve Sedgwick has pointed out, that the word 'queer' has its etymological roots in the linguistic terms for 'across', and that to be queer is to be always in motion.[22]

On the danger side, Muñoz leads us back through the Althusserian Michel Pécheux, whose concept of disidentification is neither an embrace nor a rejection of the dominant ideology but rather an accommodation within it, a position similar to a degree to the way that cultural studies understands the inhabited space of popular culture.[23] As theorised by Stuart Hall, the damage of the dominant would seem to be always ameliorated by the counter swing of popular culture, a paradigm understood as the 'double movement' of the popular which is able both to contain conservatively and to resist radically that which would try to contain it.[24] Cultural studies may, however, have underestimated the hegemonic danger produced by the dominant: damage to women, blacks, queers and other outsiders whose interests are never served by the culture with which they have become enamoured. The classic example of such hegemonic damage remains Frantz Fanon's account of the young Antillian who in colonial Fort-de-France identifies with Tarzan 'against the Negroes', but who in Paris finds that the white audience 'identifies him with the savages on the screen'.[25] To be caught always on the wrong side of identification is one of the situations that defines the plight of the colonial subject.

In response to such hegemonic dangers, the popular minority focus has been predominantly on underrepresentation and exclusion, a paradigm that is always silently informed by an assumption that if only blacks, Asians and women could gain access to the means of media production, then and only then could the problems of image, identity and identification be addressed, if not resolved. Queer theory has never really been involved in these debates between 'our images of ourselves' and 'your images of us'. Instead, it provides not only a keen sense of the deep potential damage, but, even more importantly, it offers an analysis of the total failure of identification. One only needs to think of James Baldwin's identificatory frustrations to gain a sense of the challenge to the child – black and queer – who searched for selves in all the wrong places. Judith Butler finds the starting point for politicisation in this 'failure of identification': 'what are the possibilities of politicizing *dis*identification, this experience of *misrecognition*, this uneasy sense of standing under a sign to which one does and does not belong?'.[26] Perhaps it is this dialectic of unbelonging that defines the delicate balance of disidentification, the characteristic situation in which the queer self 'is and is not'.

Perhaps the pleasures of identification are at their most intense with figures such as the opera diva and the glamorous star, where they are also comprehensible only through some grasp of the relationship that is camp.[27] The camp relationship that constitutes the discrepant connection between the self and the world, and the link between the 'is and is not' is central to my theoretical proposition. If there is pleasure in camp, it comes from revelling in discrepancies and appreciating a long chain of jokes enjoyed at the expense of straight culture. Something in the incongruous mismatch can reveal the makeshift structure of the most serious object of culture. To the 'is and is not' of cross-identification we therefore need to add the 'on–off', the modality that is often said to have its origins in the experience of 'passing for Straight' in a heterosexual world.[28] Richard Dyer's analysis of stars as tragic models of the too-close relationship between self and role illustrates this modality of theatricality. With the most highly theatrical sufferers, such as Judy Garland, something always slips to reveal a 'putting on' of roles, an acting art that is certainly one of the major tributaries feeding into theories of 'gender as dressing'.[29] In queer theory, the basic camp paradigm of 'acting' is also a critique that is literally 'performed', and Jimmy Baldwin finds his version of this paradigm in these cult actresses. The ironic relation between the queer and the world exhibits the characteristic equation between drag and distance in the astute sensibility of the fledgling literary critic, that produces Bette Davis as green.

White Not

With all his critical acumen, and the extra distance he has on the question by virtue of being queer, Baldwin is still tormented by the question of his blackness, now inseparable from his queerness.[30] But how does his queerness actually impinge on his blackness? And what, if anything, does queerness tell him about blackness? James Baldwin's account of his fascination with white film stars has not been a favoured text in either African-American studies or gay and lesbian studies in their recent growth periods. Is this because his recruitment of the white female stars into the process of discovering what it means to be black is seen as politically retrograde? I would argue that we need to recognise the ingenious eclecticism of Baldwin's forming a black queer identity by going deeply into whiteness and taking out the best parts. Black disidentification with white stars involves an attraction to the glamour in danger as well as to the danger in glamour, and it knows just how close to get to the flame. James Baldwin is and is not Bette Davis.

Only one critic has seriously pursued the question of the black American's relation to white stars. In a provocative essay, Arthur Knight denies neither the fascination nor the repulsion. Beginning with Aaron Siskind's 1940 photograph of a black janitor in a Harlem building sleeping with his back to a wall of movie star pin-ups, sometimes titled 'Sleeping with White Pin-Ups', Knight suggests that notions of oppression and dominance do not go very far toward explaining this image. He finds the complexity of the black response to the movies in Gwendolyn Brooks's poem, 'The Sundays of Satin-Legs Smith', in her reference to the audience members 'booing' at the kiss as well as the 'ivory' heroine. But 'booing' is coupled with the 'sinning' that for the black community has been synonymous with 'looking'. The African-American literary figures and characters who find and lose themselves at the movies, such as Toni Morrison's Pauline, Malcolm X's 'Detroit Red', Richard Wright's Bigger Thomas and Ralph Ellison's Invisible Man, are all active critics, but they are not equally critical, and sometimes they are more ambivalent than critical.[31] A black attitude or reading is by no means uniform or predictable, even though, as Jacqueline Bobo discovered in her important contemporary study of black women viewers, the black eye may be consistently jaundiced in the most productive of ways.[32] Black viewing is never exactly about appropriating whiteness, since this critical engagement seems not to be about borrowing at all.

In recent analyses, such as those of Mercer and Lott, an interest in black appropriations of whiteness has given way to a concern with the way in which white culture finds itself through blackness. The theme of whiteness as 'parasitic' on blackness has also marked the recent work of Cornell West and Toni Morrison, challenging us to look at raced relations in reverse and to invert the dominant version of the way things are.[33] By comparison, the way in which blacks 'use' white culture seems too transparent and too prevalent to warrant serious study, but it is interesting that in all the new work on black gay men, as well as the already voluminous literature on gay men and stars, there is almost no examination of white women as objects of fascination or influence in relation to black queerness.[34] The young Baldwin himself, indeed, eventually came to the conclusion that there was nothing that white folks could possibly tell him about blackness. If white culture is 'used' at all in the process of black self-discovery, it is used as a foil.

Other white people, however, figure significantly in Baldwin's adventures with the screen-mirror. Most notably, all his early movie-going experiences (with the exception of *Laughing Sinners,* which he recalls as *Dance, Fools, Dance*) appear to have been in the company of a white woman with a man's name. Baldwin understood Bill (Orilla) Miller, his young schoolteacher, in terms of Joan Crawford, the prototype for both the black as well as the white women whom he admired. Bill Miller was white but 'not white for me in the way, for example, that Joan Crawford was white'. Neither was she white 'in the way that the landlords and the storekeepers and the cops and most of my teachers were white … She, too … was treated like a nigger, especially by the cops, and she had no love for landlords' (pp. 6–7). He learned from Bill Miller that 'white people did not act as they did because they were white' (p. 7). His observation that there was no absolutely perfect correlation between whiteness and the abuse of power did not, however, lead Baldwin automatically to the idea of social class. He found the question difficult because, although it appeared that all oppressors were white, not all whites were oppressors.

Bill Miller, the young Communist, was instrumental in teaching the boy about victimisation and its operations irrespective of colour, illustrating through her own life that one could still experience oppression even if one was characterised by a colour normally considered as emblematic of control.[35] 'Thus', Baldwin recalls, 'she tried to suggest to me the extent to which the world's social and economic arrangements are responsible for [and to] the world's victims' (p. 12). Eventually, another white woman, Harriet Beecher Stowe, would be instrumental in this lesson in the concept of victimisation. Baldwin links his attending *A Tale of Two Cities* (MGM, 1936) at the Lincoln Theater with Bill Miller to reading *Uncle Tom's Cabin,* which he would later rail at for its dishonesty.[36] From Bill he learned something about revolution: 'Revolution was the only hope of the American working class – the proletariat: and world-wide revolution was the only hope of the world' (p. 17). It is not, however, clear to Baldwin that he understood this as a boy. If he did grasp what was meant, he understood it 'negatively': as blacks were not in the picture, 'I could not see where I fit in this formulation, and I did not see where blacks fit' (p. 17).

Blacks do not easily fit into the Marxist formulation and, unlike his more radical contemporary Richard Wright, Baldwin the historical figure was not exactly interested in actively searching for that fit over the course of his lifetime. The question of where and how class figures, however, is salient in the context of this essay on mass culture and the construction of identity. Let us consider the countless ways in which race has been theorised in relation to class during the past century, with the explanatory burden placed first on one, then the other. At times, the two categories vie for ascendancy. Stuart Hall has described the explanatory strain produced by the pressure on race and class, each expected to account for so much, as a situation in which 'both feel required to produce a single, determining [explanatory] principle'.[37] Finding ways of formulating the critical relation between the two has been difficult enough for political theorists. In some models, race and class are lived hierarchically, with one on top and the other on the bottom. In others, they are lived sequentially, with one pre-dating the other, and in still others they are lived asymmetrically, with class victimisation cutting one way and race oppression another.[38] The fact that class and race are never congruent means that, in historical circumstances, class affinities and race solidarities divide and tear, wreaking havoc within communities and groups. Within the individual, these are the historical conflicts that translate into identities that war within one small human body.

Not seeing how class could fully explain himself to himself, Baldwin continued with his search, concluding that blackness was determining and must do the explaining. He concluded that Bill Miller 'could not instruct me as to blackness, except obliquely, feeling that she had neither the right nor the authority, and also knowing that I was certain to find out' (p. 11). Having discovered that Bette Davis was ugly and white, not black, Baldwin had reason to believe that the skin system was not as straightforward as adults claimed. Since the peculiarity of his blackness was not, however, accounted for by blackness alone, he was left with the question of who is and who is not 'black like me', with no hope of finding the 'black' and the 'like me' always in the same place.

Melodrama and the Unfathomable Question

From Bill Miller and Harriet Beecher Stowe, the young Baldwin wanted an answer to his 'unfathomable question': 'what, under heaven, or beneath the sea, or in the catacombs of hell, could cause any people to act as white people acted?' (pp. 6–7). He turned to melodrama, the form that specialises in the unfathomable, the incalculable and the inexplicable. Not a form that answers questions, melodrama assuages fears and manages fantasies, often by organising inexplicable events in ways that appeal to the dispossessed, among them blacks and women.[39] In its biblical proportions, its rhythms of confrontation and release, its intense clash of villainy with righteousness and its miraculous righting of wrongs, melodrama enhances the point of view of the powerless. Feeling the powerlessness of his existence, Baldwin was drawn to the great tumultuous narratives of English and American literature – *A Tale of Two Cities* and *Uncle Tom's Cabin* – narratives that spoke to him despite his not knowing what either was about, 'which was why he read them both so obsessively'. He continued compulsively reading *Uncle Tom's Cabin*, 'trying to find out something, sensing something in the book of some immense import for me' until his terrified mother hid the book above the bathtub on a high shelf (pp. 16–17). But what the white author had to tell him was limited. In another essay, he later rails against Stowe and her book because she left 'unanswered and unnoticed the only important question: what was it, after all, that moved her people to such deeds'.[40] Obsessively reading *Uncle Tom's Cabin*, he says, 'was this particular child's way of circling around the question of what it meant to be a nigger' (p. 12). Still circling, still obsessively reading, not only did he not see where blacks fit (and not daring to ask Bill Miller, whom his father 'distrusted and disliked'), he continued 'partly because I hadn't really accepted, or understood that I was black' (p. 17).

We are given the sense that Baldwin's resolution in favour of blackness came finally with the rewarding mirroring experience of live black theatre. Bill Miller took him to the Lafayette Theater to see the Orson Welles production of *Macbeth*, set in Haiti with an all-black cast. This, he says, was the 'first time he ever really saw black actors at work: and it is important to emphasize that the people I was watching were black, like me' (p. 33). Just as formative was another, later, experience in which he saw the African-American actor Canada Lee as Bigger Thomas in the Orson Welles production of *Native Son* (p. 40). For Baldwin, the crucial difference between his earlier motion picture-going and the experience of live black theatre was one of 'shadows' as opposed to 'living black actors on a living stage: we are all each other's flesh and blood' (p. 36). The difference was a matter of distance: the distance between audience and screen is 'paradoxically absolute'; a paradox created by the illusion of closeness in the face of the actuality of separation. The motion picture is only 'masquerading as intimacy' (p. 34).[41]

Baldwin's quarrel with the cinema is not just that it fails to return his own image to him. The motion picture creates the illusion of intimacy but holds the viewer at a distance. In his hierarchy, flesh and blood theatre is superior to shadowy film, the 'like me' of theatre over the 'not-like me' of film. For the theatre offers him a continuity of liveness and blackness, and provides a lifeline between his black body and that of the actors on stage, while the closest thing to Baldwin's own face on the screen is the frog-eyed face of Bette Davis. And part of what angers him is that, in a mixed-race society, to understand that one is black is to understand what one is not. Sometimes one is black and at other times one is not-white. The politics of mirroring only compounds the problem, since the African-American child is doubly separated from the already distant screen. Not only is there no 'me' on the screen, as with all spectators, but there is no 'like me' there either.

Conclusion

Film theory has historically had an ambivalent relationship to the concept of identification, divided between the Brechtian condemnation of the identification that sucks us in and the Metzian fascination with psychological mechanisms. I have been sceptical, in this chapter, of the concept of identification that, since the 1970s, has provided the foundation for the prevailing theory of spectatorship in the cinema. Recently, some film theorists have begun to rethink earlier positions. Criticising the hostility toward identification on the part of an earlier film theory, Kaja Silverman suggests that 'political cinema for today must be one which, rather than lamenting the identification at the center of the cinematic experience seizes upon it as a vehicle for taking the spectator somewhere he or she has never been before, and which discourages the return journey'.[42] Identification may be seeing ourselves in places we would least expect to find recognition, on the model of James Baldwin, who saw his own face in the face of Bette Davis. And if we are all finding ourselves in strange places, what about the phenomenon of white people who, enthusiastically viewing new black cinema as well as rediscovering 'race movies' from the silent era, have the opportunity to see themselves *as blacks*? [43] Recommending a far more fluid concept of identification than we have previously seen, Stuart Hall offers this caution: 'Remember: identifications, not identities. Once you've got identification, you can decide which identities are working *this* week.'[44] Spectatorship inevitably engages with the most pressing of contemporary questions of identity. Sometimes, the subject seizes the self (or selves) from the image. Since the screen is never a true mirror, selves will always be formulated through, across and between others. Identification, if nothing else, is an invitation to be other than ourselves.

Notes

An expanded version of this essay will be published in Jane M. Gaines, *Fire and Desire: Mixed Race Movies in the Silent Era* (Chicago: University of Chigago Press, 2001).

1 Christian Metz, 'The Imaginary Signifier', *Screen* vol. 16, no. 2 (summer 1975), p. 54.
2 For a good discussion of the politics of using high theory in African-American literary criticism, see Diana Fuss, *Essentially Speaking* (New York and London: Routledge, 1989), pp. 82–3.
3 Anne Friedberg, 'A Denial of Difference: Theories of Cinematic Identification' in E. Ann Kaplan (ed.), *Psychoanalysis and Cinema* (New York and London: Routledge, 1990), also notes (p. 40) that Metz appears to assume that Lacan's mirror has all the functions of an empirical mirror.
4 Metz, 'Imaginary Signifier', p. 48.
5 Umberto Eco, *Semiotics and the Philosophy of Language* (Bloomington, IN: Indiana University Press, 1986), p. 207.
6 Joan Copjec has pointed out that film theory has often misunderstood Lacan, particularly when conceiving of the screen as a mirror. I am less concerned here about

misconstruction of Lacan and more interested in the fascination film theory has had with the metaphor. See Copjec, *Lacan Against the Historicists* (Cambridge, MA: MIT Press, 1995), pp. 15–16, 21–2.

7 Metz, 'Imaginary Signifier', p. 49.

8 Ibid., pp. 48–9.

9 Friedberg, 'Denial of Difference', p. 40.

10 Isaac Julien and Kobena Mercer, 'Introduction: De Margin and De Centre', *Screen*, vol. 29, no. 4 (winter 1988), p. 9.

11 Mary Ann Doane, *Femmes Fatales* (New York and London: Routledge, 1991), has argued (p. 211) that psychoanalysis is 'radically destabilized by those excluded'. Lillian Smith, *Killers of the Dream* (New York: W.W. Norton, 1949), remarks (p. 131) on the 'dual relationship which so many white southerners have had with two mothers, one white and one colored and each of a different culture that, centered in different human values, makes the Oedipus complex seem by comparison almost a simple adjustment'. For a discussion of the radical difference of child-rearing under the 'peculiar institution' of slavery see Hortense Spillers, 'Mama's Baby, Papa's Maybe: An American Grammar Book', *Diacritics*, vol. 17, no. 2 (summer 1987), pp. 65–81.

12 I have been influenced here by Kwame Anthony Appiah and Henry Louis Gates, Jr., 'Introduction: Multiplying Identities', *Critical Inquiry*, vol. 18 (1992), pp. 625–9.

13 Stuart Hall, 'Minimal Selves', in *Identity: The Real Me*, ICA Document 6 (London: The Institute of Contemporary Arts, 1987).

14 James Baldwin, *The Devil Finds Work* (New York: Dell, 1976), pp. 3–4. [Hereafter, page numbers from this work appear in the text.]

15 I would like to express my thanks here to Tom Doherty, who discovered Baldwin's confusion.

16 Michelle Wallace, 'Race, Gender, and Psychoanalysis in Forties Film: *Lost Boundaries, Home of the Brave,* and *The Quiet One*', in Manthia Diawara (ed.), *Black American Cinema* (New York: Routledge, 1993), p. 264.

17. Eric Lott, *Love and Theft: Blackface Minstrelsy and the American Working Class* (New York and Oxford: Oxford University Press, 1993), p. 197.

18 Kobena Mercer, 'Skin Head Sex Thing: Racial Difference and the Homoerotic Imaginary' in Bad Object Choices (ed.), *How Do I Look?: Queer Film and Video* (Seattle: Bay Press, 1991), p. 207.

19 The reference is to Judith Butler's provocative suggestion that gender is 'worn', but the origins of the concept are certainly in Esther Newton's groundbreaking anthropological definition of drag as both distance and costume. Newton, *Mother Camp: Female Impersonators in America* (Chicago: University of Chicago Press, 1972), p. 109.

20 José Esteban Muñoz, 'Photographs of Mourning: Melancholia and Ambivalence in Van Der Zee, Mapplethorpe, and Looking for Langston', in Harry Stecopoulos and Michael Uebel (eds), *Race and the Subject of Masculinities* (Durham, NC: Duke University Press, 1997), p. 351. See Kobena Mercer, *Welcome to the Jungle* (London and New York: Routledge, 1994), Chap. 6.

21 See, for instance, Eve Kosofsky Sedgwick, 'Across Gender, Across Sexuality: Willa Cather and Others', in Ronald R. Butters, John M. Clum and Michael Moon (eds), *Displacing Homophobia: Gay Male Perspectives in Literature and Culture* (Durham, NC: Duke University Press, 1989).

22 Eve Kosofsky Sedgwick, *Tendencies* (Durham, NC: Duke University Press, 1993), p. xii.

23 José Esteban Muñoz, 'Famous and Dandy Like B. 'n' Andy: Race, Pop and Basquiat', in Jonathan Flatley, Jennifer Doyle, and José Esteban Muñoz (eds), *Pop Out* (Durham, NC: Duke University Press, 1996), pp. 147–8. See Michel Pêcheux, *Language, Semantics, Ideology* (New York: St Martin's Press, 1982).

24 Stuart Hall, 'Notes on Deconstructing "The Popular" ', in Raphael Samuel (ed.), *People's History and Socialist Theory* (Boston: Routledge & Kegan Paul, 1981).

25 Frantz Fanon, *Black Skin, White Masks* (New York: Grove Press, 1967), pp. 152–3.

26 Judith Butler, *Bodies That Matter* (New York and London: Routledge, 1993), p. 219.

27 Probably the best basic definition of camp is the one that Esther Newton draws from the subjects of her early ethnography: 'Camp is not a thing. Most broadly it signifies a relationship between things, people, and activities or qualities, and homosexuality' (*Mother Camp*, p. 105). Newton finds her most vivid examples of camp juxtaposition in apartments decorated by her subjects: 'One queen said that *TV Guide* had described a little Mexican horse statue as campy. He said there was nothing campy about this at all, but if you put a nude cut-out of Bette Davis on it, it would be campy'. Ibid. p. 107.

28 One of the earliest discussions of this phenomenon in relation to stars is Jack Babuscio, 'Camp and Gay Sensibility', in Richard Dyer (ed.), *Gays and Film* (New York: Zoetrope, 1984), pp. 44–7.

29 Richard Dyer, *Heavenly Bodies* (London: BFI/Macmillan, 1987). See Chapter 3, 'Judy Garland and Gay Men'.

30 It was not until after Baldwin's death in 1987 that Marlon Riggs would proclaim that 'Negro faggotry is in fashion'. See 'Black Macho Revisited: Reflections of a SNAP! Queen', p. 253, and also in the same collection, Joseph Beam, 'James Baldwin: Not a Bad Legacy, Brother', and Carlyle R. Black, 'James Baldwin (1924–87)', in Essex Hemphill (ed.), *Brother to Brother: New Writings by Black Gay Men* (Boston: Alyson Publications, 1991).

31 Arthur Knight, 'Star Dance: African American Constructions of Stardom, 1925–60', unpublished paper.

32 Jacqueline Bobo, *Black Women as Cultural Readers* (New York: Columbia University Press, 1995).

33 Cornell West, 'The New Cultural Politics of Difference', in Russell Ferguson, Martha Gever, Trihn T. Minh-ha and Cornell West (eds), *Out There* (New York: The New Museum/MIT Press, 1990), p. 29; Toni Morrison says that, historically, for whites , 'a real or fabricated Africanist presence was crucial to their sense of Americanness'. Morrison, *Playing in the Dark* (Cambridge and London: Harvard University Press, 1992), p. 6.

34 Perhaps it is just assumed that racial crossing over, one way or the other, is such a part of the queer appropriation of female stars that it is always just an enhancement of the fascination. Alexander Doty refers to 'even less-analyzed queer readership positions formed around the nexus of race and sexuality, or class and sexuality, or ethnicity and sexuality, or some combination of gender/race/class/ethnicity and sexuality', and footnotes the work of Richard Fung, Kobena Mercer, Essex Hemphill, Marlon Riggs, Isaac Julien and one black lesbian, Jackie Goldsby. Doty, *Making Things Perfectly Queer* (Minneapolis: University of Minnesota Press, 1993), pp. 7, 108. It is worth noting that his comprehensive list of the spectacular female personalities around whom gay male

cults have grown includes a mix of white and black women, from Maria Callas to
Beverly Sills and from Bette Davis and Joan Crawford through Bette Midler and Barbra
Streisand to Diana Ross. Ibid., p. 6. One would assume that it is not just that gay male
fascination knows no bounds but that the cross-race dimension makes its contribution
to glamour-as-danger.

35 Baldwin refers to his 'young white school teacher who was a Communist' in his
conversations with Margaret Mead. See James Baldwin and Margaret Mead, *A Rap On
Race* (New York: Laurel Books, 1971), p. 22. David Leaming, in his biography of
Baldwin, identifies Orilla Miller as the daughter of a Farmer's Co-operative organiser
who had attended Antioch College until forced to leave school because of the
Depression. She later married Evan Winfield, a seaman she met in New York during a
strike, and the couple continued to draw Baldwin, off and on, into their radical
activities for the short time they were in New York before moving to Los Angeles. *James
Baldwin: A Biography* (New York: Knopf, 1994), pp. 14–15.

36 James Baldwin, 'Everybody's Protest Novel', in James Baldwin, *Notes of a Native Son*
(New York: Grove Press, 1949).

37 Stuart Hall, 'Gramsci's Relevance for the Study of Race and Ethnicity', *Journal of
Communication Inquiry*, vol. 10, no. 2 (1986), p. 24.

38 Marxist theorists have tended to put class first, on top of race. An interesting example is
Eugene Genovese's theorisation that racial subordination 'rendered its fundamental
class relations more complex and ambiguous; but they remained class relations'.
Genovese, *Roll, Jordan, Roll: The World the Slaves Made* (New York: Random House,
1976), p. 3. Ruth Frankenberg uses the concept 'race-as-class', and suggests that race
privilege must always be seen as 'crosscut by other axes of difference and inequality:
class, culture, ethnicity, gender, and sexuality'. Frankenberg, *White Women, Race Matters*
(Minneapolis: University of Minnesota Press, 1993), p. 1.

39 See Jane Gaines, 'Scar of Shame: Skin Color and Caste in Black Silent Melodrama',
Cinema Journal, XXVI, no. 4 (summer 1987), reprinted in Valerie Smith (ed.), *Black
Issues in Film and Visual Media* (New Brunswick, NJ: Rutgers University Press, 1997).

40 Baldwin, *Notes of a Native Son*, p. 14.

41 It is interesting to compare Baldwin with Metz, 'The Imaginery Signifier', on the
difference between film and theatre. Here one begins to see that Metz's theorisation of
the absence of the signifier in cinema has to do with a comparison with the theatre
where the actor is 'physically present, in the same space as the spectator' ('Imaginary
Signifier', p. 62). It would be because of this absence that the film spectacle is 'more
radically ignorant of its spectator', more, that is, in contrast with theatre (ibid., p. 64).
For all that cinema cares, the spectator is not there.

42 Kaja Silverman, *The Threshold of the Visible World* (New York and London: Routledge,
1996), p. 102.

43 See, for an overview, Pearl Bowser, Jane Gaines and Charles Musser (eds), *Oscar
Micheaux and His Circle: African-American Film-Making and Race Cinema in the Silent
Era* (forthcoming).

44 Stuart Hall, 'Subjects in History: Making Diasporic Identities', in Wahneema Lubiano
(ed.), *The House That Race Built* (New York: Vintage Books, 1998), p. 292.

8
The Sonic Playground: Hollywood Cinema and its Listeners

Gianluca Sergi

Cinema is an audio-visual medium; the consumption of films involves both our visual and aural senses. When it comes to investigating the act of experiencing films, however, scholars have concentrated almost exclusively on the visual impact of films. Rather than discussing the reasons behind this bias, this essay seeks to examine the virtually unknown figure of the spectator as listener.[1]

One of the most obvious consequences of the image-biased approach is the focusing on film audiences as 'viewers'. Theoretical accounts of spectatorship, from the mirror phase to the concept of 'the look', have reiterated the approach summarised by John Ellis: 'The spectator looks up towards the image: image dominates the proceedings. It is the reason for cinema, and the reason for the spectator's presence at the event of the film projection'.[2]

From this apotheosis of the image as the very reason why audiences all over the world flock to Hollywood movies, it is just a step to viewing the cinema auditorium as reflecting and almost underwriting this 'truth' by arranging seats so as to allow the audience to worship the screen. The undeniable fact that the cinema screen is the focus of our visual attention does not, however, demonstrate that Hollywood addresses its audiences solely through its visuals, or establish a definite hierarchy. Indeed, in the past thirty years, film sound has played a key role in Hollywood's strategies for engaging audiences and providing them with new pleasures. Hollywood sound has undergone a huge change, in both production and reproduction. This new sound is experienced by audiences in the technologically advanced space of the film theatre itself, which has become a sonic playground in which the spectator actively participates, making sense of what is around him or her, and discovering new pleasures.

Approaching audiences of Hollywood films from an aural perspective might therefore have far-reaching consequences: if we are to accept that audiences not only look at but also listen to films we must be prepared to investigate a different set of skills, pleasures and cultural implications. Film sound requires the spectator to perform sophisticated and demanding tasks, and critical recognition of this fact questions the accepted view of Hollywood audiences as 'comfortably inactive', lulled into a receptive 'dreamlike state' by a succession of continuously edited sequences – a view exemplified by Bruce Austin's description of the spectator as giving himself or herself 'voluntarily and passively to the action on the screen and to its uncritical interpretation supplied by his unconscious mind'.[3]

We Don't Hear Eye to Eye: Experiencing Films Differently

In the quest for unity in film criticism, the fundamental difference between viewing and listening has often given way to a more limiting and misleading view, which acknowledges no major conceptual difference between the two acts of seeing and hearing a film, because the image structures our perception of the soundtrack. In this predominant view, exemplified by Ellis, the image is seen as the primary, and often sole, source of audience information and pleasure.

When we pay attention to the processes through which we learn to listen and to look, however, such a view seems barely tenable. It is immediately obvious that the aural references that constantly 'update' and refine our hearing skills – radio, home hi-fi systems, car stereo, public address systems, telephones – differ substantially from our main sources of visual reference – photographs, paintings, sculpture and graphics. Only a few of these sources require the interaction of visuals and sounds. As a first step, then, it should not be too difficult to recognise that, although as spectators we bring 'one' cultural patrimony to the filmic experience, we perceive sounds and images differently and, as listeners, we employ different strategies and skills and refer to a different set of references. In short, our way of listening to a movie is different from our way of viewing it: this is true in technological terms (they use different systems of production and reproduction), in physical terms (we have a different set of sensual expectations) and in mode of address (the soundtrack and the image track, although obviously working within the same narrative framework, cannot but differ in the way they address audiences).[4]

These sources provide us with an incessant flow of aural and visual 'experiences', both in a narrative and historical sense of things learned and stored for future reference, and in a more interactive and dynamic sense: the way in which we react to those experiences according to our circumstances. These not only guarantee us a 'vocabulary' of images and sounds, but also provide us with the necessary confidence with which to articulate them. They shape our visual and aural expectations and our way to approach films. Although visual and aural sources often work together, they remain profoundly different. When we go to the cinema, our experience of the event is informed and aided not only by past cinema attendance, but also by our culturally specific understanding of sounds and images and the way they interact. Hollywood film-makers understand this particular dynamic and integrate it in their approach to film sound. According to sound designer Cecilia Hall, one of the key emotional aspects of John McTiernan's 1990 film *The Hunt for Red October* was to create a sound environment for the American submarine featured in the film that would feel somehow more familiar and less threatening than its Russian counterpart.[5] To achieve this, she appealed to the audience's aural cultural background:

> We wanted to create a friendly atmosphere. We used familiar-sounding computers. The dot matrix printer you are used to hearing in offices and that people recognize is exactly the kind of equipment that exists on those submarines.[6]

Pleasures on Offer, Tasks to Perform

The late 1960s and early 1970s saw a great advance in all areas of sound technology. Audiences now had access to home hi-fi systems, and they could attend concerts and experience earth-rattling amplification. As improved sound reproduction became affordable for consumers on a mass scale, Charles Schreger observed that 'In 1978, America seems sound-obsessed. You can feel the full impact of a symphony or a rock concert in your living room; you can take it with you in your car or in a pocket-size radio'.[7] Hollywood lagged conspicuously behind this new 'sound wave'. Indeed, the conditions of reproduction in cinemas were at a low point in the early 1970s. The huge costs of upgrading from mono to magnetic stereo (the only 'real' alternative to mono) had frozen any meaningful development of the relationship between Hollywood films and their 'new' listeners. Both in America and abroad, audiences of Hollywood films could enjoy better sound in their cars than at the local cinema.[8] Critically, the new 'sound obsessed' generation who went to concerts and owned hi-fi systems was roughly the same 15 to 30 demographic group which Hollywood was targeting, and had been doing so for some time.

This meant two things. First, in order to achieve the same aural appeal for young audiences that the new consumer technologies seemed to have, Hollywood had to play 'catch-up' with sound quality once again, as it had on several occasions since the inception of sound in the cinema. Second, this 'reaction' would have to address a set of aural expectations that was now higher than ever, born as it was out of the availability of increasingly sophisticated means of sound reproduction. Perhaps not surprisingly, these two key aspects were perfectly clear in the minds and intents of the emerging generation of film-makers, such as George Lucas, Steven Spielberg and Francis Ford Coppola, who were aware of the importance of addressing their listeners' demands and expectations in a 'direct' manner. As Lucas observed in 1993, 'The audience today know what good sound is, and they expect it. They don't expect to walk into a theater and hear static and hiss and no low end. They know good sound, and they respect it'.[9]

Although the process of change that began in the early 1970s was in part driven by the availability of new technology and the internal innovations introduced by the 'movie brat' generation of film-makers, it was mainly a response to the external pressures of market considerations and audience expectations. The introduction of new sound technologies and the rise of cultural phenomena such as the rock concert had a huge impact on increasing film audiences' aural expectations. These developments focused on several aspects: the quality of sound reproduction, the sonic pleasures on offer, and the kind of experience which could be expected by an audience. Schreger's 'sound-obsessed' new generation of spectators craved and obtained a change which affected the whole axis film–theatre–audience.

Audiences, especially young audiences, now expected and demanded powerful sound, capable of reaching the listener from a multiplicity of perspectives and in a more tangible/physical manner. They expected the hardware available in theatres to be able both to match the characteristics that they had rapidly become accustomed to hearing at live concerts, and to compete with the kind of quality they heard not only at these events but also in their homes and increasingly in their car.

Although a long time coming, Hollywood's response to these demands was comprehensive.[10] From the mid-1970s onward, films began to employ multi-channel technology capable of delivering extremely detailed sound from a multiplicity of perspectives. The extension of frequency and dynamic range available in film sound, which used to lag a long way below human capability, was also dramatically increased by the introduction of first the Dolby system of noise reduction and later, digital sound. As sound designer Walter Murch has observed, contemporary digital systems employing up to eight discrete channels achieve the opposite effect to those of the late 1960s: 'We've actually got too much dynamic range. We have to control it in the mixing or we will blast people out of the theaters'.[11]

When we look at the developments in the place where these new Hollywood films met their audience, the magnitude of this change becomes even more noticeable. Cinema architecture began to address the acoustic demands of the new sound systems. As Tomlinson Holman, the inventor of THX, has pointed out, 'There's a fundamental difference between a concert hall, which is a space for production ... and a movie theater which is a space for reproduction'.[12] The old movie palaces had been built to accommodate concert orchestras; their smaller relations had not been designed to cope with severe acoustic demands: stereo was a rarity and confined by the late 1960s to a few first-run theatres in big cities.

The new architecture developed during the theatre-building boom of the 1970s and, aided by the development of shopping-mall cinemas and multiplexes, needed to address a series of well-documented problems and worked to a precise brief. It had to reduce the possibility of unwanted echoes by employing better phono-absorbent material and avoid too many 'bouncing' surfaces; it had to minimise the background noise created by the noise of the projector and air ventilation systems, and sound spillages from adjacent theatres in multiplexes; it had to accommodate surround speakers correctly by arranging the placement of the speakers, bearing in mind the layout of the seating plan and the needs of surround sound. The attention and care given to producing sophisticated soundtracks, and spaces capable of reproducing them in all their dynamic potential, showed an evident shift in the weight given to the figure of the spectator as listener. This change was made all the more significant by the lack of any comparable development in the film image during the same period.

In an extension of this development, the lure of sound was also exploited outside the auditorium itself, by installing speakers throughout the cinema complex and playing back music and trailers from present and forthcoming films (in some cases even in the cinema toilets). Far from being only a marketing device, these developments increase audience expectations by addressing audiences directly as listeners, and by extending the sonic playground beyond the actual auditorium and the film projection, so that it pervades the whole of the theatre experience, heightening our expectations and enticing us to 'come in and play' from the moment we enter the cinema complex.[13]

Once inside the auditorium, we are confronted with a situation where we are placed 'inside' the filmic space, not simply in front of one. The invitation to explore these new surroundings is emphasised by the way sound designers have approached the concept of audience space and the reproductive environment. As Gary Rydstrom points out, 'People love surround in movies ... it opens up the space'.[14] This awareness of the correlation between audience involvement and cinematic space is a key factor. Working on the soundtrack as a kind of architectural construct, Hollywood sound 'architects' have treated sound as an increasingly tangible expanse in which to arrange a series of sound objects for the audience to engage with. As Walter Murch explains, 'You (the sound designer) are given an architectural space and you put things in it and make it look good'.[15]

The audience's powerful sensual involvement with this three-dimensional sonic space is clearly designed to fulfil their high aural expectations, to heighten the cinematic experience and to provide audiences with a constant source of pleasure. The contemporary Hollywood aural experience elevates the spectator to a state which we may define as that of a super-listener, a being (not to be found in nature) able to hear sounds that in reality would not be audible or would sound substantially duller. These spectators expect screen objects to fly above their heads into, and out of, the auditorium.

Most importantly, however, all this is not simply given to the audience, but has to be earned by the listener. As a consequence of contemporary recording-practices, where conditions on the set may require sounds to be recorded afresh in the acoustically-friendly studio environment, film sound is very often not produced by its visual source on (or off) screen. Indeed, most of the sounds we hear in Hollywood movies are literally designed. This is mainly because their real equivalent would often simply not sound 'right' for the kind of emotional and narrative impact that they are meant to achieve. For example, try to describe what the sound of one of Indiana Jones's punches actually sounds like. Its texture could never be produced by a fist hitting a face (or any other part of the body); its duration and 'width' greatly outlast the length of any impact. The goal of such sound effects is expressiveness rather than accurate reproduction. Audiences are asked by the film-makers to accept an 'interpretation' of that sound that bypasses the original features of the sound (that is, the actual straightforward sound recording of a punch) in favour of narrative effectiveness (that is, the 'designed' sound punch). This would at least seem to suggest that, regardless of how improbable this 'interpretation' may be, audiences show a remarkable willingness to give more 'latitude' to sound than they seem prepared to do with the image (is it possible to imagine Indiana Jones's fist growing in size, as in a cartoon, just as it is about to strike?).

To make matters even more complicated, some of these sounds are themselves produced by a combination of sounds aimed at achieving that kind of 'filmic eloquence' mentioned above: from a soufflé of animal noises (employed in the creation of countless effects, including Jake LaMotta's punches in *Raging Bull*, ET's voice and even the fighter jets in *Top Gun*) to bicycle chains and plastic bags (famously, some of the helicopter sounds used by Murch and Coppola in *Apocalypse Now*). Most Hollywood sound is not only 'artificially' constructed, it is also not at all a unique event, but rather a combination of events that the audience has to 'splice' together and make sense of.

Moreover, all these complex and sophisticated actions (from processing hundreds of different sounds to linking them to their visual source, no matter how improbable) are performed while under fairly extreme physical conditions. Contemporary sound systems are powerful enough to move a significant amount of air. As a consequence, the spectator can be 'hit' with sound, and experience the film with a far greater degree of physical involvement than ever before. This creates a situation where audiences have to deal with enough constant sound pressure to lead to physical exhaustion, if exercised over time. Sound designers are aware of the physical demands they place on their listeners. Describing the soundtrack to *Top Gun,* Cecelia Hall explained that 'Our biggest fear was that we were going to pound them [the audience] into oblivion. We knew the sound effects could not be unrelenting because by the time you got to the end of the movie, you'd be so exhausted that you'd have no energy'.[16]

A listener is required to sustain physically aggressive soundtracks, to process dozens (sometimes hundreds) of different tracks in any single moment of a film, to navigate in this ocean of sound by correlating sound direction and its visual source, and to constantly update his or her own personal sound databank with sounds never heard before. All this, as Automatic Dialogue Replacement (ADR) supervisor Juno Ellis correctly points out, requires a great deal of engagement and discernment: 'Audiences have gotten more sophisticated in what they want from sound.'[17] Indeed, this combination of heightened expectations and increased aural sophistication has produced a highly demanding, active and discerning listener of Hollywood films. This new generation of listeners expects to enter a playground where sound objects are, to follow Murch's analogy, placed around for him/her to play with. The promise is a world of sonic wonders and pleasures which is appealing precisely because this requires a certain degree of physical and mental participation.

Chaos in the Hall: Who is in Charge of the Soundtrack?

Despite Hollywood's careful 'orchestration' of all these issues, the relationship between films and their listeners is far from being devoid of blurred areas. There are contradictions to be found, both in the theatre and outside, and as a result this is a rather difficult partnership to assess.

On the one hand, Hollywood has been investigating the potential of film sound thoroughly: from the introduction of new technologies (such as Dolby, THX and digital sound) to their use in production (multi-channel, increased dynamic range, multi-layered soundtracks), from sound reproduction in theatres (now built with sound demands in mind) to its home dimension (where the circle has now closed again and home consumers can enjoy cinema-like sound quality after the recent introduction of Home THX and digital sound systems), the signs of the industry's desire to explore its spectators as listeners are all too apparent.

On the other hand, there are aspects of this relationship which betray a rather more chaotic situation than might appear on the surface. Most noticeably, the concept of a unique soundtrack experienced by a 'unified' audience is a famous casualty. We can identify at least two other 'parallel soundtracks' to the film's own: the 'structural' soundtrack, which includes sound produced during the film performance by the cinema structure itself, and the audience's soundtrack, of sounds emanating from the audience itself. The structured soundtrack is directly dependent on the conditions of reception within each individual theatre. Sound spillages from adjacent theatres, noisy ventilation systems, lack of proper insulation of the projection booth, and distortion due to excessive volume levels or inadequate speakers inevitably interact with the film's own soundtrack, creating a hybrid effect that varies from theatre to theatre. While this would still seem to be a problem mainly of a technological/architectural nature and therefore in some ways 'adjustable', it is worth noting that Lucas's Skywalker facility takes the structural soundtrack into serious consideration by adding background noise during the mixing of its productions.

Far more complex, however, is the situation in relation to the 'audience' soundtrack. As in any respectable playground, those who visit it wish to be more than just 'observers'. They want to interact with it. Theatre architecture, in particular the arrangement of seats, has limited the spectator's visual interaction with the screen. It is impossible not to acknowledge the 'restraining' nature of the cinema seat, limiting physical movement and obliging the audience to face the screen. This is not, and could not be, the case with sound, given the latter's modern dimension as multi-perspectival and generated from various points in the auditorium. As a result, audiences are relatively free to establish a complex interaction with the film soundtrack. This begins outside the auditorium, from the usual socialising conversation to talking about the film one is about to see; eating food and sipping drinks, and then continues inside the auditorium itself. Once inside, this 'interaction' takes a different form. The talking may stop, but the munching, drinking and, more importantly, the laughing, crying and screaming does not. The different relationship between audiences and sound is also institutionally acknowledged by the fact that, although the audience is made well aware that there is to be 'no talking' during the projection, there is no perceived need to adopt a similar strategy for the image (perhaps with a similar request that there should be 'no jumping up and down in front of the screen'?). By laughing at the 'wrong' time, screaming when prompted through a scary moment, applauding or booing at the end of the film, the audience's own soundtrack can support, undermine, reinforce or even contradict the film's own.

Hollywood film-makers seem to be aware of this 'threat' to the integrity of their soundtrack and have tried to address it. A good example of this attempt is Lucasfilm's revolutionary and comprehensive sound programme which includes THX and Theatre Alignment Programme (TAP). The THX programme aims to recreate in the theatre the same conditions and sound quality which can be found in Hollywood mixing studios. Its stringent criteria also address the issue of the 'parallel soundtracks' by demanding that a series of parameters regarding 'structural' conditions, such as background noise and sound insulation, must be met if certification is to be awarded. Acknowledging that a print may encounter acoustic differences between theatres, the TAP programme was created to complement the THX treatment. As well as sophisticated quality controls on the film's sound and image tracks, the TAP programme also comprises a 'print policing' strategy, which includes a 1-800 phone line and a website for cinema customers to report any problems encountered when viewing/listening to a TAP-managed print). Behind this unprecedented interest in the quality of both recording and reproduction of the film soundtrack lies the awareness that regardless of the individual efforts of the film-maker, a variety of factors 'outside' their control interact at the point of reception. Hence the desire to minimise the 'damage'. According to James Cameron, 'all that stands between us and entropy is TAP. We work so hard to create quality, it is a relief to know that there exists an organization whose sole purpose is the preservation of quality at the actual place where the film and the audience first meet.'[18]

Paradoxically, this glaring contradiction of Hollywood film-makers creating a very 'inviting' and playful sonic environment, while at the same time hoping to standardise the condition of reception and thus regulate the audience's reaction to sound, presents us with the most conclusive piece of evidence that audiences as listeners are indeed active and constantly involved in an interactive relationship with the film's soundtrack. This view of an active listener is also reinforced by the situation existing in the other, often overlooked, place of receiving of Hollywood films: the home.

At home, audiences of Hollywood movies are free to manipulate virtually all aspects of a film soundtrack, such as sound direction (by arranging speakers at will), loudness (simply by pumping the volume up or lowering it down), the relationship between surround and front channels (most home surround processors have separate controls for them) and, perhaps most importantly, their talking and commenting over the film soundtrack are no longer 'forbidden' and they are free to achieve levels of sonic interaction with the film unobtainable in a cinema.[19] Given these considerations, it would seem unwise to address the interaction between Hollywood films and their listeners/viewers as a unified event or to talk of a passive, uniformed spectator of that event.

The Comfortably Active Spectator

The concept of being active or passive spectators is one that much film scholarship has firmly located in the spheres of meaning and interpretation. The argument is deceptively simple: a film that is 'easy' to understand will not call for an active involvement on the part of audiences. On the other hand, a movie whose meaning is somewhat 'cryptic' (or open to alternative interpretations) will solicit an active response from the spectator. Leaving aside for a moment the rather slippery notions of meaning and interpretation, this view overlooks other dimensions of movie-going where audience behaviour may be categorised as 'active'.

Film sound is one such dimension. As we have seen in the case of the 'audience soundtrack', audience members interact aurally with each other and with the film in many ways. In the former case, there is talking to each other, commenting on the film, and so on; in the latter, the same interaction is achieved through clapping, booing, munching, sipping, laughing, crying, and other responses. While the level of sonic interaction varies considerably from culture to culture (clapping and cheering at the actors/events on screen, for example, is a practice more commonly accepted in some countries than others), this interaction is too evident to be unnoticed.

Similarly, as we have seen, contemporary sound systems are capable of producing intense sound pressure on film audiences, thus involving the latter also on a physical level. This is more than just about being 'loud'. Unlike the bi-dimensional image, the three-dimensional nature of sound allows soundtracks to be enveloping. Moreover, multi-channel, multi-directional sound is today organised around the auditorium, not around the image on screen. This is not to underestimate the importance of the image: images clearly suggest sounds (although the degree of this relationship clearly varies from film to film). However, sound is directed to and orchestrated around the seats to put the spectator literally 'inside' the film, reducing the distance between audience and narrative world. Audiences are invited to share the same sonic dimension as the characters on screen: as Michael Cimino once remarked, 'sound can demolish the wall separating the viewer from the film'.[20]

On yet another level, the popularity throughout the world of theatres bearing the THX logo or boasting the latest digital sound systems, not to mention the remarkable diffusion of home sound systems, suggests a third dimension where the contemporary

Hollywood listener can be seen as active. By choosing the cinema in which they see a film, audiences actively seek the best comfort available. In this respect, sound again plays a key role: audiences know that a cinema showcasing the THX logo will almost inevitably guarantee comfortable seats and large screens, as well as high-quality sound. The commercial success and huge popularity of high-end sound reproduction systems (all mainstream Hollywood productions are now released in digital sound format) testifies to the relevance of this particular audience choice.[21]

This combination of technological comfort, physical involvement and social interaction suggests a figure of the Hollywood listener that we might be tempted to define, in opposition to the view originally expressed in the quotes by Austin and Ellis at the beginning of this chapter, as 'comfortably active'. Indeed, the film industry has long acknowledged the importance of providing audiences with the necessary aural comfort and choice: film-makers provide enough visual clues to facilitate the process of linking image to sound (no matter how improbable that link might be), and cinemas provide all the necessary 'creature comforts' to make sure that contemporary audiences enjoy an aurally-sophisticated environment in which to be active (in the ways outlined above) and not merely passive 'spectators'.

Film scholarship, however, has rarely turned its eye (and ear) to the relationship between film sound and spectatorship. When it has, it has often been in a rather hostile climate towards Hollywood cinema at large. Echoes of old (but never forgotten) critiques of Hollywood clearly still haunt these accounts of Hollywood and its relationship with its listeners. In particular, scholars have gone to considerable pains to emphasise the role of contemporary sound technology as just another way that Hollywood has to hide its ideological and economic 'apparatus'. It is, however, perfectly possible to construct a view of contemporary Hollywood listeners which is far more positive than the ones expressed so far. Indeed, far from being 'hidden', today's sound technology is showcased, advertised and exploited in as 'open' a manner as possible. Newspapers carry adverts of exhibitors keen to boast about their latest sound system. Once inside the cinema complex, posters and plaques often remind us that this or that theatre is equipped with Dolby Digital (EX, DTS, etc.). The THX logo has even become a recognisable stamp of approval for the ultimate quality cinema.

Today's Hollywood listener is a discerning, demanding auditor, whose aural expectations film-makers attempt to appease. Whether this makes for 'better' soundtracks or rather leads down a path towards theme-ride style soundtracks is a debatable issue. What appears certain is that contemporary audiences have at their disposal an unprecedented array of choices and possibilities to be actively involved in the movie-going experience, and that sound plays a key role in this situation. Recent developments point towards an even greater attempt to position audiences inside the sonic playground. The introduction of the new Dolby EX sound system is one good indicator of this continuing trend. Developed by Lucasfilm and Dolby Laboratories, Dolby EX is the brain child of sound designer Gary Rydstrom. It basically adds a channel to the surround (centre surround), allowing sound to be much better placed around the auditorium: now audiences are within a sonic environment where sound can reach them from no fewer than six different directions. The sonic playground is becoming ever more playful and there appears to be plenty of audiences ready to play.

Notes

1   See, for example, Rick Altman, 'Introduction: Four and a Half Film Fallacies', in Altman, *Sound Theory, Sound Practice* (New York and London: Routledge, 1992). In this piece, Altman outlines what he sees as the key theoretical 'fallacies' on which the image-bias of mainstream film theory is based. The fallacies of his title are: the historical, the ontological, the reproductive and the nominalist (with 'indexicality' accounting for the 'half').

2   John Ellis, *Visible Fictions* (London and New York: Routledge, 1982), p. 41.

3   Hugo Mauerhofer, as quoted in Bruce A. Austin, *Immediate Seating: A Look at Movie Audiences* (Belmont, CA: Wadsworth Publishing, 1988), p. 46.

4   It is worth remembering that where the image is two-dimensional, sound is a three-dimensional construct.

5   Cecelia Hall has been responsible for some of the most innovative soundtracks of the last twenty years, including *Beverly Hills Cop, Top Gun* and *The Hunt for Red October,* for which she won an Oscar.

6   Cecelia Hall, in Vincent LoBrutto, *Sound-on-Film: Interviews with Creators of Film Sound* (Westport, CT: Praeger Publishers, 1994), pp. 191–2.

7   Charles Schreger, 'Altman, Dolby and the Second Sound Revolution', in Elizabeth Weis and John Belton (eds), *Film Sound: Theory and Practice* (New York: Columbia University Press, 1985), p. 349.

8   It is interesting to note that regardless of the advances made in the past few years by large-screen televisions, the depth, width and quality of the cinema image stands virtually unchallenged by any consumer products.

9   George Lucas, in John Young, 'Sound Revolution', *Hollywood Reporter* (22 June 1993), p. T-12.

10 It is important to acknowledge here that it would be virtually impossible to conduct a meaningful empirical study of the many kinds of audiences of Hollywood cinema. Therefore, these considerations are more based on Hollywood's own perception of audiences needs, with all the risks and omissions that this inevitably entails.

11 Walter Murch, in LoBrutto, *Sound-on-Film,* p. 99.

12 Ibid., p. 204.

13 Obviously, conditions of reception can vary widely from cinema to cinema, but I am mainly referring here to muliplex cinemas.

14 Gary Rydstrom, in LoBrutto, *Sound-on-Film*, p. 238.

15 Walter Murch, in ibid., p. 92.

16 Cecelia Hall, in ibid., p. 195.

17 Juno Ellis in ibid., p. 218.

18 James Cameron, quoted in TAP publicity material *Aligned Success* (Lucasfilm, 1992), available from LucasArts Entertainment Company, THX Division, PO Box 2009, San Rafael, California 94912, or at THX website (www.thx.com).

19 Obviously, television is perfectly aware of this issue and has attempted to incorporate, at least partly, the audience soundtrack in programmes by giving it an 'institutional' role. The best example of this is to be found in the use of audience laughter in sitcoms.

20 Michael Cimino, in Charles Schreger, 'Altman, Dolby and the Second Sound Revolution', p. 351.

21 In this sense, it is interesting to notice that audiences are active also in the sense of demanding regulation on issues like sound levels. Following audience complaints about sound level in film trailers, Dolby Laboratories have now designed a 'Soundtrack Loudness Meter' to prevent trailers from being too loud.

9
The Contemporary Cinephile: Film Collecting in the Post-Video Era

Barbara Klinger

> Let us grant that our everyday objects are in fact objects of a passion – the passion
> for private property, emotional investment in which is every bit as intense as
> investment in the 'human' passions. Indeed, the everyday passion for private
> property is often stronger than all the others, and sometimes even reigns supreme,
> all other passions being absent.
>
> Jean Baudrillard[1]

Since the 1970s the term 'cinephile' has conjured very definite meanings and associations for film scholars. Christian Metz and other psychoanalytic theorists characterised the cinephile as an extreme but logical extension of the regular film-goer who loved the cinema with a 'passion for seeing' that was tied inextricably to the movie hall's 'theatre of shadows' and the technology that made it possible (i.e. the camera, projector and screen). Ultimately, 'enchanted at what the machine is capable of', the film devotee entered the theatre not just to encounter a particular film, but to take ardent, fetishistic pleasure in the viewing conditions themselves. The cinephile thus vividly realised the capacity of the cinematic apparatus to transfix its spectators through the darkness of the theatre, the brilliantly lit screen, and other conditions that constituted cinema's spellbinding nature and its array of visual fascinations.

Given these characterisations, it is not surprising that scholars have subsequently regarded cinephilia as essentially and exclusively a big-screen experience, absolutely dependent on the projection of celluloid within the public space of the motion picture theatre. As Roland Barthes insisted, in the case of the televised film, film pleasure arises expressly out of being 'submerged in the darkness of the theater … Consider … the opposite experience, the experience of TV, which also shows films: nothing, no fascination; the darkness is dissolved, the anonymity repressed, the space is familiar, organized (by furniture and familiar objects), tamed …'[2] Because of its domestic setting, television represented the antithesis of the movie theatre as an exhibition site for films, a prime example of the 'death' of rapture caused by removing film viewing from its proper context. In the wasteland of affect defining the home and its subdued, private entertainment space, the exercise of cinephilia would be unimaginable.

While claims about the impoverishment of non-theatrical screening venues for the cinema have always been problematic, recent developments in the home exhibition of films in the United States offer a particularly interesting challenge to such long-standing

assumptions. Since the appearance of television, innovations in entertainment technologies have made this venue into the main focus of film viewing. The video revolution alone has resulted in more viewers watching films at home than in the movie
theatre.[3] The development of cable movie channels, home theatre, laserdiscs, satellite
delivery systems and other notable evolutions in home entertainment have further
emphasised and redefined television's significance as the prime viewing site for films.

At the same time, these technologies have helped to reconstitute dramatically film
spectatorship. Among other things, they have inspired the creation of new film cultures
in the home, shaped both by institutional practices and the rituals of domestic space.
As we shall see, such cultures should encourage us to reconsider the image of the
'domesticated' spectator bereft of viewing pleasure. While the dynamics of 'household'
film viewing may not replicate the psychic parameters of spectatorship in the motion
picture theatre, home film cultures raise the distinct possibility that passion for the cinema within domestic space is not anomalous. Further, these cultures suggest that the
home has been equipped and acculturated to produce its own kind of connoisseurship
and intense spectatorial investment.

The pervasive presence of new technologies in the home has encouraged the emergence of a variety of ardent spectators. One of the most avid of these is the viewer who
collects films on video, laserdisc and other formats to create a media library. Seated in
front of their television sets, collectors represent a corps of impassioned film devotees
who are, like Metz's cinephile, 'enchanted at what the machine is capable of', that is,
mesmerised by the machines of reproduction that deliver the cinematic illusion. The
contemporary film collector's romance with these machines suggests that cinephilia has
been broadened to encompass the 'forbidden' territories of television and the mediated
home. Cinema's domestication has not obliterated cinephilia; rather, the conditions
fuelling cinephilia have been relocated and rearticulated within the complex interac-
tions between commodity culture and the private sphere.

The contemporary film collector vividly represents a domestic version of the
cinephile, embodying the substantial effects that new technologies have had on how
films are consumed in the home. Examining the phenomenon of collecting helps us to
explore ultimately cinema's fate as private property. What happens to the cinema when
it becomes the viewer's possession within systems of value and affect not only characteristic of the home (family relationships, etc.),[4] but of the technoculture responsible for
the increasingly prominent place films occupy in households? While media industries
do not control the activity of collecting, they have played a significant role in inspiring
its growth as a routine activity, a commonplace aspect of the viewer's relation to film.
In league with other social forces, these industries have had a dramatic impact on the
reception of 'collectible' films in the home.

Before addressing the specific implications of contemporary film collecting for the
domestic reception of films, two preliminary questions must be addressed. How has
collecting become such an integral part of the spectator's media landscape in the United
States? How do we situate this pastime, traditionally regarded as personal and idiosyncratic, within a cultural frame?

Why Rent When You Can Own?

Since the widespread introduction of the VCR in the 1970s, video-cassettes and other surrogate forms of cinema, most notably the laserdisc and digital video disc (DVD), have dramatically transformed the spectator's relationship to film. They have, for the first time, made film an accessible commodity. Viewers can now own and operate what was once essentially an unapproachable medium that hovered in the distance on the silver screen, its transient appearance guaranteed by the end of its run. They can, as Timothy Corrigan remarks, 'adopt movies', instantly transforming public objects into home furnishings that respond to the concerns and rituals of domestic space.[5] Today cinema can be contained in small boxes, placed on a shelf, left on the coffee table or thrown on the floor. Spectators can pause, fast-forward, rewind or mangle images through the VCR; they can program a laserdisc player so that it shows only the desired scenes. In these alternative forms, films can be viewed repeatedly at the spectator's whim and achieve an indelible place in everyday routines. This previously physically remote, transitory and public medium has thus attained the solidity and semi-permanent status of a household object, intimately and infinitely subject to manipulation in the private sphere.

At the same time, there is an unprecedented availability of cinema. Beyond the motion picture theatre, films are shown on network, cable, pay and satellite television channels and on the Web. They appear in such public places as stores, airplanes and classrooms. They can also be rented or purchased in various formats from video to CD-ROM. Far from oversaturating the audience with the parade of films in multiplexes and other exhibition formats, cinema's omnipresence has served to broaden the horizons of public and private film cultures. Cinema has become not only a commonplace element of leisure, but an inextricable component of everyday life. As a reporter for the *New York Times* comments in an article entitled 'Land of the Cineplex, Home of the Cassette', 'Americans are watching movies any way they can ... watching movies has become something of a national pastime'. Further, within this pastime, there is a marked trend toward purchasing, rather than simply renting videos: consumers do not just want to watch films, they want to buy them, take them home, and see them repeatedly.[6] The presence of cheaper home entertainment equipment and lower sell-through prices of films on video and laserdisc have helped spur this movement toward film acquisition.[7] In addition, media industries have successfully marketed films for sale by tapping into a middle-class consensus about the superiority of ownership. As an ad for the video edition of *Star Trek: First Contact* (1996), priced at $14.95, puts it, 'Why Rent Space When You Can Own It?'[8] Thus, the growth of legitimate film purchases joins the existing and often more suspect practices of taping films off-air or dubbing them from prerecorded tapes as a significant means of possessing the cinema.

The contemporary film collector is then no longer the eccentric recluse who lives in the Hollywood hills surrounded by hundreds of prints or the academic who screens films on a 16 mm projector in the basement. Film collecting has been dramatically democratised by cinema's availability in venues that are both more accessible to the consumer and less expensive than celluloid. Viewers collect films on video and on laserdisc, with DVD beginning to make its impact on the market.[9]

Media industries have stimulated the growth of film collecting as part of their never-ending attempt to find new markets for their products. Film production companies, electronics firms specialising in home theatre, laserdisc and video vendors, and other businesses have explicitly targeted collectors as a niche audience.[10] As a symptom of

Special Collector's Edition of *Platoon* (1986)

their pursuit of specialised audiences, these industries routinely promote home theatre, the exhibition format that promises to replicate the experience of the movie theatre in the home, as designed for the 'serious' film viewer.[11] Similarly, such widely available audio-visual hardware magazines as *Home Theater, Widescreen Review* and *Video Magazine* aim their articles at the movie buff. More directly, films are marketed as collectables.[12] A typical ad asks the reader to 'Accessorize Your Evening' by buying *The First Wives Club* (1996), *Clueless* (1995), *Sabrina* (1995), *Harriet the Spy* (1996), and *Evening Star* (1997) as 'the perfect additions to your home video collection'.[13] While various companies frequently promote contemporary films as collectables, there is also widespread advertisement of reissued older films on video, laserdisc, and DVD. These 'classics' are films the discerning collector should add to his or her archive (e.g. the 1997 ad campaign for the 25th anniversary video edition of *The Godfather* trilogy [1972; 1974; 1990] hails them as '3 Masterpieces That Belong In Every Video Collection').[14]

    There are yet more focused appeals to this audience in the form of film reissues referred to as 'special collector's editions'. Pioneered by 'The Criterion Collection' in 1984, special collector's editions reproduce films in their original widescreen formats (if appropriate) and provide accompanying background material about various stages of production. Once available only on laserdisc, special collector's editions are now sold on video as well. For example, the 1996 big-screen re-release of *Vertigo* (1958) was quickly followed by collector's editions on both video and laserdisc. These video editions signal the growth of this market beyond laserdisc player owners into a larger sector of the viewing public.

Though they represent a specialised audience for media products, film collectors do not comprise a uniform or homogenous community. The activity of collecting is undertaken by numerous kinds of viewers, from those who buy just a few of their favourite films to rabid devotees who pursue titles systematically in order to create an extensive library. In addition, the media industries have targeted men, women and families alike. As the sales charts for videos indicate, families consistently purchase titles for their children and grandchildren. For example, *Entertainment Weekly* reported in November 1997 that of the top ten videos sold in the previous week, six were children's fare.[15] While there is a strong male presence in the collecting world, the activity is not restricted to male consumers. As the 'Accessorize Your Evening' ad suggests with its display of films aimed at female audiences (against a backdrop consisting of clothing, jewellery and roses), the industry recognises women as collectors as well. There are also 'high-end' and 'low-end' collectors. High-end collectors buy expensive entertainment equipment and concentrate on acquisitions of laserdiscs or good quality videos. Low-end types indulge in obscure and sometimes trashy titles that may be several or more generations removed from their original video versions (available, for example, from such vendors as 'Mondo Movies' or 'Something Weird Video').[16]

Each of these kinds of viewers deserves further scrutiny, since they are very much a part of the phenomenon of film collecting in the post-video era. However, to explore the most vivid connections between cinema, new technologies and home exhibition, I concentrate here on dedicated, high-end collectors intent on building a film archive within an upscale entertainment environment. In addition to their passion for the cinema, this group is particularly engaged with technological developments that mimic the conditions of the movie theatre within the home. Paramount among these developments is home theatre, an entertainment centre that promises improved image and sound reproduction through big-screen television sets, A/V receivers to deliver both audio and video signals, Dolby digital surround sound (and other multi-channel sound options), and quality playback systems like hi-fi VCRs and laserdisc players. As the direct legatees of the so-called digital revolution, contemporary film collectors are very much a part of the 'high-tech' film culture that has emerged over the last few years. For this group of collectors, the desire for cinema is inextricably linked to the desire for the newest and the best technology.

Media industries often refer to this type of collector as a 'phile' of some sort – an audiophile, cinephile, videophile or laserphile. These 'philes' are hailed as serious viewers and media specialists who exhibit a zealous preoccupation with sound and image that can only be satisfied through the purchase of the most refined electronic systems. A passion for cinema is aligned with a passion for hardware, intimately associating cinephilia with technophilia. As we shall see, film collectors often discuss questions that have more to do with technology than with other aspects of the cinema, such as which films have the best digital transfers in their re-released laserdisc versions. Such hardware 'philes' have typically been considered predominately male (e.g. the male adolescent who knows how to choose stereo speakers on the basis of the best available subwoofers and tweeters or where to procure a rare import version of a particular record).[17] There appears to be a preponderance of males involved in the type of film collecting that has a substantial technological dimension, but given the diverse audiences who buy films in alternative formats and use new entertainment technologies in the home, such generalisations should only be offered tentatively.

Male or female, the zealotry of the 'phile' is undoubtedly characterised by the whims and obsessions of the individual. But it is also inextricably tied to the practices and ideologies of an array of social contexts.

Unpacking the Film Library

Walter Benjamin's essay, 'Unpacking My Library', speaks elegantly about the private pleasures of collecting. In Benjamin's meditation on his own fascinations with book collecting, he admits that amassing a library has very little to do with actually reading the purchased texts. As he writes, 'the most profound enchantment for the collector is the locking of individual items within a magic circle in which they are fixed as the final thrill, the thrill of acquisition, passes over them'. Ownership, 'the most intimate relationship that one can have to objects', enables an intensely personal relationship to develop between collector and collectibles. The books do not, as we might expect, 'come alive' in the collector, rather it is 'he who lives in them'. The book conjures memories of its own past, from its original period and region to its former ownership. It also invokes memories of when the collector purchased the book – the time, the city, the store. Ultimately, the possession of a book produces a host of recollections that mingles personal autobiography with the book's history. As Benjamin asserts, 'to renew the old world – that is the collector's deepest desire when he is driven to acquire new things'. The collector 'disappear[s] inside' his collection, at once his possession, his intimate terrain but also his connection to the past.[18] Book collecting, then, becomes a form of personal reverie, a means to re-experience the past through an event of acquisition.

Benjamin's account clearly presents the passionate, subjective nature of collecting. Yet, his essay also suggests strong associations between collecting and external considerations, between what appear to be strictly private practices and broader cultural systems. While Benjamin does not explore some central issues, such as why certain objects in this world of connoisseurship acquire value in the first place, he highlights the linkage of collectables and collecting subjectivities to commodity culture ('the thrill of acquisition'), to the private sphere (as the collector 'disappear[s] inside' the collection), and to memory and history ('to renew the old world'). Benjamin's essay, then, invites us to entertain questions left unraised in his meditation about the book collector and to pursue provocative allusions to the social forces latent within the act of collecting. Despite its inescapable personal dimension, collecting cannot be entirely removed from broader dynamics in the public sphere. Like other aspects of the private, it is crisscrossed with the concerns of the external culture in which the individual dwells.

As James Clifford notes of personal collections in general, 'The collection and preservation of an authentic domain of identity cannot be natural or innocent … inclusions in all collections reflect wider cultural rules – of rational taxonomy, of gender, of aesthetics … the self that must possess but cannot have it all learns to select, order, classify in hierarchies – to make 'good' collections'.[19] Any kind of collecting – stamps, war souvenirs, art, books, toys, etc. – is affected at the very least by notions of value, systems of classification and other frameworks utilised by larger cultural provinces and institutions. In the case of post-video-era film collecting, classification systems from academia, video and laser vendors, and the media industries intervene in the collecting process. Thus, a collector might arrange films by period, genre, nation, director, studio, actor, or simply alphabetically, demonstrating some modicum of familiarity with procedures of arrangement that have been employed by other institutions. In the age of computers, there is even software available to 'catalog, search and sort your collection by title, director, genre and other categories'.[20]

Similarly, a collector's selection of particular artefacts may be shaped by the perceived value those artefacts have acquired as classics, rarities, oddities and other marketable categories of collectables. For instance, media industries define most of what they sell in special editions as 'classics'. The Goldwyn Classics Library advertised a series of Eddie Cantor films under the slogan, 'These classics just got more classical'; *Vertigo*, available from MCA/Universal Home Video, is Alfred Hitchcock's 'masterpiece'; and according to its collector's edition, *Alien* (1979) became an 'instant classic' upon its original release.[21] Special-edition marketing in particular provides an opportunity to elevate film to the status of high art, either by cashing in on an existing canon or by attempting to create one by affixing the classic label. In addition, through the often extensive background materials that accompany it, a special edition appears to furnish the authenticity and history so important to establishing the value of an archival object.

Since videos, laserdiscs and DVDs are mass produced and hence widely available, there would seem to be little potential in this type of collecting for pursuing the ultimate collector's commodity – the rare artefact. Scarcity of the precious collectible – an elusive first edition of a book, for example – is a condition that appears to be sorely lacking in this context. Nonetheless, the language of scarcity permeates the discourses around film re-releases. In a move not uncommon for the media business, Pioneer Entertainment reissued the seven *Star Trek* feature films on laserdisc. Its ad for this reissue states that these 'deluxe box sets are numbered and *limited to just 8000* to satisfy the true collector'. This type of limited special edition seeks to define itself as outside of the excesses of contemporary mass reproduction and therefore more 'rare'. It attempts to carve out an aesthetic place by appealing to the conditions of scarcity, conditions so important to constituting an aura of value for collectibles. The rare item is complemented by a showcase housing and the highest standards in audio-visual reproduction, finessing the associations between collecting, value and aesthetic experience. The box that contains the discs for *Star Trek: Generations* (designed as a 'Space Dock') is 'deluxe'. The discs themselves are 'encoded with Dolby Surround AC–3 Digital' and 'utilize THX technologies for the ultimate audiovisual experience at home'.[22]

There is a rarer market in laserdiscs and videos than that represented by promotional efforts. *The Laser Disc Newsletter* regularly lists hundreds of titles imported from overseas, which include such items as concert laserdiscs (e.g., 'Sex Pistols: Winterland'), boxed sets of US television series (e.g., *Lost in Space*), and foreign films often not readily available in the United States (e.g., certain Hong Kong releases). Like other sources of its kind, *The Laser Disc Newsletter* also advertises 'rare out-of-print discs' such as John Ford's *The Long Voyage Home* (1940) and Jean-Luc Godard's *Hail Mary* (1985), cult favourites such as *Honeymoon Killers* (1970) and *Cannibal Holocaust* (1978), titles not released on commercial video, and imported letter-boxed versions of films available only in pan-and-scan versions in the US. Thus, out-of-print, cult, non-commercial, letter-boxed, and other more marginal offerings help constitute the uncommon, sought-after media object, suggesting that the collector's trade has found a way to construct the categories of authenticity and rarity for mass-produced film artefacts. The existence of these artefacts also helps to stimulate the competitive gamesmanship and 'sport' characteristic of this enterprise (i.e. to see who can procure the rarity). As Charles Tashiro points out, it is particularly in the acquisition of rare items 'where we can locate the bravado in video collecting'.[23]

We can begin to see, then, how contemporary film collecting is situated within already charged systems of classification, selection and value, engaged in a *pas de deux* with market forces. To more fully unpack the film library, however, we must explore further how collecting passes through the 'the filter of culture'.[24] How, for example, is a sense of membership in the world of film connoisseurs cultivated? What kind of aesthetics dominates film collecting and how do they renegotiate established values for media objects? How have the discourses of new media technologies penetrated contemporary home film culture and affected the way films are seen and discussed? What, finally, are the relations between the enterprise of collecting, consumerism and the private sphere? At the very least, contemporary cinephilia is shaped by an 'insider' identity for the devotee and a 'hardware' aesthetic. Both of these dynamics are strongly influenced by new technologies within the framework of consumer culture.

The Insider

Media industries attempt to appeal to the collector as a film industry 'insider', privy to a secret world of information about film-making. Insiders have obtained apparently special knowledge, possessed by relatively few others, which is manifested in diverse ways. These individuals may carefully choose and install the audio-visual components of home theatre in their entertainment spaces. Similarly, they may be caught up in debates about the comparative virtues of emerging technologies that reproduce the cinema – for instance, whether laserdisc is superior in quality to DVD or whether Dolby Digital Sound surpasses Dolby Pro-Logic in surround sound capabilities. Insiders know when certain films will be reissued on video, laserdisc, or DVD and amass information about the quality of their transfers. Culling data from various sources that cater to the cinephile–collector (from magazines to the Internet), these viewers can also recite the facts of cinema. Such facts include behind-the-scenes stories about the making of particular films, gossip about stars and directors and myriad other specific historical, technological and biographical details. To concentrate on only one of these sources for a moment, the special collector's edition on laserdisc, we can see how such reissues school the viewer in just this type of information, helping to create a cognoscenti among collectors.

Special collector's editions are frequently quite intricate affairs. They present the feature film in its original screen ratio and may offer the director's cut of the film, including additional footage that did not survive the studio's final release cut (e.g. the laserdisc version of James Cameron's *The Abyss* [1989], which restores approximately thirty minutes of previously unseen material). While there are other items that may find their way into these reissues (such as a documentary about the film's production or commentary over the feature film provided by its directors, writers, producers and/or stars), special editions showcase what they refer to as the 'Collector's Supplement'. The supplement often provides quite extensive pre-production, production and post-production information about the film, from storyboards and different versions of the script to problems with the shoot and mastering the special effects to trailers designed to promote the film.

For example, in the special edition of *Citizen Kane* (1941) the viewer learns that Orson Welles had to wear a prosthetic nose designed by the film's make-up artist, Maurice Seiderman. Apparently, Welles's nose was deemed unphotogenic due to an 'underdeveloped' bridge and 'unusually large' nostrils. Delighted with the change in his appearance, Welles went on to wear the 'Seiderman nose', as it was referred to, in later films, including *Journey into Fear* (1942), *Touch of Evil* (1958), and *Compulsion* (1959). Similar disclosures occur in the commentary to the *The Graduate* (1967) laserdisc, where we are informed that the leg that graced the famous cover of the soundtrack album for *The Graduate* (an image that came to stand for the perverse links between the generations in the late 1960s), belonged not to Anne Bancroft but to Linda Gray, an actress who later played Sue Ellen Ewing in the prime-time television soap opera *Dallas*. In the special edition of *Alien*, we discover that director Ridley Scott's children took the place of the principal actors in the extreme long shots of the astronauts' first encounter with the 'Space Jockey' aboard the derelict spaceship, so as to make the creature and entire chamber seem larger. Since the replicas of space helmets were not fully operational as efficient oxygen-pumping devices, the children were overcome by carbon monoxide fumes and passed out on at least one occasion.

These few examples begin to suggest how media industries address the collector as an 'insider'. The revelation is the key ingredient of the collector's supplement on laserdisc. Each example exposes an assumption (e.g. that it is Welles's actual nose) by providing the viewer with behind-the-scenes information which reveals the cinematic tricks behind appearances. Let in on the 'secret', the viewer enters the world of filmmaking to reside in the privileged position of the director and other production personnel – the puppet-masters – who are responsible for such effective illusionism. Far from demystifying the production process, these revelations produce a sense of the film industry's magisterial control of appearances. Rather than inciting critical attitudes toward the industry, then, behind-the-scenes 'exposés' vividly create its identity as a place of marvels brought to the public by talented film professionals. As the viewer is invited to assume the position of the expert, s/he is drawn further into an identification with the industry and its wonders. But this identification, like any identification the viewer may have had with the apparently seamless diegetic universe of the film itself, is based on an illusion. Viewers do not get the unvarnished truth about the production; instead, they are presented with the 'promotable' facts, behind-the-scenes information that supports and enhances a sense of the 'movie magic' associated with the Hollywood production machine.

This kind of appeal to viewers suggests that one of the major foundations of fandom – the accumulation and dissemination of the smallest details involved in the production of media objects – is substantially informed (though not wholly determined) by industry discourse. In Henry Jenkins's study of television fans, he argues that 'we need to reconsider the importance of "trivia" as unauthorised and unpoliced knowledge existing outside academic institutions', as 'a source of popular expertise for the fans and a basis for critical reworkings of textual materials'.[25] While trivia may seem a culturally disenfranchised kind of knowledge in comparison to academic or other 'official' sources, we should also keep in mind that it has a substantial presence in popular culture as a source of vital information that often seems more important and authentic than the 'stuffy' intellectual accounts issuing from official sources. Thus, while film trivia may lack a certain cultural capital, it is not genuinely marginalised.

As the example of the special collector's edition suggests, it is also not a phenomenon that is completely 'unauthorised' and 'unpoliced'. From the earliest days of the film industry to the present, entertainment facts have achieved a particular visibility and viability as a type of knowledge and discourse in mass culture. Crossword puzzles, board games such as 'Trivial Pursuits', and television game shows are just a few of the popular forums that ask participants to marshal their knowledge of Hollywood trivia.[26] While fan's individual uses of trivia may have an idiosyncratic or even subversive dimension, there is a traffic in trivia, created, authorised and policed by various culture industries, that plays a very strong role in negotiating the audience's relationship to the media. As purveyors *par excellence* of such micro-data, special collector's editions give viewers a still-mystified account of the cinema as a part of the cultural capital they possess as 'masters' of the cinematic fact. The identity of trivia as a kind of subrosa knowledge possessed by the privileged few only enhances the effects of this mystification. Viewers are encouraged to become subjects of popular media discourse, disseminators of trivia, a process which inevitably helps to secure the place and importance of the media industries in culture.[27]

Beyond the appeal to the collector as insider, the collector's culture is also shaped by the various machines designed to reproduce films in the home. The technological aspect of the collector's world is particularly responsible for creating a film aesthetic that can transform a film's previous value (created through film reviews or academic criticism, for example) for domestic consumption.

The Hardware Aesthetic

The secret world of the collector is enhanced substantially by the primacy of technology. Technology already figures as a major component of the insider identity, since it is the various technologies of film-making that are responsible for creating the illusionism so enthusiastically elaborated by the collector's section of the special edition. Technology also plays an important role in the collectors' culture as a series of commodities to be purchased. Discourses on home entertainment technologies, which circulate in mainstream magazines as well as within the community of collectors themselves, have penetrated film aesthetics dramatically. Through what we might call a 'hardware aesthetic', the evaluation of films through the lens of hardware priorities transforms them according to imperatives drawn from technological considerations. Past film identities mutate: films regarded either as classics or failures incur reversals of aesthetic fortune; films are reread through the ideology of the spectacular; and form triumphs over content.

In his essay entitled, 'The Contradictions of Video Collecting', Charles Tashiro reveals the critical importance of technology in the mentality of the collector. Inspired by Benjamin, Tashiro is primarily interested in elaborating Benjamin's 'lyrical approach' to collecting, which he regards as 'the only legitimate one to what remains a highly private process'.[28] None the less, Tashiro's discussion of his own collecting habits demonstrates a telling shift from Benjamin's reverence for books as gateways to the past to a reverence for technological excellence and the preoccupation with the present embraced by this standard. Like many contemporary film collectors, Tashiro prefers laserdiscs over video-tapes, which are 'second-class citizens' because they degenerate. Unlike books or videos, laserdiscs do not embody their own histories by showing age. It is the physical appear-ance of laserdiscs forms a large part of their appeal: 'Discs fascinate as objects, their clear, cool surfaces promising technical perfection … discs promise modernism at its sleekest, the reduction to pristine forms and reflective surfaces'. Age, rather than being the signifier of worth, becomes a signal that a replacement disc should be put on order.[29]

Tashiro contends that this preference for new versions of the old, a distinct departure from other collecting aesthetics, is partially driven by a faith in 'the potentially perfect copy … expressed in the exploitation of ever-newer technologies, striving always to get closer to the film's original … As a result, change is valued for itself, and with each new technical capability, both collectors and producers feel compelled to improve on what has come before'. Progress is defined not so much in terms of the films themselves, but in terms of 'the technical capabilities of the disc medium'. Quality is judged in terms of 'the number of dropouts, the amount of hiss, the degree of fidelity in digital reproduc-tion. The logic of the surface of the disc spills over into its production and consump-tion: the cleaner, sleeker, shinier the image, the purer, richer, clearer the sound track, the better the disc'.[30] As Tashiro continues, this technical '*reason* serves as a perfect rational-ization, and through it I stake an emphatic claim to the importance of picture and sound over story and character, to those *technical* aspects of film best served by laser disc reproduction. By that claim, I lay the groundwork for the overall structure of the collection, its bias toward those films that favor visual style'.[31]

I quote Tashiro at length because his essay is one of the richest and most thought-provoking on the subject of contemporary film collecting. Though striving to depict collecting as irrational and subjective, his work demonstrates how techno-centric film collecting often is. The value of films is often largely determined by the quality of the transfer, the aura of the digital reproduction of sound and image, and even the pristine surface of the laserdisc itself. These priorities in turn lead to a preference for certain kinds of films over others – that is, films that have visual surfaces and technical features that appear to highlight and reinforce the capabilities of digital technology (even when the processes involved are still analogue-based, the term 'digital' functions as a catch-all term to describe quality playback).

Both producers and collectors put a premium on obtaining the newest and best tech-nological rendition of a film. Given this shared emphasis, it is not surprising that each group discusses film and film aesthetics in remarkably similar ways. Typical ads for home theatre components mix technical details with promises of spectacular effects. For example, Faroudja's Laboratories' TV enhancer offers adaptive colour processing, edge detail processing and colour alignment correction to 'make images from big screen TVs jump off the screen!'. Polk Audio's LS f/x high performance surround speakers 'can transform the surround channel from a typically flat monochromatic noise to a detached, spacious, and coherent soundfield' and 'are excellent for space-ships flying overhead or the growls of moving tanks and cranes, just the stuff of which impressive home cinema is made'.[32] The technical considerations that dominate promotions for home theatre systems or playback components make reproduction itself into the prime aesthetic criteria, while privileging a type of reproduction that favours verisimilitude mingled with spectacle. In this context, the film experience is composed of spectacular visuals and sound that bring seemingly authentic sensory perceptions into the forefront.

To explore how this kind of aesthetic affects film reception in the home, we can turn to the evaluation of films in a variety of forums that cater to collectors, from consumer electronics magazines to Internet newsgroups. 'Classic' films comprise a major category of collectables in these sources. The hardware aesthetic may entirely displace the canonical status of the legendary film or reify it to suit its demands for spectacle.

For instance, the 1995 laserdisc reissue of Akira Kurosawa's *Sanjuro* (1962) occasions this comment from a critic for *Widescreen Review*: 'The Tohoscope framing has been recomposed at 2.11:1, although the transfer credits proclaim "its original aspect ratio of 2.35:1". The picture lacks detail and sharpness, shadow detail is poor, and generally negative dirt artefacts are prevalent throughout'. In addition, 'the original soundtrack theatrically was Perspecta Stereophonic Sound … but this edition has been dubbed from a mono optical track which is undistinguished and characteristically noisy'.[33] A review for another classic film, *The Fly* (1958), re-released in 1997, similarly addresses the fine points of its reproduction. The film is 'framed at 2.35:1, exhibits inconsistencies in color fidelity with mostly dated and subdued colors and fleshtones. Overall the picture is out of focus, except for the occasional close up shots of a fly. Noise and artifacts are apparent …The overall sound is on the bright side and never sounds quite right'.[34]

Such unfavourable criticism is not, of course, the fate of all classics. If the transfer is good, the 'old' film can more successfully negotiate the requirements of the aesthetic. Thus, a reviewer judges a 'lavish' box set of a trio of Judy Garland films (*The Harvey Girls* (1946), *The Pirate* (1948), and *Summer Stock* (1950)) entitled, 'Judy Garland: The Golden Years at MGM', as looking 'absolutely gorgeous'. This is especially true of *The Pirate*, which accents director Vincente Minnelli's exotic use of colour in lighting, sets and costumes, greatly intensifying the mood of scenes like the fiery 'Pirate Ballet'. 'The excess and grandeur of Minnelli's trademark style of *mise-en-scène*, preserved and perhaps even heightened in the transfer process, co-ordinates felicitously with the superior, vivid visual experience associated with digital entertainment technologies. But in this case the experience is qualified, due to the flawed reproduction of the musical's soundtrack. The reviewer notes that 'the audio track for *The Pirate* was often marred by a harsh, scraping, practically vibrating tone'.[35]

A film widely considered to be a 'dud' in its initial run can also be reappraised. In *The Laser Disc Newsletter*'s review of *Last Man Standing* (1996), the reviewer explains that while he had not cared for the film in the theatre, listening to the laserdisc reissue 'in our home, with the sound turned way up, made it a lot more appealing, regardless of the ridiculous plot'. The new digital soundtrack makes the difference: Ry Cooder's score 'takes on more detail and omnipresent vibrancy … Throughout the film, subtle touches of sound – the wind seeping through a crack or a creaking door down the street – are given more clarity, stimulating your senses and making the tough questions, like what is a sheriff doing in a town that doesn't have any people in it, not matter'.[36]

In the land of new technologies, the past is reborn to very exacting standards demanding pristine visuals in original aspect ratios and crystalline soundtracks. It is not enough for a film to be made by Akira Kurosawa – the terms of the transfer must reproduce the correct aspect ratio, picture resolution and sound quality of the celluloid version. Furthermore, the classic film must live up to another set of standards, standards that are an integral part of the home theatre experience with its big-screen TVs and surround sound components. Ideally, films from the past should have lively, vigorous visuals and a bold (or subtle and nuanced) soundtrack amenable to digital enhancement. In some cases, this kind of updating proves to be difficult since, aside from the practice of sloppy transfers, the original inter-negatives may have deteriorated or be possessed by 'dirt artifacts' and other demons involved in the improper storage or ageing process of celluloid. As we have seen in the reviews of *Sanjuro* and *The Fly,* there is little place in the hardware aesthetic for the cinematic equivalent of the dusty, dog-eared volume. Thus, while recapturing the standards of the original remains important to high-end collectors, their sense of authenticity is more compellingly influenced by the nature of the upgrades performed on a film to render it suitable to the digital eye and ear.

In these estimations of films, sound and image displace other tried-and-true critical criteria, such as auteurism and existing canons, and, in the case of *Last Man Standing,* box-office status. This not to say that such traditional critical criteria are unimportant in the world of collecting. Auteurism and the canon carry enormous weight as a means of marketing reissues and as factors that enter into a collector's decision about which films to select for the archive. Collectors may indeed buy videos or laserdiscs that are inferior in quality just to own a coveted title or complete a sector of their media libraries. But quality transfer issues and the question of whether a film delivers the kind of audio-visual spectacle that best exhibits the prowess of the machines in question are pervasive and potent aspects of the hardware aesthetic shared and propagated by collectors.

Prizing technology and the spectacular, this aesthetic harbours a certain disregard for content. As one reviewer in *Video Magazine* writes of *Forrest Gump* (1994), since it is 'a certified phenomenon ... let's not fret over "What It Says About Us" and get right down to the chocolate, er, heart of the matter'. The heart of the matter is that '*Gump* ... boasts a wide-screen transfer of about 2.1:1, and though it's done up to THX standards (the image is quite good, if not exceptional), it displays a tendency toward soft colours. *Gump* isn't much of a surround-sound showcase, either, since the intimacy of the storyline dictates that most of the dialogue, musical score, and ambient sounds must be positioned front and centre'.[37] Similarly, Pioneer Entertainment's special edition of *Platoon* (1986) presents 'a motion picture that defined for many Americans the inhuman, hostile and futile act of the Vietnam War' as an 'impossible-to-resist hardbound, display-quality volume designed with the look and feel of a Vietnam Veteran's scrapbook, complete with embossed silver images of "dog tags" hanging from the top edge of the cover'. Further, the film is 'matted at 1.85:1. Detail and sharpness are exemplary ... Fleshtones are accurate and blacks are deep and solid for an exceptionally natural rendering. The soundtrack also is impressive over that of the theatrical mix ... the original discrete six-track elements have been re-mixed and encoded for a more potent surround effect and greater dynamics'.[38] Within this orientation, the issue of content is swept aside as secondary by more pressing concerns, i.e. the quality of the transfer, the film's suitability for maximising the capabilities of home theatre and the opportunity the reissue presents for commodification – in the case of *Platoon*, the packaging features of the laserdisc set.

Such modes of evaluation differ significantly from those characteristic of Anglo-American moral criticism. This tradition, personified in the 1950s by such critics as Bosley Crowther of the *New York Times* and Arthur Knight of the *Saturday Review* and still pervasive in contemporary writing on film in the popular press today, judges films on the basis of the relevance and worth of their social messages. In the above reviews, the collecting sensibility clearly sees such messages as a mere backdrop or even as a potential distraction to what is really noteworthy about the films – accurate fleshtones and resonant multi-track sound. Despite the fact that both *Forrest Gump* and *Platoon* concern the 1960s, one of the most hotly debated eras in US history, and that both were subject to protracted discussions in the press about their depictions of this era, reviewers of their laserdisc re-releases produce a detailed technical vision of these films, describing them in an alternative language seen as vital to their consumption by the cinephile.

It is important to point out that the reviews in consumer electronics magazines and other sources do not just echo the industry's unqualified hype about all of its re-releases; they exist as guides to buyers and collectors. Internet newsgroups devoted to laserdisc and video collecting take this role of consumer watchdog especially seriously, spreading the word about superior or deficient discs, debating the comparative merits of playback equipment and generally soliciting advice from fellow subscribers. As one newsgroup participant writes, 'I remember renting *The Silence of the Lambs* Criterion/THX CAV version and the rolling dropouts were the worst I have ever seen. I want the new CLV Criterion version. Does anybody know if this disc suffers from the same HORROR?'. Another writes, 'I have just purchased the new THX *Apocalypse Now* and I am VERY impressed with the EXCELLENT transfer video and audio wise it is beautiful, but I am concerned with the 1.9:1 ratio. I always thought the film was 2.35:1. It does not state anywhere on the disc why the director of photography recomposed the film to the ratio it is at on this transfer …'. Another subscriber answers the question: 'The transfer is presumably the same as the older version. Storaro (the DP) felt that the 2.35:1 ratio would shrink the image too much, resulting in loss of detail … Incidentally, the film wasn't necessarily 2.35:1. The 70mm version would have been 2.2:1'.[39]

The detailed interrogations of industry products by newsgroups and other consumer guides provide an alternative source of information for consumers. Industry promotions, consumer magazines and Internet groups tend to embrace technology unquestioningly, however. Most of the debates in the above newsgroup during 1997 concerned aspect ratios, transfers and home theatre technologies – the pros and cons of laserdisc versus DVD, the superiority of AC-3 sound systems to Dolby Pro-Logic, etc. Films become vehicles for the performance and assessment of these technologies (as one newsgroup participant succinctly puts it: 'You want to test your THX and AC3 hardwares? Watch *Strange Days*').[40] What is noticed, valued and appraised about films in this part of their after-life is how their display of characteristics – *mise-en-scène*, special effects and sound – maximises (or fails to deliver) the capabilities of the machines of reproduction. This aesthetic mechanism allows the generic horror of *Silence of the Lambs* (1991) to become the technological horror of the rolling dropout.

The Thrill of Acquisition

In the constitution of the 'insider' identity and the co-ordinates of the hardware aesthetic, we glimpse part of the elaborate world inhabited by the high-end film collector. Positioned by the industry as a privileged subject and captivated by the machines of reproduction, the collector is the new film connoisseur, the cinephile existing outside of the motion picture theatre. The niche audience represented by collectors offers a distinct instance of the impact that new technologies have had on film reception in the home. Recent technological developments have helped this mini-film culture to flourish, providing bountiful films for sale and shaping the terms of their consumption within a domestic environment in which both the television set (via home theatre) and the cinema have been reinvented to meet the expectations of digital quality. Within the sensibility of high-end collecting, films from different national traditions, different canons and different eras are transformed into signs of the technical proficiency and potential of the contemporary arts of mechanical and electronic reproduction. In this sense, cinephilia is inextricable from technophilia.

The domestic world of the cinephile is constructed from a series of relatively simple acts of purchase – the purchase of tapes, discs, AV receivers, speakers, big-screen television sets, etc. The fact that cinema can be acquired and taken home opens up vast possibilities for its use and its meaning in the post-video era, of which collecting is just one example. Patrons not only *see* films, they also *invest* in them, *own* them and situate them in relation to their entertainment centres and other less luminous household items. Owners who are collectors intensify this sense of possession by selecting films on the basis of their technical quality (and other criteria) and then organising individual titles according to personal systems of classification. There is an excitement about both of these processes that signifies the thrill of acquisition and the accompanying pleasure involved in creating a home-made universe out of such cinematic trophies. In this sense the collection is a sterling example of what Baudrillard refers to as the peculiar 'passion for private property' that marks our relationship to the objects populating our home environments, a passion that can be every bit as intense as that more commonly associated with other human relationships.

This kind of possession imposes a certain abstractness on collected media objects. Specifically, the collected object loses both its historical origins and its public status. The historical context in which a film initially appeared does survive in its reissue; this context functions to identify the film's appeal and to sell it, just as it invites the viewer to re-experience the past through the purchase. But this kind of reified history obscures the power the contemporaneous context has on perceptions of the object. In contradistinction to Benjamin, renewing the old world in this form of collecting suggests an unapologetic concern with the present that glories in its acquisition of the past only if the past has been renovated through contemporary technological standards.[41] This is not to say that systems of evaluation based on sentiment or nostalgia are innocent of effect. But in the displacements and strange alchemies that mark the temporal disposition of the high-end film collection, contemporary technological standards are particularly privileged as the rationale for selection and as the basis of value. It is the technology that resurrects films from the past and gives them to the audience, ideally realising each film's potential to present vivid imagery and stirring soundtracks.

Just as films achieve a vexed relation to their original historical contexts within the collection, they also experience a dramatic change in exhibition conditions. They are removed from the public sphere to become part of a private totality. Within this private totality, the role of the owner–collector assumes an importance that appears to surpass and obscure his or her initial role as a consumer in the marketplace. As Susan Stewart remarks, the collecting self generates a fantasy in which it becomes 'a producer by arrangement and manipulation' of those objects. In 'subsuming the environment to a scenario of the personal' the collection thus 'acquires an aura of transcendence and independence' in relation to larger economies of value which it actually mirrors.[42]

The joys of collecting, then, are not only bound up with the act of consumption, but with the powerful sense the collector has of being the source, the origin of the objects he or she has purchased and organised into a system (a psychology that clearly recalls Metz's cinephile).[43] The collected objects ultimately refer to the collector as auteur, as the producer of an intelligible, meaningful universe – a dynamic that occludes the relations the collection has to the outside world, particularly to the social and material conditions of mass production. There is a chain of logic between property, passion and self-referentiality that helps to explain the zeal of the collector and also the significant place films have attained within the home as private possessions.

Removed from history and public space, the abstracted artefact becomes a household object. Subject both to the particular organisation of the collection and to the apparently self-contained world of the collector, it offers the radiant pleasure that an investment in one's domestic space can bring. At the same time, cinema's domestication within this particular film culture, relying as it does on a slippage in the collector's identity from consumer to producer, tends to minimise awareness of the alliances between cinema and public institutions, between home film cultures and broader spheres of influence.

Of necessity, then, cinema's entanglement in this solipsistic environment represents a paradox. As we have seen, while the world of the collector seems exclusive and personal, it is strongly influenced by discourses of media industries and their technologies. Consumption in general provides an intense link between private and public spheres (obviously, one purchases mass-produced objects so as to make them personal possessions). At the same time, media industries offer consumers the rhetorics of intimacy (i.e. 'secrets' of the cinema) and mastery (i.e. technological expertise or media knowledge) to enhance consumers' sense of owning a personalised product. In such a situation, the leisure behaviour of the collector seems very much implicated in what Jürgen Habermas has referred to as 'the floodlit privacy' of the home, wherein the home is simultaneously constructed as a private sphere and a domain under the influence of 'laws of the market' and 'semipublic authorities'.[44]

Whether or not one fully embraces Habermas's position, collecting definitely emerges as a complex activity situated suggestively at the fluid intersection between public and private. Far from being bankrupt effectively and aesthetically, this type of viewing invites us to consider further both the implications of domestic film cultures for understanding spectatorship in the post-video age and the increasingly dynamic interplay between film, private life and public enterprise.

Notes

1   Jean Baudrillard, *The System of Objects,* trans. James Benedict (London and New York: Verso, 1996), p. 85.

2   See Christian Metz, *The Imaginary Signifier: Psychoanalysis and the Cinema,* trans. Celia Britton *et al.* (Bloomington IN: Indiana University Press, 1977), pp. 74–5, 79; and Roland Barthes, 'Upon Leaving the Movie Theater', trans. Bertrand Augst and Susan White, in Theresa Hak Kyung Cha (ed.), *Cinematographic Apparatus: Selected Writings* (New York: Tanam Press, 1980), p. 2.

3   As Janet Wasko reports, by 1990 the business of renting or buying video-cassettes had outgrossed theatrical box-office revenues by almost $10 billion. Wasko, *Hollywood in the Information Age* (Austin, TX: University of Texas Press, 1994), p. 114.

4   For analysis of the impact of family relationships and gender on home viewing, see Valerie Walkerdine, 'Video Replays: Families, Films, and Fantasy', in Victor Burgin *et al.* (ed.), *Formations of Fantasy* (London: Routledge, 1989), pp. 167–99; and Ann Gray, *Video Playtime: The Gendering of a Leisure Technology* (London: Routledge, 1992).

5   Timothy Corrigan, *A Cinema Without Walls: Movies and Culture After Vietnam* (New Brunswick, NJ: Rutgers University Press, 1991), p. 81.

6   Peter M. Nichols, 'Land of the Cineplex, Home of the Cassette', *New York Times,* 13 July 1997: sec. 2, 1. Nichols also reports that 'consumers increasingly want to buy and not just rent the biggest movies ... which they can then watch more than once' (22). Nichols had noted earlier that 'video viewers [are] collecting more movies on tape', attributing this development to the fact that 'more videos [are] being offered in their original widescreen versions' ('Home Video', *New York Times,* 11 October 1996: B17). Thus, the trend toward buying films has not only changed the way audiences watch movies by allowing multiple viewings, it has affected the suppliers, who now provide more films in widescreen or 'letter-boxed' formats to respond to collectors interested in purchasing a title in close to its original screen ratio.

7   On the growth of a sell-through market for films on video-cassette, see Wasko, *Hollywood in the Information Age,* pp. 135–6.

8   Advertisement, *Entertainment Weekly,* 7 November 1997, p. 17.

9   In 1996, there were roughly two million laserdisc players purchased by consumers in the United States. Lawrence B. Johnson, 'While Digital Video Dithers, Laser Disk Just Gets Better', *New York Times,* 10 November 1996, p. 22. Since the present essay was written, laserdiscs have been phased out in ths U.S., while the DVD has assumed more prominence. As of 2000, there were approximately 10 million DVD players in American homes. While technologies have shifted, my observations about the way that technology is valued remain unchanged in relation to this newer medium. If anything, DVD has enhanced the hardware aesthetic and, by routinely featuring collector's edition information on discs, the existence of 'secret knowledge' that makes viewers feel like experts.

10 There are many additional signs of the film-collecting trend throughout the media industry. A typical ad in a home theatre magazine reads: 'For the discriminating movie fan. 3 laserdiscs/$1.00 each ... Here's a great way to build a collection of your favorite movies – on laserdisc' (*Video Magazine,* July 1995, p. 25). 'Dave's Video, the Laser Place' encourages its customers to build 'Your Own Film Archive'. *The Criterion Collection*

advertised its 1997 collection by telling its patrons: 'The cornerstone of any movie collection is the work of a few great filmmakers'. They add that their list of 'popular favorites, lost treasures, and landmark films from around the world [will provide] the closest thing we know to a perfect shelf of movies' (pp. 3, 37). Companies releasing film 'classics' will routinely remind potential customers of the value these classics have to a film collection. For example, with the reissue of 'long-awaited Hammer titles on laserdisc, a void will be filled in LD libraries everywhere' (Mel Neuhaus, 'Hammer Hits Home', *Home Theater*, 4 June 1997, pp. 106–12). These promotions provide more evidence of the media industries' assumption that collectors are now an official part of mainstream media culture.

11 As we shall see, there is a definite connection between collectors, laserdiscs and home theatre technology. As Lawrence B. Johnson suggests, collectors, as purists, often 'want to replicate the movie theater experience in home theater systems with big-screen televisions and hi-fi sound'. See 'While Digital Video Dithers, Laser Disk Just Gets Better', p. 22.

12 That collecting has become a pervasive part of film culture in the United States is also signalled by the presence of independent, non-industry consumer guides to film collectables, from mail-order forums (such as *The Laser Disc Newsletter*, edited by Douglas Pratt and published out of East Rockaway, New York) to the Internet (such as newsgroup 'alt.laserdisc.video').

13 Advertisement, *Entertainment Weekly*, 31 October 1997, p. 21.

14 Ibid., 5 December 1997, p. 7.

15 The top-ten videos sold for the week ending 26 October 1997 were: *Batman and Robin, The Jungle Book, Liar Liar, Sleeping Beauty, Star Wars Trilogy: Special Edition, Wild America, It's The Great Pumpkin, Charlie Brown, Casper: A Spirited Beginning, Set It Off,* and *Halloween: Special Edition. Entertainment Weekly*, 7 November 1997, p. 93; statistics for this report obtained from *Video Business*, 26 October 1997. Robert Allen has analysed the significance of family-oriented film purchases to the movie business today in 'Home Alone Together: Hollywood and the "Family Film"', in Melvyn Stokes and Richard Maltby (eds), *Identifying Hollywood's Audiences: Cultural Identity and the Movies* (London: BFI, 1999), pp. 109–31.

16 For an essay that calls attention to the existence of 'low-end' audiences, see Jeffrey Sconce, '"Trashing" the Academy: Taste, Excess, and the Emerging Politics of Cinematic Style', *Screen*, vol. 36 (winter 1995), pp. 371–93.

17 For a work of fiction that plays off of a strong association between stereophilia and masculine subjectivities, see Nick Hornby, *High Fidelity* (New York: Riverhead Books, 1995). But, again, it is not so clear that this association is as 'pure' in relation to video and post-video technologies.

18 Walter Benjamin, 'Unpacking My Library', in *Illuminations*, ed. Hannah Arendt, trans. Harry Zohn (New York: Schocken Books, 1969), pp. 60, 67. For other work Benjamin did on the subject of collecting see 'Edward Fuchs: Collector and Historian', in Andrew Arato and Eike Gebhardt (eds), *The Essential Frankfurt School Reader* (New York: Urizen Books, 1978), pp. 225–53.

19 James Clifford, 'On Collecting Art and Culture', in Simon During (ed.), *The Cultural Studies Reader* (London: Routledge, 1993), pp. 52–3.

20 'Laser Disc Collector for Windows' from 'The Obsessive Collector', *Laser Disc Newsletter*, February 1997, p. 17.

21 Advertisement for Goldwyn Classics Eddie Cantor Series, *Home Theater Technology*, 2 July 1995, p. 119.

22 Pioneer Entertainment advertisement for 'Star Trek: The Movie Voyages', *Home Theater Technology Buyer's Guide* (1995), p. 29.

23 *Laser Disc Newsletter*, February 1997, pp. 13–17; Charles Tashiro, 'The Contradictions of Video Collecting', *Film Quarterly*, vol. 50 (winter 1996–7), p. 15.

24 Roland Barthes, *Camera Lucida: Reflections on Photography*, trans. Richard Howard (New York: Hill and Wang, 1981), p. 16.

25 Henry Jenkins, *Textual Poachers: Television Fans and Participatory Culture* (New York: Routledge, 1992), p. 87.

26 There are many other examples of official trivia sources sold to the public. For example, a mail-order catalogue selling children's goods, *Store of Knowledge*, has a section devoted to movies and television. From this section parents can buy 'The Movie Mania Trivia Game', 'The Six Degrees of Kevin Bacon Game', the 'I Love Lucy' book and game, and 'The Star Wars Chronicles Collector's Edition'. These are sold as 'a sheer adrenaline rush for avid Hollywood fans and movie buffs' or are 'exclusively for the die-hard ... fan' (pp. 4–5).

27 Scholars differ on how to assess the fan's relation to media knowledge. There appears to be no simple answer to questions concerning this aspect of the fan/media industry relation. While some scholars such as Jenkins see the fan's intimate knowledge of and ability to produce criticism of television shows as an empowering development, others see the popular cultural expert's status as a 'semi-fantasy' entertained by fans to compensate for their lack of power within larger political and social systems (e.g. Bernard Sharratt, 'The Politics of the Popular? From Melodrama to Television', in David Bradby, *et al.* (eds). *Performance and Politics in Popular Drama* (Cambridge: Cambridge University Press, 1980), p. 283.

28 Tashiro, 'The Contradictions of Video Collecting', p. 11.

29 Ibid., pp. 15–16.

30 Ibid., p. 16.

31 Ibid., p. 13.

32 Advertisement, *Home Theater*, June 1997, p. 9; Advertisement, *Widescreen Review*, May/June 1995, p. 9.

33 Review of *Sanjuro*, by Akira Kurosawa, *Widescreen Review*, May/June 1995, p. 129.

34 Review of *The Fly*, by Kurt Neumann, *Widescreen Review*, May 1997, p. 156.

35 Review of *The Pirate*, by Vincente Minnelli, *Video Magazine*, July/August 1995, p. 70.

36 Review of *Last Man Standing*, by Walter Hill, *The Laser Disc Newsletter*, July 1997, pp. 1–2.

37 Review of *Forrest Gump*, by Robert Zemeckis, *Video Magazine*, July/August 1995, p. 69.

38 'Platoon: Oliver Stone's Epic Vietnam War Masterpiece', *Widescreen Review* May/June 1995, p. 110.

39 Internet newsgroup 'alt.video.laserdisc', 24 June 1997.

40 Ibid.

41 Scholars who analyse the phenomenon of collecting are often deeply concerned about the effects collecting has on time and history. However, they are divided about what

these effects are. Some argue that collecting represents a serious loss of origins for the object in question as it is repositioned within the logic of the museum or personal collection (see, for example, Susan Stewart, *On Longing: Narratives of the Miniature, the Gigantic, the Souvenir, the Collection* (Durham, NC: Duke University Press, 1993), pp. 151–4). Conversely, others, such as Maurice Rheims, claim that the 'passion for collecting is joined to a loss of any sense of the present time' – that is, the collector, in seeking immersion in the past through the historical references offered by his/her artefacts, is of necessity disconnected from the present (quoted in Baudrillard, *The System of Objects*, p. 95). In the same text, Baudrillard argues that the collection 'abolishes time', that is, '*the organization of the collection itself replaces time*'. Because the collection reduces 'time to a fixed set of terms navigable in either direction', it represents an opportunity for the owner to travel anywhere historically with complete control (p. 95). Thus, the collection's temporal dimension points neither to the present nor to the past, but ultimately to the logic, the order of the collection itself. For the moment I am regarding the dynamics of film collecting as operating ultimately in the 'presentist' mode, especially given the nature of evaluation within the high-end film collecting world. But the issue of time is a complex subject that bears further reflection in relation to contemporary film collecting.

42 Stewart, *On Longing*, pp. 158, 162, 159. This displacement of material conditions of production to serve consumer fantasies recalls Theodor Adorno's discussion of commodity fetishism in mass culture in 'On the Fetish-Character in Music and the Regression of Listening', in *The Essential Frankfurt School Reader*, pp. 270–99.

43 This domestic cinephile is reminiscent of Metz's theatre-going figure. The enchantment with machines, the sense of false mastery that indulges a fantasy of control by blocking the 'reality' of the machines and the recognition of 'I' as the origin of the show are all characteristics of contemporary film collecting that dovetail with 'big screen' cinephilia. As this similarity suggests, self-referentiality appears to be a key ingredient in the individual's relationship to and pleasure in commodities. Similarly, many who study collecting see it as a prime instance of narcissism and regression, also components of Metz's argument about cinephilia. See, for example, Werner Muensterberger, *Collecting: An Unruly Passion* (New York: Harcourt, Brace, and Company, 1994).

44 Jürgen Habermas, *The Structural Transformation of the Public Sphere: An Inquiry into a Category of Bourgeois Society*, trans. Thomas Burger (Cambridge: MIT Press, 1991), pp. 159, 161.

10
Virtual Hollywood and the Genealogy of its Hyper-Spectator

Alain J.-J. Cohen

This chapter deals with the recent development of a 'virtual' Hollywood in which the line of demarcation between film and spectator has been elided, with the latter now able in some respects to enter and shape the filmic universe rather than simply to observe it. This contemporary, flexible approach to spectatorship is contrasted with its origins at the beginning of cinema, when audiences programmed for theatre, opera, paintings and photographs gave way to the first audiences programmed, *en masse*, for the cinema. These spectators were positioned by the cinematic apparatus in a number of ways. In the 1960s and 1970s, how this positioning occurred was to become one of the major concerns of film theory. The same period, however, saw the emergence of directors (especially those of the French new wave) who were historians as well as cinema auteurs, privileged spectators who, in their knowledge of the particulars and intertextuality of films provided a foretaste of what would happen in later years. I shall argue that the theories of spectatorship developed during these years have been outmoded by the arrival of new technology. As access to cinema in its various forms has exploded over the past two decades, the spectator has, in effect, been replaced by another, equally theoretical figure: the hyper-spectator. If film theory of the 1960s and 1970s encouraged the notion of a mind model in which spectatorship was, in essence, about passive subjectification, the rise of new ways of viewing Hollywood films suggests the need for a new mind model wherein the spectatorial subject actively helps to create the simulacral world of 'virtual' Hollywood, as well as being created by it.

'Virtual' Hollywood and its Spectators

The virtualisation of Hollywood can be seen to have expressed itself in several trends. Reports in the press and on the Internet have recently begun keeping score of Hollywood's major film openings and of the weekend's competing cinematic business successes or failures, nationwide and worldwide, as if the industry's financial performance had become a spectator sport. These economic reports now include number of tickets sold, million-dollar receipts at the box office, number of theatre screens and gross per screen, number of weeks the films hold up among the top ten, as well as the anticipated profits and losses for the studios and their shareholders.[1] Projections for national movie theatres, worldwide distribution, home-video rentals and sales have now become obsessional pastimes, with these business reports as veritable cliffhangers indicating the producers' return (or lack of it) on their sky-rocketing investments for each new major film. 'Insider-knowledge' and film-connoisseurship used to refer to those who were on the movie set and had been at a 'shoot' and thus had access to directors and their crews. Instead, the media are now riveted by marketing questions raised each week over which film by Disney, Sony, Universal or Warner Bros. beat the competition, or which studio head is likely to roll next. On the Net, websites and chatrooms are equally full of this type of discussion. In such a situation, 'Hollywood' has taken on the mantle of a simulacral business in which the knowledge of (frequently illusory) profits and losses attests to the 'insidership' of the film fan, who may, or may not, have any other expertise in film culture.

Together with this growing popular attention to the minutiae of Hollywood's business dealings, certain major changes have taken place in the relationship between Hollywood and the cinema generally and between Hollywood and its spectators. Shortly before he died in 1993, Federico Fellini commented that, for his generation, 'Hollywood' was synonymous with cinema. Many of his contemporaries would have echoed this view, which amounted to a recognition of the extent to which 'Hollywood' had conquered the world with its images, technologies and powerful film distribution system. But, like the Roman Empire before it which was conquered by its own conquest, Hollywood's supremacy over the world has undergone a number of mutations. It is possible to argue that if the world was conquered iconically, it retaliated by virtualising Hollywood. The filmic universe first constituted by cinema in Hollywood studio sets ended up being shot anywhere in the world. The value systems, and the ways of shooting, editing and storytelling, were replicated and proliferated in exponential seriality. In the meantime, 'Hollywood' itself morphed into a counterpart, a virtual Hollywood-effect of creations and products, indifferent and oblivious to geographies

This development of a 'virtual' Hollywood has had a range of implications so far as the filmic spectator is concerned. A number of films exist in which the borderline between the filmic and spectatorial world is transgressed or undermined: actors walk out of the screen to join the spectator in Woody Allen's *The Purple Rose of Cairo* (1985), while exactly the opposite happens in Jean-Luc Godard's *Le petit soldat* (1964), in which the spectator walks into the screen. The architecture of City Walk, designed for Universal Studios by Jon Jerde, is effectively a play upon these possible permutations.[2] City Walk is a recreation of a fictionalised studio backlot city – a simulacrum of what was itself already a simulated world. It encourages tourists to switch interchangeably back and forth from spectator to actor, and also endeavours to persuade them to become ideal consumers of film-related products in the designer-set of their choice. Life and art thereby become interwoven, with infinite situationist performances in a permanent 'society of the spectacle' offering convincing testimony of the effective virtualisation of existence.[3] We now have not just movies, but also mega-malls and mega-hotels playing on movie references, manifesting Moebius-like actualisations of the spectatorial experience in the continuum inside and outside the movie space.

Classical Hollywood's continuity system had the effect of placing the viewer in the ideal viewing position, wherever that happened to be in relation to the diegetic space of the action. Thus, diegetic space was presented as being constantly permeable by the camera/spectator. The viewer is simultaneously inside and outside the diegetic space of the action, and the play with this paradoxical position remains one of cinema's great pleasures. Richard Maltby has pointed out that as both physical environment and as institution, the cinema itself creates a 'safe space' in which the spectator may become involved in such play.[4] Theme parks and their more sophisticated successors are actualisations, in a 3-D space that spectators occupy as participants, of this concept of 'safe space', and also of the idea of the viewer's mobility not just between levels of fiction but between participation and spectatorship, which is part of the everyday experience of watching classical Hollywood.

If 'Hollywood' has become, in some respects, 'virtual', what of changes in the profile of the figure who has sustained the medium structurally and financially since the beginnings of the cinema: the film spectator? An analysis of this subject suggests that, just as Hollywood has changed, so too has its film-constituted spectatorship.

The Rise of Spectatorship

Film spectatorship's cognitive origins have been traced by Jean-Louis Baudry back to the prisoners in Plato's cave who mistook – and enjoyed – the shadows and simulacra in place of the world of ideas, to which Plato was anxious to orient them.[5] Its emotional roots can be linked to Aristotle's elaboration upon the cathartic effect of representation, or the passions of the 'purged' spectators. In more modern times, there were vast audiences for theatre and opera, for painting and music, that both mapped and modelled the path for the emergence of audiences for moving pictures. Any attempt to trace the history of film spectatorship in the industrial and post-industrial eras must, however, necessarily begin with the simultaneous invention of photography by Daguerre in France and Talbot in Britain in 1839, followed by the various developments towards the inscription of motion and locomotion in photographs in the famous experiments of Marey and Muybridge as they tried to photograph 'speed' – groping towards a sense of continuum, despite the discrete images, by moving towards the principle of multiple frames per second of running men or horses (albeit using batteries of cameras). These experiments led to the invention of fantastic machines that can now only be seen in museums of the cinema or science encyclopaedias: the zoopraxiscope, the phénakinéstiscope, the kineto-phonograph, the chronophotograph (which went from glass to paper and could record up to forty images at the same time), the kinetoscope, the vitagraph,[6] and the Lumière brothers' crowning achievement, the cinématographe.

Among these new inventions, only the cinématographe (and its American counterparts, the vitascope and the mutoscope) began to create mass audiences and a film spectatorship. Even photography, in its first years an expensive hobby for the fortunate few, did not reach a popular audience until the first Kodaks of the 1890s rendered its use more widespread. Walter Benjamin's famous remarks about photography and the 'aura' of the artwork in the age of mechanical reproduction emphasised the major distinction between the painterly and photographic modes. A painting is a unique artefact, whereas a fairly large number of identical photographic stills may be reproduced serially from the same negative. Cinematic reproduction increased this photographic seriality exponentially: identical reels can be reproduced from a negative and marketed all over the world to be seen by mass audiences in many different places.

The Construction of Spectators by Early Cinema

An analogy may be drawn between the invention of a cinema spectatorship and the momentous invention of perspective and of the consequent geometrisation of space that resulted in the Italian Renaissance. From the early experiments of Brunelleschi, to the mastery of Piero della Francesca and Laurana, artists learned from the increasing sophistication of their craft how effectively they could discipline their spectators into looking in certain ways through their technical manipulations of perspective.[7] The perspectival effect in paintings constructs the specific ways in which the spectator may enter the pictural apparatus. Similarly, as the early cinematic pioneers struggled with light and the motion of pictures, concerned with the processing of a cluster of frames in order to produce the foundational flashes of the medium (the arrival of a locomotive at a station or a fantasmatic trip to the moon), they were at the same time beginning to feel their way towards the use of mechanisms for positioning spectators in certain ways. Such positioning, and the spectatorial alignment leading to obligatory technical identification with a what (a setting) or a who (one character or a cast of characters rather than another) was, of course, far from new in cultural terms.

During the first years of motion pictures, there were no normative cinema spectators. Exhibition circumstances for early films varied enormously. They were shown in vaudeville theatres, exhibition and church halls, opera houses, cafés, department stores, schools, fairgrounds and many other locations. Motion pictures themselves shared the billing at these venues with other forms of entertainment, including dancers, acrobats and singers. What Miriam Hansen has termed the 'variety format' extended also to the selection of the (short) films themselves, which were chosen to be as diverse as possible.[8] Films shown might include comic acts, dances, scenes from well-known plays and operas, representations of historical events, travelogues, and 'actualities' based on news events and sports, including prize-fights. The kind of spectatorship offered by such a type of entertainment, therefore, essentially involved 'a mobilization of the viewer's attention through a discontinuous series of attractions, shocks, and surprises'.[9] Early cinema was very much – in Tom Gunning's phrase – 'a cinema of attractions', much closer in spirit to the display and showmanship of the music hall (and fairground) than to the later narrative conventions associated with the 'classical' style of film-making.[10] Before the latter could come into existence, the cinema had first to acquire its own dedicated physical space, which it did with the mushrooming of store-front theatres or nickelodeons from 1907 onward. It also had to evolve its own narrative strategies for storytelling. One of the first steps towards the emergence of such strategies taken by early film-makers was the comic gag. Its proliferation throughout the first years of cinema was intimately linked to the structure of brevity in tandem with the rapid conquest of audiences by actors (soon to become stars) and the relentless exploration of humorous expression. The ubiquitous early appearance of the gag and its enduring power may well be accounted for by its combination of the medium's formal visual wit and the dramatic performances of actors. At the same time, the gag requires an elementary *mise-en-scène* and the strategic editing which was later to characterise the art of montage. Above all, since the gag establishes stylised and minimal narrativity, it points to how cinema evolved afterwards into the next logical step of more and more sophisticated narrative processes, far from its original syntax.

Between 1907 and the late 1910s, the 'cinema of attractions' was largely replaced by what has come to be perceived as 'classical' cinema. Instead of a spectator being offered a discontinuous series of amusements, the spectator of the classical period was encouraged to become involved (and vicariously participate) in the world of space and time as represented on the screen. In effect, the spectator was bound into the film though a series of techniques that, collectively, would come to be known as the 'continuity system'. The objective of these techniques was to further the narrative of movies by securing smooth and continuous transitions between shots. They included eyeline matches, in which a shot of a character looking off-screen was immediately followed by a shot of what the character concerned 'saw', if not from his/her precise standpoint; shot/reverse-shot structures, in which a shot of a character looking off-screen in one direction was succeeded by a shot of another character looking in the opposite direction; and cut-ins, when a longer shot was followed by a close one, effectively bringing the spectator closer to the scene of action. Contiguity editing, or ensuring that characters in successive shots moved constantly in the same direction, helped ensure that the spectator perceived a smooth flow of action. The editorial technique known as inter-cutting, in which alternate shots focused on different locations, helped spectators understand that the action in these locations was (in most cases) happening simultaneously. Dissolves were used to suggest to audiences that expanses of time of no significance to the story had occurred between shots. While the narrative film was becoming, in the years after 1907, the emblematic American movie, to be succeeded after 1912 by the feature film, therefore, a particular kind of cinema spectatorship was being constructed – a spectatorship that understood the narrative conventions of this new art form and could consequently identify with and become involved in the fictional world depicted on screen.

Jeff Bridges as Kevin Flynn/Clu in *Tron* (1982)

Film Theory and the Spectator

Although the history of cinema is inseparable from the history of theories of cinema, the field of film theory emerged in earnest only in the mid-1960s under the pioneering leadership of Christian Metz. As I have noted elsewhere, there were three different phases in Metz's career, each of which expressed itself in the publication of a significant work: a semiotic–rhetorical approach to film analysis in the young Metz (*Film Language: A Semiotics of the Cinema,* 1968), followed by a Lacanian phase (*Psychoanalysis and Cinema,* 1977), followed in turn by a last phase in which he was concerned with the question of filmic enunciation (*L'énonciation impersonnelle ou le site du film,* 1991).[11]

In his first phase, Metz was not directly concerned with the question of spectatorship, even if his discussion of methods would prove of fundamental importance to film analysis. The second, psychoanalytical, Metz did not analyse any particular film or film sequence; he gave careful attention to the questions of identificatory processes at play in the filmic processes or to the import of psychoanalytical categories (condensation and displacement) in the filmic image – all of which would prove useful in the forming of a philosophy of cinema, but would not seem of primary significance to the technical analysis of film *per se.* The second Metz discussed dream and film and the application of the language model previously applied to the iconic. He engaged in an exegesis of the Freud of *The Interpretation of Dreams* in synergy with the Lacan of *Ecrits* (1966). He explored the psychology of the lap-dissolve, the issue of fetishism in cinema, Freud's topographic, dynamic, economic and structural models of the psyche, as well as their Lacanian elaboration. The second Metz was thus apparently searching for an understanding of what anthropologists and psychoanalysts alike call the 'mind model'. A powerful version of spectatorship was sketched and constructed from the propositions of the second Metz. Led by *Screen* (Laura Mulvey, Stephen Heath, *et al.*) and the translators of Lacan in the 1970s, a whole general psychology of the spectator came into being, and was then explored in the late 1970s and 1980s through extensive elaborations upon a gendered spectator/spectatrix.

Auteur-Directors as Spectators and Historians of Cinema

The theories of spectatorship developed by Metz and his successors have, however, been challenged by the arrival of new technologies and the emergence as a consequence of a new theoretical figure who might best be thought of as the 'hyper-spectator'. Such a spectator, who may have a deep knowledge of cinema, can reconfigure both the films themselves and filmic fragments into new and novel forms of both cinema and spectatorship, making use of the vastly expanded access to films arrived at through modern communications equipment and media. The hyper-spectator is, at least potentially, the material (which here means virtual) creator of his or her hyper-cinematic experience. Appropriately enough for a reconfiguration of cinema in which the spectator assumes the place of the auteur, the human prototypes for the hyper-spectator were film directors. The best American directors of recent years (Scorsese, Kubrick, Woody Allen, etc.) have themselves also been remarkable historians of cinema. This trend may have started with the French new wave directors of the 1960s (Godard, Truffaut, Resnais, Varda, Rivette, Chabrol), who were historians of cinema in their own right. Some of them had initially demonstrated their passion for cinema as film critics in *Cahiers du cinéma* in the 1950s. They were more Hollywoodian than most in Hollywood, and working encyclopaedias of the film medium. Since directors have in many ways a reversible role – privileged participants in the history of cinema, they also testify as shrewd spectators of that same history – some offered a foretaste and premonition of the coming hyper-spectatorship in their treatments of such history.

Jean-Luc Godard gives centre stage to the history of cinema, in most of his films, with cascades of (often witty) references, allusions and citations. *Breathless* (1959) is a homage to the once-neglected Hollywood B-movies, to which it made dozens of explicit references.[12] Other directors – Jean-Pierre Melville in *Breathless*, Fritz Lang in *Contempt* and Sam Fuller in *Pierrot le Fou* – often play themselves in his films, thus making his approach to the history of cinema vibrantly alive. Between 1988 and 1997, Godard produced his eight-part *Histoire(s) du cinéma*. This history is not presented in narrative or chronological form. Using to the full the ambiguity of the title (history/histories; story/stories), Godard announced in the opening part that he intended 'to recount "all the stories" in the history of cinema'.[13] His 'history', comments Emma Wilson, is 'deconstructive', being both 'multilayered and disassociative' in form.[14] In this work, Godard devised a strategy of flash shots, often with superimposed clips, barely giving time for recognition and leaving identification for later construction, using quick allusions to frame Hollywood and the world of the cinema. He thereby paid homage to many known and much lesser-known films. Godard's series – its text published in book form, with many illustrative stills in 1998[15] – epitomised a dialogue with film history that was the product of his own spectatorship as well as his participation in that history.

Aside from making several films which revolve around Hollywood, Agnès Varda shows, even in a very short feature such as *T'as de beaux escaliers, tu sais?*, with recursive images of imposing staircases from a series of Hollywood films (e.g., *Gone With the Wind, Citizen Kane, et al.*), how Hollywood inhabits her imaginary. More comprehensive is her long 1995 feature, *Les cent et une nuits du Cinéma*, celebrating the centennial of cinema itself, in which the wheelchair-bound Monsieur Cinéma (Michel Piccoli) introduces, with blurred memories, selected clips from glowing images highlighting Hollywood (and world) cinema.

Among the work of other European film-makers, Wim Wenders's tribute to Hollywood in *The State of Things* also deserves attention. The Munich School director of the 1970s travels to Hollywood, but only to meet his on-screen demise. Friedrich, the film-within-the-film director, shoots with his crew in Portugal (a stylish film called *The Survivors*, itself paying homage to Ford's *The Searchers*), before running out of film stock and money. He flies to Hollywood to look for his producer, who is hiding from the Mafia after his failed investment in a new wave film without a story. After a quest involving a shot of Fritz Lang's star in front of the old Grauman's Chinese theatre, a theatre marquee advertising Ford's *The Searchers* and a visit to Sam Fuller, Friedrich finds the producer, and the two drive around together in a mobile home. Theirs is a depressing miscommunication. The producer sings, in effect, an *unheimliche* funeral litany to Hollywood, mumbling clichés about Hollywood film history, confusing actors (Garfield and Hodiak), films and genres ('Was it *They Drive by Night?*'... 'or rather *Thieves' Highway, He Ran All the Way*...') pell-mell in his blurry memory (not unlike Varda's Monsieur Cinéma) as he and Friedrich themselves drive by night on Hollywood Boulevard. At the end of the night, both producer and director are shot to death as the director records in jump cuts and tilting angles the record of his 'own' death, symbolising perhaps the death of both the new wave and the Munich School at the heart of a Hollywood they both knew so well.

In a sense, what Godard, Varda and Wenders also deal with metaphorically in these works is the death of the classical Hollywood spectator. With all its instabilities, the memory belonging to that spectator necessarily fails to deliver an adequately clear and linear history to correspond with the structures of classical Hollywood. The ground is thus prepared for the advent of a more self-consciously indeterminate (and eclectic) figure in the shape of the hyper-spectator.

The Emergence of the Hyper-Spectator

While what may be thought of as the 'classical' film spectator was very much a product of technological change (the emergence of moving pictures in the 1890s, the advent of sound at the end of the 1920s and the arrival of colour film in the 1930s), the film theory surrounding spectatorship has been undermined and rendered largely out of date by the escalating pace of technology in the last two decades of the twentieth century. VCRs and laserdisc-players or newer DVDs have produced, and are still producing, a Gutenberg-type of revolution in relation to the moving image. There is evidence that scholars and historians of cinema (along with countless unknown spectators) have fast been building film libraries patterned upon their book libraries.[16]

The easy availability of a host of filmic images competing for a brief moment of attention suggests not so much the conventional spectator of film theory as a new mind model: the hyper-spectator with the memory (or hyper-memory) of the whole history of cinema. Contemporary technologies are in the process of creating a virtual and universal digital-cinémathèque, constituting an imaginary museum of cinema under our very eyes. In the coming years, digital cable systems plan to offer to their subscribers not only a few hundred choices of films every week (as cable TV presently does) but ready access to any and every film in their immense film libraries. Band width offers a digitised hyper-space, in which all films are stored and ready to roll at the punch of a code number assigned to any film or TV programme, running side by side all the time on their separate or interactive screens. The (much-debated) must-films of the history of cinema, the sleepers, the epiphanic films unseen for lack of distributors, the cult films with unaccountable followings but devoted audiences, the unavoidable mega-million productions, will all attract their virtual spectators. The hyper-spectator's random access memory (RAM) scans any and every detail of filmic dialogues, iconic configurations, conventions and narratives, and relates them to the universal history of cinema.[17] Categories, genres, nations, eccentricities, all find their place in this Olympian archive and labyrinth of compressed hyper-space.

The Hyper-Spectator and Film Theory

The advent of the hyper-spectator, of course, reframes completely the questions raised with reference to the enunciative apparatus and the theoretical spectator. In film analysis, three coexistent systems have normally been perceived to be at play.[18] System I comprises the filmic enunciative apparatus itself (director, screenwriter, stars, editors, camera, music, soundtrack, etc.); System II points to a spectatorship principle; System III designates the diegetic interactants, the characters whose narrative manipulates the logic and the emotions of the spectatorial principle of System II. For example, in a sequence of Howard Hawks's *To Have and Have Not* (1946), Lauren Bacall pauses in the doorway and looks seductively at Humphrey Bogart (both stars are part of System I, together with director Hawks); Bacall's character (thus System III) then comes on with the (immortal) lines which enthrall both Bogey's character (System III) and the spectator (System II): 'You know you don't have to ask with me, Steve. You don't have to say anything … Not a thing. Oh, maybe just whistle. You know how to whistle, don't you, Steve? You just put your lips together and blow'. A cut to Bogart ensues, leaving room for a chorus of implicit whistles for all the virtual simulacral positions – Bogart's character, Bogart the star (who was to marry Bacall soon thereafter), the spectator's, maybe even the cameraman's whistle would join in this virtual chorus. The spectator's enthralment is polymorphous, of course, titillated by these role-reversing, well-written, well-delivered lines as their tactical ambiguity outsmarts the (resented) Hays Code. The vector in Bacall's gaze includes simultaneously Bogart's character, Bogart the actor and the spectator, in these direct (albeit cool) seductions. The seduction of these gender-defying lines (and gaze) is itself part of the camera's structural manipulation ('structural' in the sense in which Hitchcock, who wanted to direct actors and spectators alike, made his famous quip to Truffaut referring to *Psycho* and his earlier films: 'I want to make the spectator holler'). This spectatorship principle, or this filmically-constituted (and whistling or hollering) spectator, is thus structurally endowed with a delayed apprehension and intelligence of System I's work and project. In effect, the constitution of its spectatorship corresponds to the ways in which a film provides the rules of its own self-interpretation.

The enunciative filmic apparatus and its constructed spectatorship should be conceived as two simulacral positions thus engaged in an exchange, perhaps a dialogue. The parameters of their dialogue are delineated by System III (the object of fiction *per se*, a third simulacral position), the diegetic cast of characters thus invested with passions, involved in their drama and their narrative programmes, and upon whom Systems I and II project their own passions and dramas, aesthetics and histories. Three heterogeneous histories are now interconnected: the history of the filmic enunciative apparatus (which, if it were confined to the film director, would involve style, psychology and evolution); the complex history of the spectator; and the particular film object (part of a vast repertoire of culture, with its stock of narratives and images). These three histories overlap and intersect. Philosophically, the dialectic of the self/object dyad or, psychoanalytically and more precisely, the subjectivation and objectivation processes, may be represented as a Moebius loop. System III is, so to speak, the object structurally necessary for the subjectivation of the enunciative apparatus to take place. Vice versa, its (time-delayed) mirror-image spectatorship becomes involved in its own subjectivation when aligned according to the vectors, or the delusions, snares, traps, or manipulations provided by System I. This elaborate triangularity is at play within every single film, perhaps within single shots.

Complex as the relationships between the different systems whose interaction has formed the basis of traditional film analysis have been, that complexity is greatly increased when the hyper-spectator appears on the scene. For the hyper-spectator can be seen both as a series of typologies (consumer spectator, cognitive spectator, artistic spectator and so on) and a syntax of rules for the combination of these different spectatorships. He/she/it is both plastic and modular, sexually polymorphous and transnational, switching sex, class and anthropology at a click of protheses – the mouse or remote control. The hyper-spectator morphs alternately into Westerner and/or Japanese and/or Chinese, etc., male and/or female and/or child, criminal and/or detective, or combinations thereof, according to the aesthesis of the iconophilic filmic object and especially according to the designer-spectatorship programmed and aligned by the filmic apparatus.

If changes in the creation and positioning of subjects are seen in terms of Foucauldian epistemic shifts, it could be said that the classical (and baroque) era posited a subject's involvement in the mastery of its object. The industrial (and modern) era posited the dialectics of the subject/object dyad. In our postmodern era, however, objects posit the construct of simulacral subjects. Lacan spoke eloquently of a fragmented 'subject-effect' swept by linguistic codings, split into different orders of personality. For Lacan, the 'subject' is not the old-fashioned self, but is rather the subject-of-the-unconscious. Lacan spoke persuasively in *The Four Fundamental Concepts of Psychoanalysis* (1973) about paintings looking at us when we think that we are looking at them. Thus, by analogy, the 'prothetic' hyper-spectator sitting at the computer interconnected with films-by-cable and his DVD-player, pressing buttons and having lots of fun digitising everything in sight and rearranging it for pleasure is, of course, a well-disciplined subject working at the whim of *2001*'s big HAL (or is it 'Deep Blue'?) – all for the glory of virtualising the universal cinémathèque of digitised hyper-space whilst virtualising herself/himself/itself in the process.

The hyper-spectator 'surfs' 'hyper-films' (moving cross-referentially from film to film, from one director to another or from genre to genre, and into trans-national cinemas) with the same ease as we presently surf 'hypertexts' cross-referentially on the Net (without changing CD-ROMS in the course of a search). In a mind-model hypothesis, this exponential hyper-spectatorship is a differential variant of the (time-deferred) mirroring of filmic apparatus itself, one of the multiple facets of the complex mind, split into its dual programmes of doing and its programme of self-observing, or its multiple structure switching back and forth between exhibitionism and voyeurism. To return to the example of *To Have and Have Not*: who whistles, then, in this new and infinitely more complicated theoretical terrain? Bogart? his character? the spectator? the cameraman? Hawks? Well, in fact, all of them, including naturally Bacall and her character, narcissistically enjoying the performance.

Writing about Hollywood and its impact on spectators in the 1960s, 1970s and 1980s centred for the most part on how the cinematic apparatus positioned spectators by various forms of filmic address. The spectator was himself (or later herself) always the spectator of a classical Hollywood cinema that had, by then, largely ceased to exist. S/he viewed films in a building dedicated to the showing of films as a commercial enterprise. For such commercial reasons, however, 'Hollywood' had already begun to metamorphose by the 1960s into a 'virtual' Hollywood of effects and commercial products. In a world in which 'spectatorship' might be expanded as a concept to include buying consumer goods associated with particular films, and visiting malls and hotels 'based on' Hollywood associations, pursuing the classical film spectator became an increasingly questionable enterprise. Since the 1960s, the spectator watching films in a cinema had in any case become a member of a small minority of film enthusiasts. Most spectators watched films increasingly at home, first in reruns on television, then through the VCRs mass-marketed in the 1980s and DVDs in the 1990s. Access to movies through vast numbers of cable and satellite channels, videos, laserdiscs and DVDs increased exponentially, as has the capacity of the spectator to influence where, when and how s/he chooses to watch such films. But the digital revolution that has now begun to take place, and the advent of band-width compression technology, promises a greater revolution still, leading to a universal cinémathèque in which the whole of cinema is instantly available. Effectively, the advent of a 'virtual' Hollywood is now being followed by the emergence of a virtual spectator, creating – and at the same time created by – the digitised world of hyper-space. In postmodern terms, this virtual ('spectated') spectator bears a remarkable resemblance to the de-centred Lacanian 'I-effect' taken over by its concentration of signifiers. Any future attempts to study spectatorship, therefore, will need to deal with the new and infinitely complex model of this simulacral hyper-spectator.

Notes

1   The cost of a Hollywood studio film has increased to the point where many now commonly reach the $100 million mark. It is now several years since Jean-Luc Godard, thinking from a European perspective about the spiralling expense just of special effects, joked that Hollywood might end up in the future making only one film a year, but that that film would cost several billion dollars. A. Bergala (ed.), *J.-L. Godard par J.-L. Godard* (Paris: Editions de l'Etoile/Cahiers du cinéma, 1985).

2   Jon Jerde's development and conception of malls, and recently the Mirage hotel in Las Vegas, develops this design/architectural narrativity into a film-set way of life. Jerde argues that in his playful settings visitors are reversibly spectators and actors, while Disneyland is, by contrast, lethal and hackneyed 'theming'.

3   At the heart of all definitions of postmodernity, the influential trajectory of Jean Baudrillard's theories of simulation and simulacra include some elements of Guy Debord's theories albeit with a mix of Plato, Nietzsche and Lefèbvre. See Debord's concepts (e.g. his political/aesthetic 'situationism') in *La société du spectacle* (Paris, 1970, translation New York: Zone Books, 1994).

4   Richard Maltby, *Hollywood Cinema: An Introduction* (Oxford: Blackwell Publishers, 1995), pp. 20, 36, 45, 190–1, 204, 219, 240, 265, 354, 368, 492.

5   J.-L. Baudry, 'Le dispositif', *Communications,* no. 23 (1975), pp. 56–72.

6   See my discussion of the history of cinema in Alain J.-J. Cohen, 'La Méduse du Caravage/*La Jetée* de Chris Marker. Chiasmes pour Louis Marin', *Documents de Travail* (Urbino: Centro Internazionale di Semiotica, Nos. 244–5, 1995), pp. 1–19. Also see – explaining why cinema was not invented earlier than it was – Warren Buckland, 'The Delay of the Cinema Age', in W. Nöth (ed.), *Semiotics of the Media. State of the Art* (Berlin/ New York: Mouton de Gruyter, 1997); and J. L. Fell (ed.), *Film before Griffith* (Berkeley/Los Angeles: University of California Press, 1983).

7   This designated positioning is best illustrated by the positioning of the viewer in the Renaissance perspectival effect. The spectatorship is programmed for the right distance, just as was the viewer in the Brunelleschian construct. See Hubert Damisch, *L'origine de la perspective* (Paris: Flammarion, 1987), as well as his *Un souvenir d'enfance par Piero della Francesca* (Paris: Seuil, 1997), pp. 164–7. See also Alain J.-J. Cohen, 'Piero della Francesca's *Flagellation*. The painter as film-maker', *Il Cannocchiale. Rivista di studi filosofica,* 'The Cognitive Vallue of Art', no. 2 (2000) pp. 11–32.

8   Miriam Hansen, *Babel and Babylon: Spectatorship in American Silent Film* (Cambridge, MA: Harvard University Press, 1991), p. 29.

9   Ibid.
10 Tom Gunning, 'The Cinema of Attraction[s]', *Wide Angle*, vol. 8, nos. 3–4 (1986), pp. 63–70.
11 Alain J.-J. Cohen, 'Stochastics of Sex and Death in *Basic* (Filmic) *Instinct*', *Semiotica. Special Issue: Christian Metz*, 112, nos. 1–2 (1996), pp. 109–22.
12 See Alain J.-J.Cohen, 'Godard/Lang/Godard – The Film-Within-the-Film', *The American Journal of Semiotics*, vol. 9, no. 4 (1992), pp. 115–30.
13 Michael Temple, 'It Will Be Worth It', *Sight and Sound*, vol. 8, no.1 (January 1998), p. 22.
14 Emma Wilson, *French Cinema since 1950: Personal Histories* (London: Duckworth, 1999), p. 138.
15 Jean-Luc Godard, *Histoire(s) du cinéma*, 4 vols (Paris: Gallimard, 1998).
16 See Chapter 10 in this volume.
17 See Alain J.-J.Cohen, 'Ipermemoria e iconofilia. Montag tra Freud e le scienzecognitive', *Montag* Book Series, vol. 2, *La naturadella visione* (Rome: Edizioni Farenheit 451, 1997), pp. 173–85.
18 See Alain J.-J. Cohen, *Psycho. Programmes filmiques de lapsychose. Documents de travail* (Urbino: Centro Internazionale di Semiotica, 1989), pp. 1–16.

Index